DRIVEN BY DRUGS

U.S. POLICY TOWARD COLOMBIA

RUSSELL CRANDALL

LYNNE
RIENNER
PUBLISHERS

BOULDER
LONDON

Published in the United States of America in 2002 by
Lynne Rienner Publishers, Inc.
1800 30th Street, Boulder, Colorado 80301
www.rienner.com

and in the United Kingdom by
Lynne Rienner Publishers, Inc.
3 Henrietta Street, Covent Garden, London WC2E 8LU

Library of Congress Cataloging-in-Publication Data
A Cataloging-in-Publication record for this book
is available from the Library of Congress.

ISBN: 1-58826-064-X (alk. paper)
ISBN: 1-58826-089-5 (pb : alk. paper)

British Cataloguing in Publication Data
A Cataloguing in Publication record for this book
is available from the British Library.

Printed and bound in the United States of America

The paper used in this publication meets the requirements
∞ of the American National Standard for Permanence of
Paper for Printed Library Materials Z39.48-1984.

5 4 3 2 1

DRIVEN BY DRUGS

To my mom and dad, for everything

Contents

Illustrations

TABLES

FIGURES

PHOTOGRAPHS

Acknowledgments

This book is a result of the combined efforts of many individuals. I am deeply grateful to all of you.

Britta Hillstrom was an indispensable copilot during the life of this book. She was involved in this project from its embryonic stage through the final edits. It is no stretch to say that without her encouragement and collaboration I would still be in graduate school. Her continuous editing smoothed over the manuscript's many rough edges; her intellectual thumbprints are on every page.

I owe gratitude to a number of individuals at Johns Hopkins University's Paul H. Nitze School of Advanced International Studies (SAIS). Riordan Roett's support and direction were invaluable. The debt I owe him is tremendous. Fred Holborn was a wise mentor in the peculiar ways of U.S. foreign policy. Brian Burgoon and Carol Wise also provided important feedback. Guadalupe Paz, Diane Monash, and Anne McKenzie were fantastic in so many ways during my years at SAIS.

Allen Wells at Bowdoin College introduced me to Latin America and taught me the importance of thinking critically. The Smith Richardson Foundation and Davidson College's Dean Rusk International Program provided critical financial support during the manuscript's final stages. The Department of Political Science at Davidson has been a wonderful home while I finished the book. Michael Shifter, Diana Pardo, Arlene Tickner, Juan Forero, Daniel García-Peña, and Chris Chivvis read drafts or discussed issues and ideas with me over coffee.

Finally, a number of U.S. and Colombian government officials, who shall remain nameless due to the nature of their positions, provided me with firsthand perspectives on the craft of diplomacy.

—Russell Crandall

DRIVEN BY DRUGS

COLOMBIA

1

Introduction

In 1982 the United States sent the Colombian government U.S.$2.8 million in order to bolster the fight against illicit drug cultivation and production. In 1988 this figure had increased to just under U.S.$10 million, and by 1994 the figure had risen to U.S.$26 million. In August 2000, President Bill Clinton signed a bill that allocated roughly U.S.$800 million for counternarcotics assistance in Colombia, making Colombia the third leading recipient of U.S. foreign assistance in the world, behind Israel and Egypt.[1] In 2001 the incoming George W. Bush administration followed up on Clinton's request by approving another U.S.$400 million in annual aid for Colombia. Indeed, as this dramatic increase in assistance makes clear, in less than a decade Colombia has become one of the U.S. government's overriding foreign policy concerns.

What is most apparent in the story of U.S. policy toward Colombia is that U.S. concerns in Colombia remain inextricably linked with a politically volatile issue that has its roots in the domestic political arena—the war on drugs. Colombia's virtual monopoly on the export of cocaine destined for the United States since the early 1980s made it the prime focus of U.S. international narcotics interdiction efforts in subsequent years.

Complicating this foreign policy scenario is that, in addition to the drug traffickers, leftist guerrilla insurgents who have been fighting in the countryside and provincial cities since the 1960s are stronger today than ever.[2] Moreover, right-wing paramilitary groups have launched an undeclared war on suspected civilian supporters of the guerrillas, destabilizing an already chaotic situation in Colombia. The issue has been further clouded over the past decade as these guerrilla and paramilitary groups have increased their involvement in the drug trade, as well as expanded their operations in neighboring countries such as Ecuador and Venezuela.

This increasing violence and drug cultivation in Colombia has coincided with the evolution of the U.S. war on drugs. At the same time that this war on drugs was escalating in the 1980s and 1990s, the war against communists—the Cold War—was winding down. Consequently, the attention of the many U.S. government agencies dealing with intelligence and military issues quickly turned from the Soviet Union to the drug war. This shift resulted in much greater U.S. attention and scrutiny of events in drug-producing countries, especially those located in the Andes. By the late 1980s, U.S. international antidrug efforts began to focus on combating drugs at the source (i.e., the locales where drugs are cultivated) as opposed to interdicting them when they enter the United States. And since approximately 90 percent of the world's cocaine is produced in Colombia, this country became ground zero in the U.S. war on drugs. Motivated by the domestic need to solve the drug problem, the United States increasingly found itself trying to fight a drug war in the middle of a country mired in a violent and complex civil conflict.

The term that analysts have used to describe the U.S. government's seemingly unyielding focus on pursuing the drug war into Colombia is "narcotization." That is, virtually all aspects of U.S. involvement in Colombia were in some way linked to drugs. U.S. policy in Colombia has been narcotized since the 1980s, when the international component of the drug war came into full swing. In turn, narcotization has greatly influenced the U.S. stance toward other key issues of its bilateral relationship with Colombia, such as human rights, economic ties, and the Colombian government's ongoing peace process with leftist guerrilla groups.

This is not to say that the U.S. policy of narcotization was static; rather, the U.S. drug war agenda swung widely between the extreme policies of isolation to cooperation: when Washington believed that the Colombian government was cooperating on the drug front, relations were strong and the Colombian government was supported; when Washington felt that the Colombian government was not acting appropriately, relations quickly chilled or even froze, as was the case during Ernesto Samper's presidency (1994–1998). But regardless of whether relations between Washington and Bogotá were warm or cool, the underlying primacy of the drug war never wavered.

In order to fully understand the nature of U.S. policy in Colombia, it is necessary to trace the course of U.S. involvement in Colombia all the way back to the early nineteenth century, when Colombia won its independence from Spain. What is readily apparent is that, before the United States began its drug war, the normal state of the U.S.-Colombian relationship was relatively cordial in nature, free of much of the suspicion and animosity that often characterized U.S. relations with other Latin American states. While a number of factors explain this unusually high level of cooperation between the two countries, one reason in particular is that both Bogotá and Washington shared the common goals of promoting political stability, economic growth, and most important, anticommunism.

This meeting of the minds gradually broke down as the U.S. national interest in Colombia switched from fighting communists to fighting drugs. This meant that during the 1980s and 1990s cooperation was often replaced by suspicion, bilateralism with unilateralism. Today it remains to be seen whether the two countries can return to the cooperative climate that dominated the pre–drug war years. Within this analysis of the evolution of U.S. policy toward Colombia, this book will focus on the two key episodes of the contemporary bilateral relationship: the presidential administrations of Ernesto Samper and Andrés Pastrana.

U.S. POLICY DURING THE SAMPER AND PASTRANA ADMINISTRATIONS

The Samper Administration: 1994–1998

During the years of Ernesto Samper's presidency, the U.S.-Colombian bilateral relationship was deeply strained, and often a normal relationship barely existed. The drug war issue played an especially integral role in the policy process during this time, since virtually all U.S. officials involved firmly believed that Samper's presidential campaign had received several million dollars from the Cali drug cartel. This focus on Samper exacerbated an already delicate bilateral relationship as, for the first time since the drug war began in the 1980s, the United States shifted its counternarcotics strategies from focusing on arresting drug kingpins and interdicting drug production to aggressively and publicly attempting to bring down the scandal-ridden but democratically elected president of Colombia. This conflict made the relationship between the United States and the Samper administration one of the most abrasive episodes in U.S.–Latin American relations since the end of the Cold War. This fact is probably best exemplified when the United States revoked Samper's visa in July 1996, making him only the second head of state to receive this dubious honor.[3]

What also makes this particular case interesting is that during the Samper years the U.S. government did not consider Colombia a "crisis" foreign policy case, like that of Kosovo or Iraq; Colombia therefore did not receive the attention of high-level U.S. foreign policy officials such as the secretary of state or the national security adviser. In fact, during these years there were only a few episodes when then secretary of state Warren Christopher publicly addressed an issue related to Colombia. Instead, U.S. policy toward Colombia was overwhelmingly driven by upper-middle-level officials, chief among them the U.S. ambassador to Colombia, Myles Frechette, and the assistant secretary of state for international narcotics and law enforcement, Robert Gelbard.

In many ways, Frechette and Gelbard became U.S. "viceroys" in Colombia—they formulated "Colombia policy" in a way that at times adhered to their own personal political agendas as much as it was any type of clearly formulated official U.S. policy originating in Foggy Bottom. These officials gained, by default, an amount of power and influence that was inconsistent with the level of their positions. In this sense, the Samper era shows how the United States conducts policy in a client state when important domestic-driven factors such as the drug war are involved, but when the country is not considered a foreign policy priority.

While U.S.-Colombian relations were virtually frozen during the Samper years, this did not mean that the United States was unable to execute its policies. Rather, we have the interesting paradox that although U.S.-Colombian relations during the Samper administration were at their lowest point in history, the United States was able to carry out its foreign policy toward Colombia—which at this time had become almost indistinguishable from U.S. drug policy toward Colombia—quite successfully in terms of continuing to prosecute the war on drugs. The solution to this puzzle is that Samper, lacking credibility on the drug issue due to the suspected links to the Cali cartel, had little choice but to cooperate with U.S. counternarcotics efforts, no matter how much he might have personally detested them. Furthermore, since the bilateral relationship became so polarized during Samper's tenure, the United States was often able to circumvent Samper and work directly with what it believed were trusted counternarcotics allies in Colombia's armed forces and national police. Consequently, the United States was free to pursue its foreign policy goals both within and outside the Samper administration.

There is no doubt that the U.S. government was uncomfortable working with the Samper administration; but there was much more behind the deterioration in U.S.-Colombian relations than just a moral stand by the United States. Rather, the U.S. stance toward the Samper administration had almost as much to do with U.S. counternarcotics policy as it did with whether Samper did indeed receive money from the Cali cartel. First, many of the most damaging revelations related to Samper's trustworthiness came well after the United States had already decertified Colombia for not doing enough on the drug front. This leads one to believe that if Samper had better satisfied U.S. counternarcotics demands the United States would have been more willing to overlook Samper's links to the drug cartels. Second, confronted with a strategy that had failed to curb the flow of narcotics into the United States, the State Department used the drug-tainted Samper administration as a convenient scapegoat to mollify a now Republican-controlled Congress that was demanding success on the drug front.

Conversely, by putting Samper on the defensive the United States was in fact able to exploit Samper's drug links by forcing him to do even more in the antidrug arena than he normally would have done had he never been suspected of receiving payments from the drug cartels. A reflection of the irony of this situation is that Ernesto Samper carried out Washington's wishes on the antidrug front with more vigor and success than any of his predecessors, including President César Gaviria (1990–1994), who was seen by many in Washington to be the archetype of a reliable antidrug ally.

After years of pursuing a set of policies that were intended to undermine Ernesto Samper's legitimacy as president of Colombia, the U.S. government came to realize that its policies were producing unexpected counterproductive effects. Above all, the United States realized that its anti-Samper policies were weakening the institution of the Colombian presidency at the very time that, due to increased revenues from involvement in the drug trade, guerrilla groups and paramilitary organizations were becoming stronger than ever and were beginning to threaten the very survival of the Colombian state.

Indeed, by the end of Samper's term in office the civil conflict was entering into an unprecedented phase of wanton violence and bloodshed. And thus, after four years of focusing almost exclusively on how it could remove Samper from office, Washington now realized that it had to focus on the increasingly unstable situation in Colombia. Colombia had now become a crisis for the United States, mandating the need for a strong relationship with Bogotá, a move the United States had never deemed necessary during the Samper years. Fortunately for the United States, by this time Ernesto Samper's term in office was just about over and Colombian law prevented him from running for reelection.

The Pastrana Administration: 1998–2002

Anxious to forget an era that was now considered counterproductive to the overall U.S. objective in Colombia and eager to embrace a new administration that it could work with in order to manage what it now perceived to be a crisis in Colombia, the U.S. government eagerly awaited the inauguration of Conservative Party candidate Andrés Pastrana in August 1998.[4] Indeed, U.S. officials were convinced that Pastrana was the reliable and pro-U.S. president that they badly needed in order to repair the damage done to the bilateral relationship—and more important, to the U.S.-led war on drugs—that occurred during the Samper years.

Yet while the Clinton administration received the newly elected president with open arms, the overwhelming U.S. focus on drugs did not dissipate. Instead, the United States made Pastrana's cooperation on U.S.-led drug efforts an underlying component of a warmer bilateral relationship. So while many aspects of Washington-Bogotá relations were significantly more positive than during the Samper years, narcotization did not end.

In 1999 the U.S. government presented the Pastrana administration with an unprecedented U.S.$1.3 billion aid package that consisted primarily of military-related armaments intended to assist the Colombian government in rolling back the gains made by the guerrillas and drug traffickers during the previous several years. When this aid package was approved by the U.S. Congress and signed into law by President Bill Clinton a year later, the United States had embarked on the most costly and highest profile initiative in the history of the war on drugs. It is unclear what this drastic escalation in involvement will ultimately mean for the situation in Colombia and for the future of the bilateral relationship. What is more certain is that there will be tremendous bureaucratic pressure from within the U.S. government to continue the drug war in its present form and place tremendous focus on international interdiction efforts in the Andes. This is mostly due to the reality that over the past fifteen years the war on drugs has become institutionalized within the U.S. government's policy process, an occurrence that necessitates continuous annual funding for U.S. government agencies involved in antidrug efforts. The U.S. war on drugs has taken on a life of its own, an inertial drive that will continue regardless of its success in actually reducing the amount of illegal drugs that enter the United States.

Upon leaving office, President Dwight Eisenhower warned the American public of the creeping "military industrial complex," a situation where continuous expenditures on strategic weapons to counter the threat from the Soviet Union would eventually require even greater amounts of spending regardless of the strategic reality. Today, with regard to the war on drugs, U.S. policy might be characterized as the "military industrial narcotics complex": the budgets of U.S. government agencies involved in the drug war and the billions of dollars in military hardware that the United States sends to the Andes have become almost self-perpetuating.

COLOMBIA IN POST–COLD WAR CONTEXT

Most scholars of U.S.–Latin American relations agree that U.S. policies toward Latin America during the Cold War were dominantly concerned with the threat of communist infiltration and expansion in the region. Even if it meant allying itself with authoritarian regimes or helping to overthrow democratically elected governments, the United States spent considerable effort pursuing its regional security objectives, above all preventing communism from gaining a foothold in the hemisphere.[5] With the collapse of the Soviet Union and the compromise of Marxist-Leninist ideology largely across the globe, the United States can no longer use this framework to formulate policy in the region. Accordingly, there must be a new model for understanding U.S. foreign and security policies in the hemisphere.

Yet in the decade since the end of the Cold War, it has proved difficult to create convincing new explanatory paradigms.[6] This book argues that the overriding U.S. priorities—including security concerns—in Latin America since the end of the Cold War are increasingly linked to "intermestic" issues (combining international and domestic concerns), such as immigration and the war on drugs.[7] This book addresses how this intermestic-driven context has been especially influential in the case of U.S. policy toward Colombia. Specifically, in intermestic-driven cases such as Colombia, U.S. foreign policy tends to be characterized by competition among the involved U.S. agencies, personalized diplomacy, and greater intervention in the domestic political situation of the foreign country.

The debate surrounding U.S. policy toward Colombia was not as polemical as had been the case with, for example, U.S. policy toward Central America in the 1980s. If one glances at the dozens of congressional hearings that dealt with Colombia during the past ten years, one might conclude that there were sharp disagreements within the U.S. government over the nature of U.S. policies, especially between Congress and the State Department. Yet with a closer look it becomes clear that these ostensibly acerbic political disputes were actually episodes in which both sides generally agreed with each other. While some U.S. policymakers expressed concern over the human rights implications and lack of an exit strategy, the main disagreements arose, for example, not over *whether* to send helicopters to the Colombian National Police, but over *how many* should be sent.

Coexistent with this bureaucratic interpretation of U.S. policy toward Colombia is the fact that the general consensus on the drug war— that it is aligned with U.S. national interests—tends to make policy more realist.[8] Thus U.S. policy toward Colombia produces the unusual result of being at once bureaucratic and realist. On one level it is characterized by intense competition among government agencies, seemingly devoid of any type of overarching strategic policy, all reflecting a bureaucratic analysis. At the same time, U.S. policy toward Colombia is marked by a consensus that crosses ideological boundaries, united in the realist belief that the war on drugs is both necessary and vital to U.S. national interests.

That this level of agreement over U.S. policy toward Colombia almost invariably revolved around counternarcotics issues is yet another indication that drugs had so overtaken other bilateral issues (e.g., government-guerrilla peace talks, human rights, commercial ties) as to make them largely nonexistent by comparison. Thus, the answer to why the United States was willing to allow its bilateral relationship with Colombia to implode has its roots in the domestic-driven, national interest concern that is the drug war. As we will see in the analysis of U.S. policy in Colombia, ultimately it is the national interest concern, in this case the drug war, that overrides the bureaucratic political factors, thus making U.S. policy surprisingly realist.

These findings hold important ramifications for how we understand current and future hemispheric-wide trends in U.S. policy, as Colombia represents the type of potential foreign policy crisis that the United States will be confronted with in the post–Cold War era.[9] While these types of crises will not be common, when they occur they will hold

Washington's attention and the threat to regional stability will be considerable. Moreover, the U.S. response to these crises—while still highly influenced by domestic political concerns—will ultimately be characterized as realist policies, reflecting the dominance of perceived national interest over bureaucratic factors.

CONTEMPORARY U.S.–LATIN AMERICAN RELATIONS: OUT OF THE WHIRLPOOL?

U.S. policy toward Latin America over the course of the past decade can be perhaps best characterized by Peter Smith's label "the age of uncertainty."[10] This phrase reflects the fact that there is no clear way to characterize the often vague and ill-defined characteristics of contemporary U.S. policy toward Latin America. What is clear, however, is that the nature of U.S. policy in the Western Hemisphere has changed dramatically following the end of the Cold War.[11] Above all, the overriding U.S. security and diplomatic priorities in Latin America are now increasingly linked to these intermestic issues, such as immigration and the war on drugs.[12]

When the Cold War ended a decade ago, some scholars of U.S.–Latin American relations predicted that a new era would emerge in which multilateralism and dialogue would replace the coercion and unilateralism of the Cold War; others believed that the U.S. policy toward Latin America in the post–Cold War era would essentially resemble that of the Cold War, the only difference being that, instead of communists, the U.S. policymakers would surely devise new enemies to justify U.S. hegemony in the region.[13] Lars Schoultz is one of most vociferous of these scholars: "[W]hen the Soviet Union disappeared and U.S. security interests no longer required the same level of dominance, Washington identified new problems—everything from drug trafficking to dictatorship to financial mismanagement—and moved to increase its control over Latin America."[14] There are many who might take issue with Schoultz's conspiracy theory depiction of U.S. policy in Latin America in the 1990s, but there is nonetheless wide agreement that the United States no longer has the clear-cut framework of anticommunism to guide its hemispheric policies.[15]

The key to understanding the nature of the new phase in U.S. hemispheric relations lies in the analysis of a crucial causal variable—the hegemonic presumption. The hegemonic presumption is the belief on

the part of the United States that it has a right—and often an obliga-
tion—to intervene in the affairs of its own backyard, whether it be in
the name of security, economic interests, or anticommunism.[16]

As we will see, the case of Colombia suggests that the U.S. hegemonic presumption continues in Latin America, but usually only when
intermestic issues are involved. Several scholars of U.S.–Latin American relations made the assertion during the years following the fall of
the Berlin Wall that we could expect to see domestic issues like drugs
and immigration replace communism as the U.S. impetus and justification for continued influence in Latin America. Abraham Lowenthal, for
example, has written:

> Issues at the heart of U.S.-Latin relations in the 1990s will increas-
> ingly be "intermestic"—based on the international spillover of do-
> mestic concerns and involving both international and domestic aspects
> and actors. . . . In sum, Latin America will be of heightened impor-
> tance to the United States. For those who have seen the world almost
> exclusively in Cold War terms, the events of the past year have made
> Latin America seem virtually irrelevant, likely, as some say, to "fall
> off the map" of U.S. concerns. But as U.S. interests and energies turn
> inward to domestic challenges, Latin America may well be increas-
> ingly pertinent. Far from becoming irrelevant, Latin America's prob-
> lems and opportunities will be increasingly our own.[17]

While Lowenthal is correct in predicting the growing influence of intermestic issues in U.S.–Latin American relations, we will still need to
dig deeper into the U.S. policymaking process to see exactly why and
how particular intermestic issues might dominate U.S.–Latin American
relations in the coming decades.[18]

Robert Pastor's work helps open up the "black box" of government
decisionmaking in order to provide clues to the composition of intermestic issues.[19] Specifically, Pastor divides U.S. policymakers into two
camps: "conservatives" and "liberals." Conservatives uphold the national interest to the exclusion of any other and tend to see changes in
the international system as direct threats to the national interest. On the
other extreme, liberals do not believe that the national interest is inextricably linked to national identity and therefore often do not see the
need for, say, military action to deal with external issues. Pastor writes:

> Conservatives focus on a relatively narrower idea of U.S. interests and
> a military-based definition of power. They believe that the United

States should approach problems unilaterally and in a practical and forceful problem-solving manner. Liberals give higher priority to the moral dimension and to what Joseph S. Nye calls "soft power," which derives from the American model. They look at social and economic causes of the crisis, try to understand the issues from the other's perspective, and rely on multilateral, diplomatic approaches.[20]

The continual shifting of influence between the conservatives and the liberals can be clearly seen in the course of U.S. policy in Latin America during the Cold War. John F. Kennedy's Alliance for Progress, the Peace Corps, the Organization of American States (OAS), and Jimmy Carter's pro–human rights policies are just a few examples of the liberal approach to hemispheric relations.[21] The 1954 CIA-backed overthrow of Jacobo Arbenz in Guatemala, Richard Nixon's policies toward Socialist president Salvador Allende in Chile, and the Reagan administration's policies in Central America in the 1980s are examples of the conservative approach.[22]

The question then becomes one of which policy stance will dominate the post–Cold War era. The case of Colombia definitely points toward the conservative approach, as the U.S. war on drugs in Colombia definitely resembles a unilateral crusade. Yet paradoxically this might not mean that we should expect U.S. policy in Latin America in general to be conservative. Rather, when certain hot-button intermestic issues are involved we should expect the United States to act in a conservative manner; when no intermestic issues are involved, such as arms proliferation or disaster relief, we should expect U.S. policy to be more liberal.

As during the Cold War when the policy of anticommunism undoubtedly influenced liberal policies like the Alliance for Progress, conservative viewpoints in the future will have the ability to affect liberal issues. For example, in Colombia we will see how the U.S. war on drugs (a conservative issue) is heavily influencing the manner in which the United States views the current Colombian peace process (a liberal issue). Thus, today, we should expect that intermestic-driven issues—which are often conservative issues—will possess the potential to spill over into other areas where we should normally expect liberalism to hold.

Before deliberating whether U.S. policy toward Latin America in the post–Cold War era will be liberal or conservative, we first must ask whether the United States will even care about Latin America. Pastor's framework of "introversion" versus "extroversion" is useful in that it explains how the United States tends to fluctuate between the introversion of focusing solely on domestic issues (isolationism) and the extroversion of focusing on international efforts such as World War II or the 1991 Gulf War.[23] When this concept is applied to U.S. policy toward Latin America, it appears that the U.S. position will be one of introversion (i.e., neglect), unless a key intermestic issue is involved. If this is indeed the case, and if we assume that introversion tends to generate liberal foreign policies by default, we can expect U.S. policy toward Latin America to be characterized by benign neglect and liberal policies, periodically disrupted by episodes of conservative interventions.

Once the liberal-conservative framework is taken into consideration, Abraham Lowenthal's prediction that U.S. policy in Latin America will be characterized by the "unilateral activist impulse" becomes easier to comprehend, as conservative episodes will surely provoke this type of intervention.[24] Still, these impulses will be the exception and not the rule to U.S. policy in Latin America; and when they occur they usually will be driven by intermestic issues and will be intense and highly unilateral in nature. Tellingly, three of the most pressing U.S. actions in Latin America since the end of the Cold War—the 1989 invasion of Panama (the only U.S. post–Cold War invasion in Latin America), the 1994 intervention in Haiti, and the continued embargo against Cuba—can all be defined as being cases of intermestic issues driving intermittent "unilateral activist impulses" on the part of the United States.[25]

Before analyzing contemporary U.S. policy toward Colombia within this conceptual framework, we must first review the evolution of U.S. policy in Colombia as well as the roots of Colombia's narcotics trade and civil conflict.

NOTES

1. Office of Management and Budget, Executive Office of the President, 2000.

2. See Russell Crandall, "The End of Civil Conflict in Colombia: The Military, Paramilitaries, and a New Role for the United States," *SAIS Review* 19, no. 1 (Winter–Spring 1999): 223–237; and Marc Chernick, "Negotiating Peace Amid Multiple Forms of Violence: The Protracted Search for a Settlement to the Armed Conflicts in Colombia," in *Comparative Peace Processes in Latin America,* edited by Cynthia J. Arnson (Washington, D.C.: Woodrow Wilson Center Press, 1999), pp. 159–200.

3. The other head of state to have his visa revoked was Austrian president Kurt Waldheim in 1987.

4. Andrés Pastrana defeated Liberal Party candidate Horacio Serpa in June 1998.

5. For an overview of the final years of U.S. policy in Latin America during the Cold War, see Gaddis Smith, *The Last Years of the Monroe Doctrine: 1945–1993* (New York: Hill & Wang, 1994); Peter Smith, *Talons of the Eagle: Dynamics of U.S.–Latin American Relations* (Oxford: Oxford University Press, 1996); and Lars Schoultz, *Beneath the United States: A History of U.S. Policy Toward Latin America* (Cambridge: Harvard University Press, 1998), pp. 316–386.

6. See Michael C. Desch, "Why Latin America May Miss the Cold War," in *International Security and Democracy: Latin America and the Caribbean in the Post–Cold War Era,* edited by Jorge Domínguez (Pittsburgh: University of Pittsburgh Press, 1998), pp. 245–265; and Albert Fishlow, "The Foreign Policy Challenge for the United States," in *The United States and the Americas: A Twenty-First-Century View,* edited by Albert Fishlow and James Jones (New York: W. W. Norton, 1999), pp. 197–206.

7. See Bayless Manning, "The Congress, the Executive, and Intermestic Affairs: Three Proposals," *Foreign Affairs* 55, no. 2 (1977): 309. For a look at how intermestic issues have been applied to post–Cold War U.S. policy toward Latin America, see Abraham F. Lowenthal, "United States–Latin American Relations at the Century's Turn: Managing the Intermestic Agenda," in *The United States and the Americas,* pp. 109–136. For more on the U.S. security involvement in Latin America, see Jorge Domínguez, "The Future of Inter-American Relations" (Inter-American Dialogue working paper, Washington, D.C., June 1999), pp. 9–12. The two major episodes of concerted U.S. involvement/intervention in Latin America since the end of the Cold War—the 1989 invasion of Panama (drugs) and the 1994 intervention in Haiti (immigration)—can be directly attributed to domestic issues.

8. Here "realism" is defined as U.S. policymakers acting "rationally" and in general agreement in order to pursue the perceived national interest. According to Brian White, in comments he attributes to Joseph Nye, for the realist "the state, rather than any other international actor, is regarded as the foreign policy making unit. More importantly, the state, or rather the government acting on behalf of the state, is treated for analytical purposes as a unitary, monolithic actor; in other words, as a collectivity whose behaviour is broadly analogous to that of a purposeful individual." See Brian White, "Analyzing Foreign Policy: Problems and Approaches," in *Understanding Foreign Policy: The Foreign Policy Systems Approach,* edited by Michael Clarke and Brian White (Brookfield, Vt.: Gower, 1989), p. 11.

9. For the most recent analysis of contemporary U.S. security policy in the Americas, see Paul Buchanan, "Chameleon, Tortoise, or Toad? The Changing U.S. Security Role in Contemporary Latin America," in *International Security and Democracy,* pp. 266–288. For an overview of U.S. Cold War security policy in Latin America, see Lars Schoultz, *National Security and United States Policy Toward Latin America* (Princeton: Princeton University Press, 1987).

10. See Smith, *Talons of the Eagle,* pp. 217–248.

11. For a recent analysis of U.S.–Latin American security models, see Augusto Varas, "From Coercion to Partnership: A New Paradigm for Security Cooperation in the Western Hemisphere," in *The United States and Latin America,* pp. 46–63. See also Abraham F. Lowenthal, "Changing U.S. Interests and Policies in a New World," in *The United States and Latin America,* pp. 64–85.

12. See Desch, "Why Latin America May Miss the Cold War."

13. For the most current discussion of U.S.–Latin American relations, see *Journal of Interamerican Studies and World Affairs* 39, no. 1 (Spring 1997), a special issue on U.S.-Latin American relations.

14. Schoultz, *Beneath the United States,* p. xiv.

15. See Joseph S. Tulchin, "Hemispheric Relations in the Twenty-first Century," *Journal of Interamerican Studies and World Affairs* 39, no. 1 (Spring 1997): 33–38; and Jorge Castañeda, "Latin America and the End of the Cold War," *World Policy Journal* 7, no. 3 (Summer 1990): 469–492.

16. See Abraham F. Lowenthal, "Ending the Hegemonic Presumption: The United States and Latin America," *Foreign Affairs* 55, no. 1 (Autumn 1976): 199–213.

17. Abraham F. Lowenthal, "Rediscovering Latin America," *Foreign Affairs* (Fall 1990): 38.

18. See Abraham F. Lowenthal, "United States–Latin American Relations."

19. Robert Pastor, *Whirlpool: U.S. Foreign Policy Toward Latin America and the Caribbean* (Princeton: Princeton University Press, 1992).

20. Ibid., p. 32.

21. For more on the Alliance for Progress, see Smith, *Talons of the Eagle,* pp. 142–162.

22. For more on the Guatemala case, see Piero Gleijeses, *Shattered Hope: The Guatemalan Revolution and the United States* (Princeton: Princeton University Press, 1991). For the Reagan administration's policies toward Central America, see Cynthia Arnson, *Crossroads: Congress, the President, and Central America, 1976–1993* (University Park: Pennsylvania State University Press, 1993), pp. 53–227. Democratic presidents were more than willing to carry out conservative policies, with Lyndon Johnson's decision to invade the Dominican Republic in 1965 being one such example.

23. Robert Pastor, "The Clinton Administration and the Americas: The Postwar Rhythm and Blues," *Journal of Interamerican Studies and World Affairs* 38, no. 4 (Winter 1996–1997): 99–123.

24. Abraham F. Lowenthal, "Changing U.S. Interests," p. 69.

25. The case of U.S. policy toward Cuba can be classified as an intermestic issue, as it is generally accepted that a significant share of this policy is formulated under consideration of the domestic political influence of the highly influential Cuban exile community.

2

The Evolution of U.S. Policy
Toward Colombia

*More startling and less well known, when in 1857 the United States was press-
ing New Granada [Colombia] for compensation for the deaths of American citizens in riots in Panama and New Granadan leaders despaired of obtaining
British protection, President Mariano Ospina Rodríguez proposed to Washington the annexation of the entire republic of New Granada by the United States.
Ospina reasoned that in view of the United States' inexorable expansion, as
demonstrated in the war with Mexico in 1846–48 and in the filibuster adven-
tures in Nicaragua of the 1850s, New Granada would inevitably be swallowed
up sooner or later. Better to get it over with quickly, without unnecessary
bloodshed, particularly considering the probability that rule by the United
States would bring stability and security of property.*

—Frank Safford[1]

Stephen Randall has written that over the past two centuries there have
been several layers to U.S.-Colombian relations.[2] On one layer there has
been the traditional antagonism and mistrust that historically has been
characteristic of U.S.–Latin American relations in general. On another
layer, however, there is a unique legacy of bilateral treaties, resolution of
disputes, and a general meeting of the minds that ensured cordial relations between Washington and Bogotá.

While Randall's notion of several layers to U.S.-Colombian relations is accurate, it is also necessary to emphasize the international context in which these relations take place. Beginning with the many disputes over the ownership and construction of an interoceanic canal and
continuing through counternarcotics issues of more recent times, U.S.-
Colombian relations must be viewed as interaction between a growing
superpower and a relatively weak developing country. This uneven relationship was especially acute during the late nineteenth and early

twentieth centuries—a time of heightened concern in the bilateral relationship due to interoceanic canal issues—as the United States was
emerging as one of the world's strongest powers and Colombia was still
recovering from decades of devastating civil wars. As the twentieth century progressed, U.S. concerns in Colombia shifted from the Panama
Canal to issues of trade (1920s), antifascism (1930s), and most important, anticommunism (the Cold War, 1945–1990).[3]

Indeed, as the Cold War began to take hold following the end of
World War II, preventing communist expansion into Latin America became the overriding U.S. policy priority in the region. Consequently, as
was the case in many other Latin American countries, U.S. policy in
Colombia during these years emphasized national security and ideological issues. However, as we will see, unlike the often more combative
relationships that the United States held with other Latin American
countries such as Mexico and Brazil, U.S. Cold War–era relations with
Colombia were remarkably cooperative.

Yet since the advent of the U.S. war on drugs in the 1980s, this
legacy of bilateral cooperation has periodically disintegrated, generally
replaced by unilateralism on the part of the United States and suspicion
and frustration on the part of Colombia. It is within this context of narcotization that an analysis of contemporary U.S. policy toward Colombia must be viewed. Moreover, tracing the evolution of narcotization al-
lows us to better understand why the United States pursued a highly
unilateral policy toward Colombia for most of the 1990s. This chapter
will chronicle the salient episodes of U.S.-Colombian relations over the
past two centuries. Because contemporary U.S.-Colombian relations can
only be understood within the context of the war on drugs, special emphasis will be placed on the course of U.S. policy since the United
States escalated its counternarcotics efforts in the 1980s.

THE EARLY YEARS: 1820–1932

U.S.-Colombian relations began in essence in 1821 when Spanish America's independence leader Simón Bolívar and his troops defeated Spanish forces at the Battle of Carabobo, which resulted in the overthrow of
Spanish rule in Colombia. Until this point, for a number of mostly domestic political reasons, the United States had been ambivalent about
granting recognition to the Latin American rebel movements. Thus, during the wars of independence in the 1810s and early 1820s, U.S. support

of Latin American independence movements was generally limited to rhetorical statements. Yet Bolívar's resounding triumph convinced U.S. president James Monroe that it was now time to recognize the newly independent republics. In 1822 the U.S. Congress agreed with Monroe's decision and appropriated U.S.$100,000 to establish diplomatic missions in several countries in Latin America, including Colombia.[4]

But even though the United States had now recognized the new republics, the subsequent Panamanian Congress in Colombia in 1826 revealed a lack of harmony between U.S. and Latin American interests. This conference was of major importance to the newly independent republics in Latin America as many Latin American leaders—including Bolívar—hoped that the meeting would serve to promote cooperation and unity among the participating nations of the hemisphere. However, Bolívar was not in favor of inviting the United States, which was ultimately done by Colombia's vice president, Francisco Santander, while Bolívar was away.[5] The United States, not wanting to overtly support activities promoting greater independence, reacted ambivalently and belatedly to this Latin American initiative.

While the United States wanted Spain evicted from the region, it was still unsure about the idea of the "Latins" governing themselves, and many Southern U.S. politicians were worried that eventually notions of independence would apply to their slaves.[6] Additionally, the concept of pan-Americanism—whereby the countries of the Americas would form a sort of political and economic confederation—unsettled many in Washington who preferred separate Latin American republics. Also, at this time there was an incipient move to express U.S. dominion over the hemisphere, exemplified by James Monroe's famous "Doctrine" speech that addressed this issue in 1823. While at this time the United States was still too weak to actually replace Spain as the hegemonic power in the Caribbean and South America, the rhetoric served as an indication that the United States was eager to assume a more assertive role in the hemisphere. Not surprisingly, therefore, the United States played little part in the Panamanian Congress; in fact, it only sent two representatives to the conference, a gesture that might have been the first indication that U.S.–Latin American relations would not be always harmonious. To make matters worse, one representative died on the journey to Panama and the other arrived after the Congress had ended.

The disagreement over U.S. policy toward the newly independent Latin American republics fell largely along sectional lines—the North supported recognition as a way to promote a potential trading partner;

the South saw recognition as the beginning of what would become a cheap competitor to its agriculture-based economy. The South, however, was not uniformly anti-recognition, revealed best by pro-recognition Southern politician Henry Clay, although his contrarian position was mainly due to his personal anti-Spanish sentiments and his wish to embarrass the Monroe administration. Referring to the controversy—which included a duel between Clay, then secretary of state, and Virginia senator John Randolph—over whether or not to participate in the Panamanian Congress, Lars Schoultz writes:

> Boys will be boys, of course, and everyone recognized that neither this Yankee machismo nor the heated Congressional debate had much to do with the wisdom of attending an international conference. Rather, the debate was an early example of a now-common aspect of United States policy toward Latin America: the tendency of unconnected U.S. domestic political disputes to spill over into inter-American relations. This had already been seen in the Clay-Adams dispute over recognition, which was in large measure a struggle for leadership of the Whigs, and which featured both Clay's May 1821 pro-recognition speech in Lexington, Kentucky and Adams's scorching 4th of July response. In the case of the Panama conference, the disputes were over two domestic issues: slavery (the Panama agenda included consideration of the recognition of Haiti) and the Adams-Clay "theft" of the White House.[7]

While the first U.S. encounters with the newly independent Colombia did not begin auspiciously, relations remained stable for the next several decades. More than anything else, the issue of interoceanic travel came to dominate U.S. policy toward Colombia.[8] In fact, as early as 1850, even though canal-motivated U.S. involvement in Central America would not physically begin for several decades, the United States began laying the groundwork for what it hoped would be an interoceanic canal. The Clayton-Bulwer Treaty, signed in 1850 between the United States and Great Britain, was designed to mitigate competition over any possible canal construction. Most important, the Clayton-Bulwer Treaty marked the arrival of the United States as a credible international player in the region. While it would only be in the 1890s that the United States would seriously exert power in Central America, this treaty showed that the United States was becoming more assertive in its diplomacy.[9]

The geographic characteristics of Colombia's northernmost department (present-day Panama) made it one of the most desirable sites for the construction of a canal within Central America.[10] Before a canal route had been determined, U.S. commercial involvement in Colombia was largely confined to railroad construction, which eventually ferried cargo and persons across the isthmus. The 1846 Bidlack Treaty committed the United States to guaranteeing Colombia's sovereignty over the isthmus in the province of Panama in return for permission to build a bicoastal road. Increasingly, however, U.S. commercial interests in the 1860s and 1870s were subsumed by continued U.S.-Colombian tensions over canal route negotiations. Indeed, several agreements that would have granted the United States territory for building a canal broke down, usually due to Colombian opposition.

The United States that Colombia negotiated with in the 1860s and 1870s barely resembled the United States of the 1890s and 1900s.[11] The U.S. economy grew rapidly in the latter half of the nineteenth century and by 1898 it was prepared to exert this newfound power in its own backyard in the Caribbean as well as in the Philippines. After painlessly defeating the imploding Spanish empire during the "splendid little war" in 1898, the United States, under the firm guidance of President Theodore Roosevelt, finally began to seriously consider the issue of canal construction in Central America.[12] While the United States increased its power and its willingness to use this power abroad, Colombia remained fragmented and poor, characterized by the internecine civil wars in the late nineteenth century that devastated the domestic economy.[13] Thus the stage was set for the United States to wield its "big stick" against Colombia in its efforts to obtain the territory needed for canal construction.[14]

The United States made its first attempt to negotiate access to a canal route with Colombia at the start of the twentieth century, best exemplified by the Hay-Herrán Treaty of 1903.[15] This treaty would have given the United States the right to construct a canal through Panama and hold a six-mile-wide strip of territory for 100 years; Colombia would receive U.S.$10 million initially, followed by annual payments of U.S.$250,000.[16] On March 17, 1903, the U.S. Congress approved the treaty, but soon after the Colombian Congress rejected it unanimously.[17] The U.S. government, especially since Theodore Roosevelt had taken office and promoted his active, unilateral vision of U.S. foreign policy, quickly decided that if Colombia would not negotiate U.S. access for canal construction, it would have to take more aggressive measures in order to secure the territory from Colombia.

In 1903, local elites in Panama—a region with a historically uneasy relationship with the national government in Bogotá in which independence sentiments had simmered for decades—seized control of the department in a bloodless coup.[18] In a display of power politics, the

United States encouraged the secessionist leaders to revolt and almost immediately recognized the rebel government as independent.[19] Any ideas that the Colombian government had of quelling the rebellion were cut short by the presence of the U.S. gunboat *Nashville* anchored off the Panamanian coast. On November 3, 1903, the *Nashville* steamed into the harbor at port of Colón, sending a clear message: the United States would back Panamanian independence, even if it had to shed blood to do so.[20] The next day Panama declared its independence and three days later the United States established diplomatic relations.

Now that the United States finally had its friendly government in place in the form of the Panamanian rebels, it was prepared to negotiate another treaty of access to a canal route. To the surprise of few, U.S. Secretary of State John Hay signed the Hay–Bunau-Varilla Treaty with the representatives of the Panamanian "government" in 1903, and received U.S. Senate approval on February 24, 1904, giving the United States a ten-mile-wide zone.[21] In return Panama was to receive a U.S.$10 million lump-sum payment and annual payments of U.S.$250,000, as well as a guarantee that the United States would protect its newly acquired national sovereignty. U.S.-led construction of the canal started shortly thereafter and concluded in 1914, marking an extraordinary feat of human engineering.

The manner in which Panama gained its independence proved to be a sore point in U.S.-Colombian relations, continuing throughout construction of the canal and well after.[22] The matter was finally settled in 1921 with the Urrutia-Thomson Treaty, which required the United States to pay to Colombia an indemnity of U.S.$25 million.[23] Interestingly, Theodore Roosevelt, while out of the White House, had found a new vocation as one of the most vociferous and acerbic critics of long-time political rival and then president Woodrow Wilson. Not surprisingly, Roosevelt was vehemently opposed to any treaty with Colombia. But Wilson, who felt that the United States had a moral duty to settle this issue with Colombia, supported the concept of a treaty, although it was not officially ratified until after the Harding administration took office.

The 1920s saw a shift in U.S. policy toward Colombia, from the canal to commercial issues.[24] Specifically, Colombia's boom in coffee production and exports increasingly gave it greater weight on the trade front; in turn this evolution served to increase its economic ties to the United States, a relationship that endures to the present.[25] Drawn to a more stable Colombia, U.S. investors moved in, especially in the oil, mining, and agricultural sectors. By the end of the decade, U.S. investors had sent approximately U.S.$130 million in investment, a substantial amount of money when compared with other Andean countries such as Ecuador and Peru.[26] While the Great Depression of the 1930s greatly diminished U.S. imports of Colombian goods and direct investment, the economic ties created in this era withstood this tremendous shock. Colombia subsequently became one of the most reliable and efficient trading partners that the United States had in South America during the Cold War.

GOOD NEIGHBORS

Following the War of 1898, U.S. policy during the first thirty years of the twentieth century in Latin America (especially in Central America and the Caribbean) was marked by its unilateral character, one intent on preserving U.S. economic and political interests in the region. Indeed, according to Peter Smith's calculations, between 1898 and 1933 the United States conducted over thirty interventions in Latin America, often involving the U.S. Marines.[27] Whether it was in Nicaragua (1912–1933) or the Dominican Republic (1916–1924), the United States was willing to send in the marines in order to stamp out instability, to ensure that U.S. economic interests were not threatened, and, in the words of Woodrow Wilson, to teach "the South American republics to elect good men."[28] As the disputes over Panama and the canal route make clear, Colombia did not escape the long arm of Uncle Sam.

This habitual policy of intervention began to change in the middle to late 1920s as the United States began to tire of its protracted involvement in the domestic affairs of its Latin American neighbors. This was especially true in Nicaragua, where nationalist leader Augusto Sandino inflicted heavy casualties on marines who were occupying the country at that time. Disillusionment with intervention was coupled with a growing consensus within the U.S. government that it was in the national interest to improve relations with the nations of Latin America. This newfound interest in better relations with Latin America stemmed in part from the incipient U.S. economic depression that many believed could be helped by better trade relations with Latin America. The rise of fascism in Europe also led Washington to increasingly rely on better relations with Latin American nations in order to check this worrisome expansion. Begun during the Hoover administration, the result of this new perspective was the creation under Franklin Roosevelt of the Good Neighbor Policy in the 1930s and 1940s, which ushered in a period of relatively strong, cooperative U.S.–Latin American relations.[29]

Believing that Nazi influence was gaining ground in the region, during the period of the Good Neighbor Policy the United States made stopping the "German threat" the most pressing priority of its Colombia policy. The high degree of cooperation between the United States and Colombia on this issue reveals the widespread cooperation that characterized relations during this period. The United States therefore welcomed the 1938 election of the moderate Liberal Party presidential candidate Eduardo Santos, who harbored pro-U.S. leanings and was viewed as a model of the type of South American president who would help the United States check Nazi incursions into the Western Hemisphere.

One interesting example of how the United States involved itself in Colombian affairs to battle fascism revolved around Colombia's airline industry. With war against Germany seemingly inevitable as the 1930s progressed, the United States became very concerned with the presence and influence that German nationals had in the airline industry in Colombia. The United States feared that Germany might then use Colombia as a seat from which to attack the United States. While in hindsight this scenario might seem somewhat farfetched, at the time it was seen as a credible threat. In 1919 the airline SCADTA had been created as a Colombian-German consortium. In the 1930s the United States pressured the Colombian government to do something about this issue and the Colombians responded by creating a new national airline— Avianca. SCADTA was absorbed into Avianca, but not before almost all of the Germans had been purged from the company.[30] As this example shows, the Good Neighbor Policy was only partially altruistic: raw geostrategic concerns mattered as much to Washington as did the promotion of respectful bilateral relationships.

In the aftermath of World War II, the United States attempted to continue its Good Neighbor Policy in Latin America. Yet the growing fear of communism soon replaced the "good neighbor" as the motivating force in U.S. policy toward Latin America. In an act that was designed to create multilateral yet firmly anticommunist hemispheric organizations, the United States became the driving force behind the creation of the Organization of American States (OAS). In order to illustrate that Colombia was considered a strong ally of the United States, the inaugural meeting was held in Bogotá in 1948 in what the United States hoped would be seen as a commitment to promote cooperation and mutual security.

Coincidentally, during the OAS meetings in Bogotá, populist Liberal Party president Jorge Eliécer Gaitán was killed by an assassin's bullet.

The violence that erupted afterward, known in Colombia as the *Bogotazo,* shocked U.S. officials, who interpreted the episode as another example of communist agitation.[31] In statements that are indicative of the increasingly rigid view within the U.S. government that communism was at the root of all evil in Latin America, veteran U.S. diplomat Averell Harriman stated that "international communism" had attempted to exploit the assassination.[32] The State Department called the just-murdered Gaitán "a demagogic Liberal Party leader with an immense following."[33]

COLOMBIA AS COLD WAR PARADIGM

These types of hard-line comments by the United States were repeated for the next forty years throughout Latin America whenever the issue of communism was involved. But relative to many other Latin American nations that experienced heavy-handed meddling, coercion, and even interventions by the United States in the name of anticommunism, Colombia was largely immune from these pressures. This anomalous dearth of U.S.-Colombian antagonisms was driven predominantly by the fact that successive Colombian governments shared the U.S. concern about communist influence. This Western Hemisphere version of the "special relationship" between the United States and Colombia is best revealed by the fact that Colombia was the only Latin American nation to send troops, including the frigate *Almirante Padilla,* to support the United Nations (overwhelmingly run by the United States) in its efforts on the Korean peninsula in the early 1950s.[34]

During the first few decades of the Cold War the United States no doubt felt more comfortable with moderate, U.S.-leaning presidents in Latin America—especially if they were overtly anticommunist—than with the more left-leaning political reformers, such as Jacobo Arbenz in Guatemala in the early 1950s or João Goulart in Brazil in the early 1960s. The same was true for Colombia. Moderate presidents from the Liberal Party, such as Alberto Lleras Camargo (1958–1962) or Carlos Lleras Restrepo (1966–1970) were seen, in a manner similar to Eduardo Santos during the Good Neighbor years, as the type of reliable allies that Washington needed to stop communist infiltration in Latin America. Indeed, Colombia during the 1950s and 1960s was the paradigm of the relatively stable, pro-U.S. country that Washington greatly desired to encounter in the region, but that in actuality proved so elusive.

While Colombia's anticommunist stance contributed to a warm bilateral relationship, the strong U.S.-Colombian ties during the Cold War were not due solely to the fact that Colombian governments never veered toward Havana or Moscow. Rather there were a number of domestic issues that served to make Colombia a place unfavorable to communist infiltration. First, guerrilla movements sprang up throughout Colombia in the decades after the *Bogotazo,* but these movements were relatively unorganized at this time; they did not cooperate with one another and were more interested in the Colombian political scene than in promoting international communism. Moreover, if civil conflict in Colombia since 1946 is seen as the continuation of centuries-old disputes and hatreds and not as the beginnings of international communist revolution, it becomes clearer why such a violent and unstable country would actually *not* be an epicenter in the struggle against communism.

Since the United States considered Colombia to be firmly in the anticommunist camp, Washington made it a showcase for capitalist development and modernization during John F. Kennedy's vaunted Alliance for Progress, which began in 1961.[35] Between 1961 and 1965 Colombia received U.S.\$833 million in loans from the United States; the newly created U.S. Peace Corps sent approximately 700 volunteers by the mid-1960s; and Colombia became one of the hemisphere's prime recipients of U.S. military aid.

U.S. military relations with Colombia began to increase significantly in the 1950s before the advent of the Alliance for Progress. It was in that decade that the U.S. government established army, navy, and air force attaché offices in Bogotá. In 1952 the United States signed a "Military Assistance Agreement" with Colombia committing itself to helping the Colombian military in its efforts to promote hemispheric security. Following President Eisenhower's 1959 decision to increase involvement of the U.S. military in Colombia's "internal security problems," in 1961 the United States sent its first military training team (MTT) to Colombia to help train the country's military in areas related to intelligence capabilities. According to Dennis Rempe, the arrival of the MTTs signaled a significant increase in U.S. military involvement in Colombia: "Everything from supply, engineering, sanitation, and other civic actions projects, to intelligence, to counter-insurgency, psychological warfare, and special operations were taught. Indeed, more MTTs were sent to Colombia during this period than anywhere else in Latin America."[36]

As was the case on the political side, where the United States sought to cultivate its ties with moderate presidents, the U.S. military relationship with Colombia was seen as an effective and appropriate method through which to bolster the forces against communism and subversion. The reasoning was that if the Colombian military could be a respected, pro-U.S. institution, it would surely serve to promote hemispheric security against any threat that diverged from these same values. Interestingly, while communism no longer poses a threat to the U.S. notion of hemispheric stability, today U.S. military relations with Colombia are at their highest point in history, but this time over a new threat—drugs.

Because of the lack of a credible communist infiltration threat and the general pro-U.S. positions of various Colombian governments, relations between the two countries remained strong and predictable from the 1960s until the early 1980s. But if the United States did not perceive the threat of communism to be very great in Colombia, beginning in the 1970s the growing concern over drug production in Colombia caused Washington to dramatically alter its policies toward the country.

THE WAR ON DRUGS

> *U.S.-supported crop control, enforcement, and interdiction efforts in Colombia and Bolivia have not produced major reductions in coca and marijuana production and trafficking, and it is questionable whether major reductions will be achieved in the near future.*
> *—U.S. General Accounting Office[37]*

President Richard Nixon is credited with coining the phrase "war on drugs" on March 24, 1968. But while he was most likely referring only to a domestic war on drugs, this term is now mostly applied to U.S. international interdiction efforts. U.S. antidrug assistance to Colombia formally began in 1973 when the two countries signed a bilateral agreement allowing for this type of aid to be transferred. The issue of drugs followed a linear path from the 1970s to the first years of the twenty-first century, increasingly gaining importance to the United States and increasingly dominating U.S.-Colombian relations.[38] Former foreign service officer Robert Drexler describes the gradual but consistent increase in the U.S. focus on the drug issue:

> By 1978 . . . the drug syndicate had grown so powerful that the Colombian authorities had insufficient strength to overcome them. . . . [W]e had not foreseen it three or four years earlier. . . . American

authorities had become concerned about drug trafficking in Colombia
in the early 1970s and the Drug Enforcement Agency (DEA) stationed
a small number of agents in our embassy in Bogotá. There was no
sense of crisis in connection with the DEA operation, however, and
the narcotics issue was only one of several diplomatic problems facing
the embassy when Viron P. Vaky was the ambassador, never the most
important one.[39]

Viron "Pete" Vaky corroborates this point when he observes that during his ambassadorial tenure in Bogotá in the 1970s the drug issue was
growing in importance but never an integral part of the bilateral relationship: "It [the drug issue] was there. We had DEA guys in the embassy but it was not a central element of our policy. At that time there
were no cartels and little to no involvement in the cocaine trade. . . . No
one saw it [U.S. drug policy] reaching the proportions it did."[40]

The early 1980s marked a fundamental turning point in the new international war on drugs as the arrival of the Reagan administration ushered in a more assertive international drug interdiction policy. The new
administration quickly made drugs the primary focus of its relations
with Colombia. President Ronald Reagan's appointment of former Arizona State University professor Lewis A. Tambs as ambassador to
Colombia was one of the first signs that the United States was looking
to get tough on the drug issue in Latin America.[41] As a hard-liner on the
drug issue, the Reagan administration considered Tambs to be the perfect choice for Colombia. This became an important qualification for
subsequent U.S. ambassadors in Colombia as a good share of the new
U.S. antidrug resolve would be concentrated there, in a country whose
involvement in the international drug trade at that time consisted primarily in the production and export of marijuana.[42]

Colombia Tackles the Drug Issue

It was first during the administration of Liberal leader Julio César Turbay Ayala (1978–1982) that the Colombian government raised the stakes
in its war against drug traffickers.[43] Turbay was the first Colombian
president to declare war on the traffickers, prompted by the reality that
by the late 1970s Colombia had become the primary producer and ex-
porter of marijuana to the U.S. market. Some 10,000 metric tons of
marijuana were being produced annually by up to 50,000 small farmers.[44] But even if he realized that he needed to do something about the
rapidly expanding marijuana cultivation and export problem, Turbay

also realized that drug money was bringing an estimated U.S.$1.5–$4.1 billion in badly needed foreign exchange income. Nevertheless, Turbay cracked down on illicit drug cultivation, a move that ushered in an extended period of mutual cooperation between Washington and Bogotá with respect to antidrug efforts.[45]

While at this time Jamaica and Mexico were also major producers of marijuana destined for the United States, the U.S. government chose to place its diplomatic pressure on the Colombian government to become more involved in antidrug efforts. Specifically, Washington urged the Turbay administration to begin fumigating marijuana with the herbicide paraquat, which the Colombian government proceeded to do. Turbay also directed the military to increase its involvement in the antidrug campaign.

The culmination of Turbay's decision to bring a reluctant military that was more concerned with fighting the guerrilla insurgents into the fight against drugs was an operation in the Guajira peninsula, in the northernmost tip of the country, that targeted marijuana production. The operation utilized over 10,000 troops, who seized over 6,000 tons of marijuana, destroyed 10,000 marijuana plants, and confiscated 300 boats and aircraft. Yet marijuana cultivation moved to other parts of Colombia and also quickly returned to Guajira once the program ended.

In a backlash that would become common following antidrug operations, the Colombian government's operation provoked a high level of resentment from the local population, of which an estimated 100,000 persons were thought to be involved in the cultivation of marijuana.[46] However, the end result of the Turbay administration's escalation was that, in addition to moving marijuana cultivation to other areas of the country, the drug traffickers focused more on cocaine production, making it more mobile and utilizing small-scale processing labs that were much harder to detect and destroy.[47] Moreover, rampant corruption and ineptitude within the military prompted the Colombian government to shift central antidrug authority to the National Police. By 1982 the National Police had established a special antinarcotics unit, which has subsequently received the lion's share of U.S. antidrug assistance.[48]

These initial attempts to clamp down on drug production did not translate into success in stemming the amount of drugs leaving Colombia for the United States. While aerial eradication of marijuana plants was able to cut marijuana production by 22 percent, total acreage planted increased soon thereafter. Moreover, while the U.S. and Colombian governments were focusing on eradicating marijuana, coca cultivation and cocaine production accelerated, a transformation that had grave consequences for Colombian society—and U.S. drug policy—in the 1980s and 1990s.[49] However, even if the eradication efforts were not effective, this period in the drug war is of importance in understanding contemporary U.S.-Colombian relations, since by cooperating in U.S. antidrug efforts, the Colombian government was conceding that the drug issue had a large supply component. Since that time, there has been surprisingly little debate in either Washington or Bogotá as to whether supply reduction should be a fundamental component of the war on drugs.

Extradition

Another sign that Colombia was willing to cooperate with the incipient U.S. counternarcotics efforts in the Andes occurred on November 14, 1979, when the Turbay and Carter administrations signed an extradition treaty that officially became Colombian law on November 3, 1980.[50] Not surprisingly, Washington was pleased with Turbay's decision and responded by sending Bogotá an additional U.S.$16 million in military assistance.[51] Once again Turbay was ambivalent, as he knew that such a treaty was vital for the Colombian government's ability to fight drug trafficking; he also knew that the bilateral treaty signaled to those both within and outside Colombia that only the U.S. legal system was capable of dealing with Colombia's problems. Moreover, Turbay believed that by signing the treaty Colombia was probably forever losing its sovereignty over drug policy conducted within its borders. Juan Tokatlian writes how the extradition treaty posed sensitive issues for both Bogotá and Washington:

> The delicacy of the issue involved was enormous: to agree on a bilateral juridical instrument that would allow for the extradition of each country's nationals to the other directly affected each country's national sovereignty. . . . At the same time, the recourse to a specific treaty was not a question of mere tactical convenience. Treaties imply binding obligations and long-term commitments. The accord on extradition indicated the choice of a strategic mechanism that was thought to be central to the fight against drugs. The rationale behind it was that such a treaty would contribute to bring justice, to deter the drug lords, to reduce narcotics trafficking, to improve bilateral state-to-state relations and to alleviate the Colombian legal process from the burden of mounting drug offenses. The underlying implications were that tough law enforcement was the best alternative to eliminate drug supply, that the U.S. government had no confidence at all in the Colombian judicial system, and that the U.S. official diagnosis on drugs was the correct one. It also provided the U.S. administration with an instrument (a "stick") to determine unilaterally Colombian collaboration on drugs.[52]

Turbay's successor, Conservative leader Belisario Betancur (1982–1986), refused to enforce the extradition law and instead preferred to test the efficacy of the Colombian judicial system without external interference.[53] It would not be long, however, before Betancur became the first Colombian president to utilize the law when on January 5, 1985, he sent four Colombian nationals to be tried in the United States. By June 1987 the U.S. government had made 140 extradition requests, and ultimately the Colombian government sent thirteen Colombians and two foreigners to face trial in the United States. Three drug traffickers were extradited from the United States to Colombia.[54]

Betancur's change in resolve was prompted by the April 30, 1984, assassination of his minister of justice, Rodrigo Lara Bonilla. Working in tandem with the U.S. DEA, Lara Bonilla led the effort that eventually resulted in the discovery and destruction of a cocaine lab on the Yari River in the department of Guaviare; they captured seven aircraft and some fourteen metric tons of cocaine with an estimated U.S.$1.2 billion market value.[55] The narcotics traffickers took revenge by murdering Lara Bonilla. Drug kingpins also placed a U.S.$500,000 bounty on Ambassador Tambs's head, and offered a U.S.$300,000 reward to anyone who captured a DEA agent. In addition to stepping up the extradition efforts, Betancur gave the green light for more extensive uses of herbicides in order to fumigate illicit crops.[56] Like Turbay, Betancur's tough stance was not overlooked in the United States: U.S. antidrug assistance tripled from 1983 to 1985, and President Ronald Reagan publicly praised Betancur's efforts during his April 1986 visit to the White House.[57]

On June 25, 1987, the Colombian Supreme Court ruled that the extradition law was unconstitutional, putting an end to the extradition of Colombian nationals. Nevertheless, the August 18, 1989, murder of Liberal Party presidential candidate Luis Carlos Galán prompted President Virgilio Barco (1986–1990) to utilize emergency decrees in order to extradite certain drug traffickers to the United States.[58] Between August 1989 and December 1990, the Colombian government extradited twenty-four suspected drug traffickers to the United States. President Barco's decision to extradite drug traffickers prompted the Medellín drug cartel to unleash a brutal campaign of violence against the Colombian state and political class.

Upon taking office in 1990, Liberal Party president César Gaviria implemented a policy whereby extradition would be used as a discretionary tool.[59] In practical terms, this meant that the government would reduce the drug traffickers' prison terms by one-third and not extradite them if they agreed to turn themselves in and confess to at least one crime.[60] By mid-1991 almost all of the top leadership of the Medellín cartel had agreed to the surrender in return for a reduced sentence and a guarantee of no extradition.[61] In 1991, under intense pressure from the drug cartels, the Constituent Assembly approved Article 35 of the newly promulgated constitution that banned extradition.[62] Soon after the constitution was approved, Medellín drug lord Pablo Escobar turned himself in, correctly believing that he now was no longer threatened with extradition to the United States. In 1997 the constitution was amended to allow for nonretroactive extradition and in 2000 the first Colombian in nine years was extradited to the United States.[63]

Narcotization and Militarization

In contrast to the more combative stance of the 1970s, the early 1980s were marked by more cooperation between Colombia and the United States on the drug issue. Tired of battling Washington, the Betancur administration was looking to find a more cooperative position vis-à-vis the U.S. antidrug policies. According to Tokatlian:

> Bogotá had gone full circle from 1983 to 1984: from a distant, conflictual position vis-à-vis Washington on drugs to friendly, nonfrictional cooperation with the White House on narcotics matters. Both the United States administration and the U.S. Congress praised Colombia for its "frontal" attack on drug trafficking: the three pillars of the anti-narcotics offensive—extradition, militarization, and eradication—were working.[64]

While others place the date at the end of the 1980s with the advent of the Andean Initiative, Tokatlian believes that it was during the mid-1980s that U.S.-Colombian relations became narcotized, when virtually all bilateral issues became dependent on the drug issue: if Colombia wanted good relations or support from the United States on a certain issue, it was clear to all that it first had to be perceived by Washington as cooperating in the war on drugs.[65] For example, when Betancur's attorney general, Carlos Jiménez Gómez, declared the 1979 extradition law to be unconstitutional, the reaction from Washington was one of anger and frustration, manifested by Congressman Charles Rangel's move to sanction the import of Colombian flowers. Tokatlian writes that by the end of the Betancur administration, "Drugs had permeated every aspect of the Bogotá-Washington relationship. Moreover, the U.S. antinarcotics policy was, by now, a permanent component of Colombian domestic politics and Colombia's relative international leverage was seriously constrained by the centrality of drugs in U.S.-Colombian narcopolitics."[66] Robert Drexler echoes Tokatlian's view when he writes:

> President Reagan, and, even more, President Bush wanted to demonstrate to the American public that they were going personally (trips to Colombia) to what they contended was the source of our narcotics problems—Colombia—to press for tough action there. . . . Failing, or declining, to perceive American drug abuse as primarily a social problem, they were naturally unreceptive to their Colombian counterparts' emphasis on the social context of Colombia's narcotics problem and were almost deaf to Colombian complaints about the insatiable American demand for drugs.[67]

The roots of this rapid escalation in the war on drugs, and subsequent fruition in the 1990s, can be traced back to April 8, 1986, when President Reagan issued National Security Directive no. 221, which stated that drug production and trafficking threatened U.S. security and that the United States needed to place greater emphasis on source control.[68] This directive is also thought to have authorized the CIA's involvement in international drug interdiction efforts.[69] Since that time the CIA has significantly increased its presence in Colombia as it seeks to gather more information on the drug trade as well as on the guerrilla insurgents and paramilitary groups. In the early 1990s, for example, the agency played an instrumental—albeit highly secretive—role in the search for and eventual killing of Medellín cartel kingpin Pablo Escobar.[70]

Also in 1986, the United States launched its Andean military–based antidrug program Operation Blast Furnace, which primarily focused on counternarcotics efforts in Bolivia. Among other actions, this initiative sent six Black Hawk helicopters and 160 U.S. troops to help the Bolivian narcotics police destroy cocaine laboratories. Sewall Menzel has written that the small scope and time period of Blast Furnace ensured that the program was not very effective. In fact, the operation ended up serving as a "learning experience" for drug traffickers insofar as they could now better predict the future military tactics of the Reagan administration's source-oriented antidrug efforts.[71]

While mostly operational in Bolivia, Blast Furnace set a precedent for the increasingly militarized Andean drug policy, a trait that continues to characterize U.S. drug policy—and in turn overall policy—in Colombia. Blast Furnace was followed in 1987 by Operation Snowcap, which initially targeted its efforts in Bolivia and Peru. The program was extended to Colombia in 1989. The entire budget for Snowcap (U.S.$24 million) was insignificant compared to the 2000 budget for counternarcotics assistance to Colombia alone (U.S.$850 million; see Table 2.1), a figure that reveals just how much and how fast the United States has increased its counternaroctics efforts in Latin America—and specifically in Colombia.[72]

The Bush Administration: Escalation

By the late 1980s public concern over the U.S. drug problem had reached unprecedented levels.[73] The U.S. media reported on an almost daily basis how the scourge of crack cocaine was infecting U.S. cities and how thousands of "crack babies" were being born into a life they were physically unprepared to survive. Tellingly, a CBS News/New York Times poll published in March 1988 showed that 48 percent of the U.S. public considered drugs to be the principal foreign policy challenge facing the United States, and that 63 percent thought drugs should take precedence over the anticommunist struggle.[74]

George Bush picked up on this "do something about our drug problem" sentiment and made international drug interdiction efforts a fundamental component of his newly declared war on drugs. But what was new was the growing emphasis on fighting the war on drugs in source countries such as Bolivia, Peru, and Colombia. During the 1980s, an-

Table 2.1 U.S. Counternarcotics-Related Assistance to Colombia (selected years, U.S.$ millions)

1978	2.49
1983	3.49
1987	11.55
1989	75.01[a]
1990	11.63
1991	126.00
1996	16.00
1997	13.60
1998	140.00
1999	289.00
2000	850.00

Sources: Office of National Drug Control Policy, various years; Office of Management and Budget, 1999; USAID, various years.

Note: a. Includes the U.S.$65 million in emergency counternarcotics aid (506 Drawdown) sent after the August 1989 assassination of Luis Carlos Galán.

tidrug efforts were more focused on interdicting drugs as they were entering the United States using agencies such as the U.S. Coast Guard. Now the United States would go after the raw materials of the drug trade, and by definition this meant the Andes.

In a 1988 campaign speech Bush declared, "The logic is simple. The cheapest way to eradicate narcotics is to destroy them at their source. . . . We need to wipe out crops wherever they are grown and take out labs wherever they exist."[75] The arrival of the Bush administration—and the concomitant end of the Cold War—underscored the fact that drugs had now replaced communism as the primary threat to the United States in Latin America. Tokatlian writes:

> Whereas from Harry Truman to Ronald Reagan, no U.S. politician wished to be considered "soft" on Communism, at the end of the 1980s no one wanted to be seen as flexible on the issue of drugs. With congressional cooperation, neoconservative U.S. think-tanks were calling for the creation of a multi-national anti-narcotic force in Latin America, thus promoting regional militarization.[76]

At the same time that the United States was making source-country drug interdiction a national security priority, events in Colombia quickly made the country a focus for heightened U.S. antidrug interdiction. Due to the partially successful peace negotiations during the Betancur administration, many guerrillas laid down their arms and integrated themselves into the orthodox political system, with a good number of them forming a new political party Unión Patriótica (UP; Patriotic Union). At the same time, however, the cocaine business in Colombia was beginning to explode and newly wealthy drug traffickers were declaring war on the ex-guerrillas, believing that their moves toward political integration were actually thinly veiled attempts to continue their revolutionary agenda through seemingly legitimate means.

This explosive mix of drug traffickers and former guerrillas resulted in the assassination of several ex-guerrillas cum politicians. For example, on August 27, 1987, former UP presidential candidate Jaime Pardo Leal was killed by orders from drug traffickers; a few years later on March 22, 1990, UP presidential candidate Bernardo Jaramillo Ossa was assassinated; and a month later Movimiento 19 de Abril (M-19) presidential candidate Carlos Pizarro Leongómez was also killed. All told, over 1,000 members of the UP, as well as countless other ex-guerrillas, were killed during the 1980s and early 1990s, with the vast majority of the deaths coming at the hands of the drug trafficker–financed paramilitary groups.

Regardless of how many ex-guerrillas were killed, it was the assassination of Liberal Party presidential candidate Luis Carlos Galán on August 18, 1989, that prompted the United States to get more involved in Colombia. Washington viewed Galán as a reliable and modernizing politician who was committed to warm relations with the United States. His violent death horrified many U.S. government officials, who now came to believe that much more needed to be done to support the Colombian government in its fight against the drug traffickers.

The United States quickly sent an additional U.S.$65 million in counternarcotics aid (U.S.$10 million was the original budgeted amount for 1989), and on September 5, 1989, President Bush announced his five-year U.S.$2.2 billion Andean Initiative.[77] This initiative resulted in making the Andes, rather than Central America (where by then most of the civil conflicts had been resolved peacefully), the leading recipient of U.S. military aid in the hemisphere. The U.S. shift in focus from stopping communism to stopping drugs made it clear to Andean governments that the war on drugs needed to become a top priority in their countries, something that caused tremendous friction between Washington and Andean governments throughout the 1990s.[78]

This firm belief that Andean governments must unconditionally cooperate with U.S. antidrug efforts helps explain the vituperative reaction in Washington whenever the United States perceived that this cooperation was not forthcoming. In the most extreme instances the U.S. government decertified countries for not adequately cooperating in the war on drugs. This happened to Bolivia in 1994 and to Colombia in 1996 and 1997. This belief in the need for source-country government cooperation also drove the U.S. government's efforts to undermine President Ernesto Samper in Colombia.

The first phase of the Andean Initiative sent U.S.$65 million to Colombia, consisting primarily of military equipment even though the Barco administration had requested intelligence devices and technical assistance for the judicial system. This began a long trend: starting with the Andean Initiative and continuing through the 1990s, almost all of the counternarcotics aid that the United States has sent to Colombia has been military related (see Table 2.2). The Andean Initiative also sent U.S. military advisers to train the Colombian military on counternarcotics efforts.[79]

In an attempt to show that as part of the Andean Initiative the Bush administration was committed to a more multilateral approach to the drug interdiction issue, in February 1990 the United States and several

Table 2.2   Andean Initiative–Assistance for Colombia (U.S.$ millions)

	FY 89	FY 90	FY 91	FY 92	FY 93	FY 94	Total
Military	8.6	40.3	60.5	60.5	60.5	60.5	290.9
Economic	0.0	3.6	50.0	50.0	50.0	50.0	203.6
Law enforcement	10.0	20.0	20.0	20.0	20.0	20.0	110.0
DEA support	4.2	4.4	4.4	4.4	4.4	4.4	26.2
Total	22.8	68.3	134.9	134.9	134.9	134.9	—

Sources: Office of National Drug Control Policy, 1990, 1992; Sewall Menzel, *Cocaine Quagmire: Implementing U.S. Anti-Drug Policy in the North Andes–Colombia* (New York: University Press of America, 1997), p. 73.

Note: FY = fiscal year.

Latin American governments issued the Declaration of Cartagena.[80] It stated that the United States would provide resources to the Andean countries that cooperated in counternarcotics efforts.[81] The declaration largely consisted of platitudes on multilateral cooperation and how the drug problem was both a supply and a demand problem.[82] Nevertheless, it maintained that a hard line on drugs would produce a victory. This conference was significant since only a few months earlier the United States had positioned an aircraft carrier off the coast of Colombia in an attempt to bolster its claim that it was serious about stopping drugs at their source. The response from the Colombian government and public was extremely negative and the carrier was quickly given orders to move away from the coast.[83]

While the 1990 Cartagena Conference did briefly boost George Bush's Andean Initiative strategy, by the end of 1992 there was widespread agreement within the U.S. government that the plan had failed in its effort to reduce the amount of cocaine and heroine entering the country. Indeed, after three years and U.S.$2.2 billion, cocaine was as cheap and plentiful as ever on U.S. streets.[84] According to Congressman Charles Schumer, "by every objective standard, the President's Andean strategy has failed."[85] Compounding this inability to stem the flow of drugs was the fact that the U.S. military's focus on the drug war had been diverted due to the 1990–1991 Gulf War, which it considered more important than antidrug efforts in the Andes.[86]

The Clinton Administration Confronts the Drug War

The subsequent election of Bill Clinton saw a reduction in U.S. antidrug efforts in the Andes. In early 1993 the Clinton administration conducted an "extensive classified review" of drug eradication and interdiction programs in the Andes and concluded that efforts to date had been ineffective. The end result was that the planned 1993 fiscal year budget of U.S.$387 million in antidrug aid for the Andean countries was slashed to U.S.$174 million.[87] The staff of the Office of National Drug Control Policy (ONDCP) was reduced from 146 positions to 25.[88]

Yet any possibility for significant long-term reduction in U.S. counternarcotics efforts in the Andes was ended when the Republicans took control of both houses of Congress following the 1994 midterm elections. While it is clear that Democrats can be as hawkish on the drug issue as their Republican counterparts, the Republican majority nonetheless turned up the heat on the drug war. This fact had grave consequences for the new president of Colombia, Ernesto Samper, who happened to be taking office at about this time. The Republican majority in Congress emboldened a number of influential legislators to take a strong stand on the drug war. Congressmen such as Dennis Hastert (R–Ill.), Benjamin Gilman (R–N.Y.), and Dan Burton (R–Ind.) were becoming vocal critics of the Clinton administration's antidrug policies and strong proponents of doing more to fight the drug war in Colombia.

These "drug hawks" viewed Clinton's antidrug policies as too soft and argued that more direct types of support for the Colombian government's antidrug efforts were needed. Yet following Ernesto Samper's inauguration in 1994 this strategy became more difficult, as support for the Colombian government's antidrug efforts meant support for Ernesto Samper, who by this time was anathema to the drug hawks in Congress. It was during this time that, led by the drug hawks, the U.S. Congress began to work directly with what it considered trusted allies in the Colombian National Police so that it could continue to fund the drug war without providing support to Ernesto Samper.

But it was not only Ernesto Samper who felt the reach of the drug hawks' wrath; rather, the Clinton administration was constantly on the defensive on the drug war, continuously defending itself against charges from Congress that it was too soft. With respect to its source-country drug war policies (which at this point were increasingly inseparable from its Colombia policy), the Clinton White House spent as much time focused on answering critics on Capitol Hill as it did analyzing how its policies would influence events in the Andes. The Clinton administration's fear that the drug hawks would inflict political damage on the drug war issue is also a significant reason why President Clinton decided to send such a massive antidrug assistance package to Colombia in 2000.

The move toward a scaled-down antidrug program in the Andes during the first year of the Clinton administration proved ephemeral, replaced by the Republican-led belief that the United States needed to continue to fight the war on drugs at its source in Latin America. Any move by Washington toward "denarcotization" was over, replaced by the revival of the war on drugs. That this shift was coupled with the election of a "narco-president" in Colombia held serious consequences for the bilateral relationship.

Tired of Gaviria, Looking Forward to Samper

Although there were suspicions about Ernesto Samper's drug involvement during the early stages of his presidency, many of the sparks between the United States and Colombia were not necessarily related to the U.S. view of Samper. Rather, in the last year of his presidency, César Gaviria's antidrug credentials were becoming increasingly suspect in Washington, which in turn cooled the bilateral relationship. This was due mainly to the perception that, after dismantling the Medellín cartel, Gaviria had gone soft on the Cali cartel. Indeed, U.S. DEA agent Joe Toft's revelations in September 1994 on Colombian national television about a country he termed a "narco-democracy" had as much or more to do with Gaviria as they did with Samper.[89]

Gaviria, who at this point was in Washington settling in at his new post as secretary general of the OAS, did not take these criticisms supinely. He began taking an openly hard line against what he saw as incessant U.S. meddling and censure of Colombian counternarcotics efforts. In one particularly sharp response to U.S. accusations that Colombia had not done enough on the drug issue, Gaviria retorted: "We disqualify as offensive the insinuations that we are not doing enough. The Colombians do much more than what is sufficient. We are practically alone in a war that is not ours but instead that of the international community in general, especially the drug-consuming countries."[90]

The most contentious issue between Washington and the departing Gaviria administration was over the policies and statements of Gaviria's prosecutor general, Gustavo de Grieff.[91] In contrast to the heavy-handed antidrug strategy that Washington promoted (and so admired in President Barco and initially Gaviria), de Grieff advocated a more conciliatory position, one that included offering softer sentences to the Cali cartel if they agreed to surrender and explore the possibility of drug legalization. That de Grieff was willing to go public with such "outrageous" policies infuriated top officials in Washington, chief among them Attorney General Janet Reno, who at one point exchanged heated words with de Grieff.

To make matters worse, de Grieff met with three of the Cali cartel's top leaders in January 1994. During the meeting he apparently offered the traffickers as little as a year in prison in return for their surrender. When news of the offer leaked, U.S. officials could not control their anger.[92] In an example that suggests how both sides of the congressional aisle could be equally hawkish on the drug issue, Senate Democrat John Kerry wrote in the *Washington Post* that de Grieff's antics served "to bring about his nation's capitulation to the Cali cocaine cartel."[93] Colombia's ambassador to the United States, Gabriel Silva, responded to Kerry's opinion editorial in a letter to the editor arguing that the Colombian government "has made enormous sacrifices to defend its democracy, so it is hasty to say that Colombia is a narco-democracy."[94]

Another acerbic episode occurred on May 1, 1994, when the U.S. Pentagon unilaterally declared that it was halting its air interception efforts in the Andes (the United States had four radar stations—one in Peru, one in Bolivia, and two in southern Colombia). It also announced that it would cease providing radar information to Colombia and Peru. These operations were intended to hinder drug traffickers' efforts to transport raw coca leaf by plane into Colombia from Bolivia and Peru. The Pentagon's decision came after the Colombian government announced a policy to shoot down planes suspected of transporting drugs.[95]

The reason for such a move was that, in a highly sensitive mood following the accidental bombing of an Iranian airliner in 1988, Pentagon officials were worried about the potential for a lawsuit against the U.S. government by relatives of anyone shot down with the assistance of the U.S.-funded radar installations.[96] So even though the Colombian government's decision to shoot down planes was a positive development in terms of fighting the war on drugs, the Pentagon considered this particular strategy to be too politically risky. While it agreed with the Pentagon's legal premise, the State Department was incensed at the handling of the matter and a nasty interagency dispute erupted. Predictably, this decision to stop the provision of radar information appeared as a form of capitulation in the war on drugs to members of both parties in the U.S. Congress. Congressman Charles Schumer stated: "The signal now is unmistakable: an American withdrawal is taking place in the drug war. . . . The U.S. withdrawal from the drug war is the most significant retreat since George Washington retreated from New York during our revolution."[97]

While this incident was essentially a dispute within the U.S. government over antidrug policy, it nevertheless did serve to worsen U.S.-Colombian relations, since the unilateral move—the State Department ultimately notified the Colombian government with no prior warning and no official explanation—indicated that Washington was increasingly reluctant to share sensitive antidrug information with its Colombian counterparts.[98] A spokesman for President Gaviria retorted that the method through which the United States changed its radar policy was "unilateral, untimely and rude."[99] The United States eventually reversed its decision in December 1994.

These types of controversies rankled the bilateral relationship and altered the U.S. perception of the Colombian government's willingness to combat drugs; but they never significantly changed Washington's confidence in César Gaviria himself. By the end of his administration, however, this would change, as Washington increasingly realized that Gaviria was not the docile ally they had once believed. In many ways, while for the first few years of his administration he was considered by Washington to be a reliable, effective ally in the war on drugs, Gaviria's increasingly tough, independent stance toward Washington on the drug issue helps to explain why the U.S. government was initially eager to work with Ernesto Samper, even though for years U.S. officials had believed that he had links to the drug cartels.

The thinking in Washington was that Ernesto Samper might not be perfect, but that he could not be any worse than Gaviria. Yet the honeymoon between the United States and Samper proved short-lived. The relationship quickly turned into a seemingly counterproductive shouting match. And much of the reason for this deterioration lay in a tightening of the U.S. stance in 1994: fueled by the Republicans in control of Congress, Washington's litmus test for strong bilateral relations with Colombia had become more stringent, a point not lost on the new president of Colombia.

THE ROOTS OF CONTEMPORARY
U.S. DRUG POLICY IN COLOMBIA AND THE ANDES

The vast majority of the counternarcotics aid sent to Colombia over the past two decades has been directed toward crop eradication. In 1988, James M. Van Wert, executive director of the U.S. State Department's Bureau of International Narcotics Matters, defined the goals of U.S. eradication policy:

U.S. government policy officials still maintain that eradication of illicit narcotics closest to the source of the raw material represents the
most cost-effective and efficient approach to narcotics control within
the overall supply reduction strategy. Illicit crops may be either erad-
icated involuntarily or destroyed through voluntary means. Eradication of illicit crops may be accomplished by physically uprooting the
plants or by chemical or biological control agents. Payment to the
farmers for the labor of willingly uprooting the plants is an important
element of the successful implementation of eradication efforts. Economic support and development assistance is a longer-range component of the overall eradication strategy. It is believed that illicit crops
constitute the cheapest link in the narcotics chain; producers devote
fewer resources to their detection, and it is easier to locate and destroy
crops in the field than to locate the subsequently processed drugs in
the smuggling routes or on the streets of U.S. cities. The Department
of State believes that the supply of narcotics being shipped from Latin
America to the United States could be reduced significantly if governments agreed to institute massive herbicidal spraying to reduce
coca cultivation by fifty percent in 1993.[100]

Van Wert's description of U.S. drug policy goals for Colombia illustrates the glaring gap between the initial stated goals and actual results of U.S. drug policy over the course of the 1990s. In Colombia
specifically, the major U.S. policy goals were to ensure that "marijuana
and cocaine cultivation are eliminated and major cocaine and marijuana
trafficking organizations are immobilized."[101] Moreover, the United
States attempted to assist the Colombian National Police in its efforts to
develop better intelligence for both eradication and interdiction activities; subsequently, aerial eradication was extended and new herbicides
were tested to measure their efficacy on coca plants. It was at this time
in the mid-1990s that the U.S. relationship with the Colombian National
Police—the military organization that usually coordinates counternarcotics efforts—began to grow and strengthen. A strong argument can be
made that between 1995 and 2000 the head of the Colombian national
police had as much or more influence in Washington than the Colombian ambassador.[102]

An important development in the U.S. war on drugs has been the
growing involvement of the U.S. military in counternarcotics operations. In the early 1980s, the U.S. military had been reluctant to get involved in the counternarcotics efforts, since it viewed them as more appropriate for police units. Furthermore, the Pentagon was much more
concerned with dealing with the threat of Soviet-led expansion around

the world. Much of this initial impetus for greater military involvement in the drug war came from Congress. For example, Republican Larry J. Hopkins of Kentucky, during a 1989 hearing of the House Armed Services Subcommittee on Investigations, stated: "We are serious about (the military's) active role in this war on drugs, even if it means we have to drag (them) kicking and screaming every step of the wary. (We) are going to have to straighten out their priorities for them. This is war. And they are going to have to lace up their combat boots and get involved."[103]

A decade later the U.S. military's involvement in Colombia is significant and permanent. In fact, the drug war—with Colombia's involvement in particular—has become one of the overriding priorities for the U.S. Southern Command (SouthCom), the U.S. military's command center that covers Latin America and the Caribbean. According to one U.S. official in Bogotá, "it seems like General Wilhelm [then commander of SouthCom] is here every week."[104]

Yet it is just as clear that the Pentagon remains ambivalent about its involvement in the war on drugs, especially now that this war seems increasingly intertwined with Colombia's civil conflict. This indifference is due mostly to the strongly held belief that the U.S. military's resources should be geared toward fighting a major war, such as the 1991 Gulf War or a potential conflagration in Asia, rather than being distracted by what is essentially a law enforcement issue. While this ambivalence is pervasive within the U.S. military, it nonetheless has not prevented the military from increasing its contacts with the Colombian military in recent years.[105]

That the U.S. military now plays a significant role in the war on drugs in Colombia represents new challenges and potential areas of controversy. This stems from the fact that Colombia's coca cultivation and cocaine production trade—the primary concern of U.S. antidrug efforts—are inextricably linked with the guerrilla insurgents and paramilitary groups. Thus, in its efforts to carry out its antidrug missions the U.S. military is also supremely aware of the military situation in Colombia and has spent considerable time analyzing different ways that the conflict could evolve.

Naturally there have been calls within some elements of the U.S. military for it to move away from counternarcotics support and more directly into counterinsurgency efforts. According to one U.S. State Department officer, "Some guys in the Pentagon complain to me that 'they don't get no respect in the sandbox' so long as they remain involved in the drug war. What they really want to be doing is anti-insurgent efforts."[106] At present the role of the U.S. military remains largely confined to antidrug efforts. Yet as the civil conflict continues to rage, there will be increasing calls in Washington for the George W. Bush administration to clarify the military's role in Colombia. Indeed, one of the biggest challenges for the administration's Colombia policy will be to determine the extent and mission of the U.S. military in Colombia.

CERTIFICATION

First made into law with the 1986 Anti–Drug Abuse Act and subsequently modified in the 1988 Anti–Drug Abuse Act, the annual drug certification process became one of the most visible (and many would argue counterproductive) aspects of the U.S.-Colombian relationship in the 1990s.[107] When, for example, the two consecutive decisions to decertify Colombia were made in 1996 and 1997, it generated an unusually hostile reaction and sense of betrayal among the Colombian populace. Ironically, however, these two decertification decisions in many ways served to bolster Ernesto Samper's faltering presidency, as he was able to champion himself as the defender of Colombian sovereignty, an antithetical result.

The contemporary use of the certification process traces back to the legislation of the two Anti–Drug Abuse Acts, when the United States began to link source-country cooperation on counternarcotics efforts with eligibility for U.S. foreign aid as well as for U.S. support within international multilateral institutions.[108] The initial concept of reviewing the counternarcotics efforts of foreign countries actually predates these two acts and began with the Foreign Assistance Act of 1961. Certification was added to this process in 1986, and the 1988 Anti–Drug Abuse Act expanded and altered the definition of certification. The act also earmarked U.S.$500,000 for the testing and use of safe and effective herbicides for aerial eradication of coca. For Colombia specifically, it authorized U.S.$15 million in 1989 for defense equipment and an additional U.S.$5 million to protect officials and members of the press against "narco-terrorist" attacks. (At the advent of the certification process, the U.S. Congress viewed narco-terrorists such as Pablo Escobar to be the main threat in Colombia; since the mid-1990s, however, this threat has become the "narco-guerrilla.")

Every year the president is required to submit to Congress a list of the countries that he has determined to be major drug-producing or drug-trafficking countries (the secretary of state sends recommendations to the president, who makes the final decisions as to which countries will be included on the list). At this point in the process, half of most types of U.S. government assistance to these countries is withheld until the president determines whether the country has done enough to combat drugs and thus merits certification. (A major drug-producing country is defined as one in which 1,000 or more hectares of illicit opium poppy are cultivated or harvested during a year; 1,000 or more hectares of illicit coca are cultivated or harvested during a year; or 5,000 or more hectares of illicit cannabis are cultivated or harvested during a year. A major drug-trafficking country is defined as being a significant source of illicit narcotic or other controlled substances significantly affecting the United States; or a country through which such drugs or substances are transported.)[109]

The president is then required to review the antinarcotics efforts undertaken by the countries most involved in these issues (the "majors") and transmit certification decisions to Congress by March 1 of the following year. The president may select from the following certification options for each of the countries on the "majors" list: full certification, denial of certification, or a "vital national interest" certification. If a country receives full certification, all aid that had been withheld is released. If a country receives "national interest" certification, assistance is provided in the same manner as if the country had received full certification.[110]

Congress has thirty calendar days to analyze the list and to enact country-specific resolutions of disapproval. The president can veto these resolutions, which would force Congress to achieve a two-thirds majority to override the veto and alter the president's decisions.

If a country is decertified and this decision is not overturned by Congress, mandatory sanctions are imposed, including 50 percent suspension of U.S. assistance for the current fiscal year (humanitarian and narcotics aid are exempted), 100 percent suspension of assistance for subsequent fiscal years (unless the country is certified in the interim), and voting against loans to a country from the multilateral development banks. Discretionary sanctions include denial of preferential treatment to a country's exports under the Generalized System of Preferences and the Caribbean Basin Economic Recovery Act, duty increases of up to 50 percent of value on a country's exports to the United States, curtailment of air transportation and traffic between the United States and the noncertified country, and withdrawal of U.S. participation in any preclearance customs arrangements with the noncertified country.[111]

The certification law meant above all that in the 1990s the U.S. Congress assumed a leading role in narcotics-related foreign policy issues. According to Raphael Perl:

> The certification process will continue to serve as an important mechanism through which the Congress can press its own assessment of specific nations in international narcotics policy. . . . This process and the role and influence of the Congress appear likely both to expand and to become more active. Although one can argue that the process may not always be effective in persuading foreign nations to cooperate in the anti-drug fight, it is difficult to argue that the certification process has not proved an effective vehicle by which the Congress has been—and is—able to exert influence upon the executive branch. Congress will not soon give up the power it has acquired in this policy area, one which has become increasingly important to the United States public. It is also likely that the Congress will continue to require new types of narco-related certification. New certification requirements concerning cooperation on money-laundering issues offer but one example of what may well prove to be an on-going trend.[112]

The certification process increases the influence of a legislative body that, more than any other governing branch in the U.S. government, is directly tied to support from its constituents. Thus certification, and the tremendous impact that it yields on foreign countries, increased the intermestic nature of the U.S. war on drugs. For example, if a local constituency is concerned about a drug abuse problem in its area, its congressperson might very well be quite hawkish on the drug war issue and thus more likely to decertify a foreign country. The certification process therefore streamlined the political channels through which members of Congress, driven by a domestic policy concern, could influence the foreign policy of the U.S. government. In an event that might serve as an indication that Washington is finally seriously considering an alternative to this controversial annual ritual, early in his administration President George W. Bush indicated that he might support a two-year suspension of the certification process.

CONCLUSION

Until recently, U.S.-Colombian relations during this century were relatively strong, best characterized by the countries' shared anticommunist positions during the Cold War. However, by the late 1980s, U.S.

international counternarcotics efforts had become "militarized" and "Andeanized" and, following the Republican takeover of Congress in 1994 and the arrival of Ernesto Samper to the presidency, U.S. policy toward Colombia became "hypernarcotized." One integral—and highly controversial—component of this new relationship was the issue of U.S. certification of whether or not certain countries were cooperating sufficiently in the area of counternarcotics. Certification became the most visible symbol of the highly unilateral, intermestic politics–driven crusade against drugs.

By the mid-1990s, after Bill Clinton had replaced George Bush Sr. in the White House, the U.S.-led Andean source-country strategy and the concomitant certification process had become a regular and integral component of U.S. foreign policy, especially for the intelligence and defense agencies. But while the war on drugs might have been good for the budgets of the relevant government agencies, it was not achieving the desired effect of reducing the amount of drugs flooding into the United States. Not surprisingly, frustration began to set in. Eventually, the U.S. drug war failures—and the resulting disillusionment in Congress and participating government agencies—provided the impetus for Washington to substantially modify its policies toward Colombia following the election of President Andrés Pastrana in 1998. But, as will be shown, much of the new U.S. policies toward Colombia looked quite similar to the old ones, reflecting the continued reality that drugs remain the overriding U.S. priority in the region.

NOTES

1. Frank Safford, "Politics, Ideology, and Society in Post-Independence Latin America," in *The Cambridge History of Latin America,* vol. 3, edited by Leslie Bethell (Cambridge: Cambridge University Press, 1985), p. 413.

2. Stephen Randall, *Colombia and the United States: Hegemony and Interdependence* (Athens: University of Georgia Press, 1992), p. 6.

3. For an overview of the evolution of nineteenth-century U.S.-Colombian relations, see E. Taylor Parks, *Colombia and the United States, 1765–1934* (Durham: Duke University Press, 1935).

4. Robert Drexler, *Colombia and the United States: A Failed Foreign Policy* (London: McFarland, 1997), p. 12. See also George Dangerfield, *The Era of Good Feelings* (New York: Harcourt Brace, 1952), pp. 269–271.

5. See David Bushnell, "The Independence of Spanish South America," in *The Cambridge History of Latin America,* vol. 3, pp. 140–151.

6. Lars Schoultz, *Beneath the United States: A History of U.S. Policy Toward Latin America* (Cambridge: Harvard University Press, 1998), pp. 10–12.

7. Schoultz, *Beneath the United States,* p. 12.

8. At that time, what are now the geographic boundaries of modern Colombia were located within what was known as Gran Colombia. Shortly after independence, Gran Colombia split apart and "Colombia" became New Granada. The 1886 constitution created the modern Republic of Colombia. To avoid confusion, this book uses the term *Colombia* in referring to the country both before and after 1886.

9. See Fareed Zakaria, *From Wealth to Power: The Unusual Origins of America's World Role* (Princeton: Princeton University Press, 1998). Zakaria argues that by the middle of the nineteenth century the United States had become a "wealthy" nation, but that fifty years would pass before it became a "powerful" nation, exemplified by events such as its victory over Spain in 1898.

10. Nicaragua was the other coveted location for a canal route.

11. See Zakaria, *From Wealth to Power,* pp. 165–168.

12. Shoultz, *Beneath the United States,* pp. 152–175. See also David McCollough, *The Path Between the Seas: The Creation of the Panama Canal, 1870–1914* (New York: Simon and Schuster, 1977).

13. David Bushnell, *The Making of Modern Colombia: A Nation in Spite of Itself* (Berkeley: University of California Press, 1993), pp. 140–154.

14. See Richard L. Lael, *Arrogant Diplomacy: U.S. Policy Toward Colombia, 1903–1922* (Wilmington, Del.: Scholarly Resources, 1987).

15. John Hay was Theodore Roosevelt's secretary of state. Tomás Herrán was the Colombian chargé d'affaires in Washington.

16. See Dwight C. Miner, *The Fight for the Panama Route: The Story of the Spooner Act and the Hay-Herrán Treaty* (New York: Octagon, 1966). See also Paolo E. Coletta, "William Jennings Bryan and the United States–Colombian Impasse, 1903–1921," *Hispanic American Historical Review* 47, no. 4 (November 1967): 486–501.

17. President Theodore Roosevelt responded to the Colombian legislature's rejection of the treaty by writing letters that referred to Colombians as "contemptible little creatures," "jack rabbits," and "foolish and homicidal corruptionists." See Schoultz, *Beneath the United States,* p. 164.

18. See Bushnell, *The Making of Modern Colombia,* pp. 148–154.

19. See Richard H. Collin, *Theodore Roosevelt's Caribbean: The Panama Canal, the Monroe Doctrine, and the Latin American Context* (Baton Rouge: Louisiana State University Press, 1990); and Howard C. Hill, *Roosevelt and the Caribbean* (Chicago: University of Chicago Press, 1927).

20. It deserves note that the United States signed the Hay-Paunceforte Treaty with Great Britain in 1901. This treaty abrogated the bilateral tenets of the 1850 Clayton-Bulwer Treaty, virtually erasing any semblance of British influence in the isthmus. The United States was now the sole imperial power in Central America.

21. Philippe Bunau-Varilla was a French national with vested interests in canal construction and concessions who was acting on behalf of the Panamanian government.

22. See Joseph L. Arbena, "The Image of an American Imperialist: Colombian Views of Theodore Roosevelt," *West Georgia College, Studies in the Social Sciences* 6, no. 1 (June 1967): 3–27.

23. Schoultz, *Beneath the United States*, p. 257.

24. See Stephen J. Randall, *The Diplomacy of Modernization: Colombian-American Relations, 1920–1940* (Toronto: University of Toronto Press, 1977).

25. In 1925 coffee constituted 80 percent of the value of total goods exported.

26. Randall, *Colombia and the United States*, pp. 112–114.

27. Peter Smith, *Talons of the Eagle: Dynamics of U.S.–Latin American Relations* (Oxford: Oxford University Press, 1996), p. 52.

28. Cited in Schoultz, *Beneath the United States*, p. 244. The long-term consequences on the economies and political systems in the countries that experienced U.S. interventions during this period continue to be a subject of debate. While U.S. policymakers at the time argued that U.S. intervention was beneficial for democracy, the fact is that the Latin American countries that saw the highest level of U.S. intervention (Haiti, Dominican Republic, Nicaragua) turned out to be some of the most repressive, economically backward countries in the region in subsequent decades. See Elihu Root, "The Real Monroe Doctrine," *North American Review* (June 1914): 841–856; Nancy Mitchell, "The Height of the German Challenge: The Venezuela Blockade, 1902–1903," *Diplomatic History* 20, no. 2 (Spring 1996): 185–209; and Lester Langley, *The United States and the Caribbean in the Twentieth Century* (Athens: University of Georgia Press, 1982), pp. 77–88.

29. It remains a debate among scholars over the extent to which the Good Neighbor Policy represents a departure from the early U.S. tendency toward intervention and control. Peter Smith believes that the Good Neighbor Policy was basically nothing more than imperialism through different means. See Smith, *Talons of the Eagle,* pp. 65–87; and Schoultz, *Beneath the United States,* pp. 290–315. The genesis for the Good Neighbor Policy began during the Hoover administration, but was mostly implemented during the Roosevelt years and for that reason has come to be associated with his term in office. See also David Bushnell, *Eduardo Santos and the Good Neighbor Policy, 1938–1942* (Gainesville: University of Florida Press, 1967).

30. See David G. Haglund, "De-Lousing SCADTA: The Role of Pan American Airways in U.S. Aviation Diplomacy in Colombia, 1939–1940," *Aerospace Historian* 30, no. 3 (September 1983): 177–190.

31. A young Cuban idealist named Fidel Castro was in Colombia during this time, adding to the intrigue behind what caused the violence associated with *El Bogotazo.* However, most historians agree that Castro had nothing to do with the assassination or ensuing events.

32. Cited in Randall, *Colombia and the United States,* p. 191.

33. Ibid.

34. For a discussion of Colombian participation in the Korean War, see Drexler, *Colombia and the United States,* pp. 63–77.

35. Colombia earned special gratitude from the United States when it identified with the United States during the 1962 Cuban Missile Crisis. Colombia remained cool toward Havana in ensuing decades.

36. Dennis Rempe, "Guerrillas, Bandits, and Independent Republics: U.S. Counterinsurgency Efforts in Colombia, 1959–1965," *Small Wars and Insurgencies* 6, no. 3 (Winter 1995): 313.

37. U.S. General Accounting Office (GAO), "Drug Control: U.S.-Supported Efforts in Colombia and Bolivia," GAO/NSIAD-89-24, Washington, D.C., September 1988, p. 2.

38. See John Fishel, "Developing a Drug War Strategy: Lessons from Operation Blast Furnace," *Military Review* 71, no. 6 (June 1991): 61–69.

39. Drexler, *Colombia and the United States,* p. 96.

40. Author interview with Viron Vaky, U.S. ambassador to Colombia (1974–1976), Washington, D.C., April 1999.

41. See Iván Orozco Abad, "Los diálogos con el narcotráfico: Historia de la transformación fallida de un delincuente común en un delincuente político," *Análisis Político* 11 (September–December 1990): 38.

42. See Kenneth Sharpe, "The Drug War: Going After Supply," *Journal of Interamerican Studies and World Affairs* 30, nos. 2–3 (Summer–Fall 1988): 77–85.

43. For more on the Turbay administration's stance toward the United States, see Rodrigo Pardo and Juan Gabriel Tokatlian, "Teoría y práctica de las relaciones internacionales: El caso de Colombia," *Estudios Internacionales* (January–March 1988): 124–127.

44. Sewall Menzel, *Cocaine Quagmire: Implementing U.S. Anti-Drug Policy in the North Andes–Colombia* (New York: University Press of America, 1997), p. 19.

45. Juan Gabriel Tokatlian, "National Security and Drugs: Their Impact on Colombian-U.S. Relations," *Journal of Interamerican Studies and World Affairs* 30, no. 1 (Spring 1988): 145.

46. Sharpe, "The Drug War," pp. 77–85.

47. Juan Gabriel Tokatlian, "The Political Economy of Colombian-U.S. Narcodiplomacy: A Case Study of Colombian Foreign Policy Decision-Making, 1978–1990" (Ph.D. thesis, Paul H. Nitze School of Advanced International Studies, Johns Hopkins University, Baltimore, 1990).

48. U.S. GAO, "Drug Control," p. 18.

49. Tokatlian, "The Political Economy," pp. 60–93.

50. Marc Chernick, "Colombia's 'War on Drugs' vs. the United States' 'War on Drugs,'" WOLA Briefing Series no. 3, Washington Office on Latin America, Washington, D.C., May 30, 1991.

51. Arnaldo Claudio, "United States–Colombia Extradition Treaty: Failure of a Security Strategy," *Military Review* 71, no. 12 (December 1991): 71.

52. Tokatlian, "The Political Economy," p. 95.

53. Claudio, "United States–Colombia Extradition Treaty," p. 71.

54. U.S. GAO, "Drug Control," p. 26.

55. At the drug laboratory there was an airstrip large enough for jet aircraft, a dormitory that housed sixty people, six generators, and heavy tractors. See Robert Filippone, "The Medellín Cartel: Why We Can't Win the Drug War," *Studies in Conflict and Terrorism* 17, no. 4 (1994): 331.

56. Tokatlian, "National Security and Drugs," p. 145.

57. Ibid., p. 146.

58. Rensselaer W. Lee III, "Cocaine Mafia," *Social Science and Modern Society* 27, no. 2 (January–February 1990): 61.

59. Rensselaer W. Lee III, "Colombia's Cocaine Syndicates," *Crime, Law, and Social Change* 16, no. 1 (1991): 15.

60. See Orozco Abad, "Los diálogos con el narcotráfico," pp. 28–58.

61. Chernick, "Colombia's 'War on Drugs.'"

62. Claudio, "United States–Colombia Extradition Treaty," pp. 71–73.

63. U.S. Department of State, U.S. Bureau for International Narcotics and Law Enforcement, 2000.

64. Tokatlian, "The Political Economy," p. 136. See also Pilar Lozano, "Los grandes 'capos' colombianos del narcotráfico escapan a la extradición pretendida por EEUU: La reforma constitucional adoptada el martes no tendrá caracter retroactivo," *El País,* November 27, 1997.

65. Author interview with Charles Gillespie, U.S. ambassador to Colombia (1985–1988), Washington, D.C., September 1999.

66. Tokatlian, "The Political Economy," p. 148.

67. Drexler, *Colombia and the United States,* pp. 135–136.

68. William Walker III, "Drug Control and U.S. Hegemony," In *United States Policy in Latin America: A Decade of Crisis and Challenge,* edited by John D. Martz (Lincoln: University of Nebraska Press, 1995), pp. 299–319.

69. Ibid.

70. See Mark Bowden, *Killing Pablo: The Hunt for the World's Greatest Outlaw* (New York: Atlantic Monthly Press, 2001).

71. Menzel, *Cocaine Quagmire,* pp. 39–41.

72. See U.S. House of Representatives, Committee on Government Operations, "Stopping the Flood of Cocaine with Operation Snowcap: Is It Working?" August 15, 1990.

73. For an overview of the Bush administration's policies in Latin America, see Robert Pastor, "George Bush and Latin America: The Pragmatic Style and the Regionalist Option," in *Eagle in a New World: American Grand Strategy in the Post–Cold War World,* edited by Kenneth A. Oye, Robert J. Lieber, and Donald Rothchild (New York: HarperCollins, 1992).

74. Juan Gabriel Tokatlian, "Latin American Reaction to U.S. Policies on Drugs and Terrorism," in *Security, Democracy, and Development in U.S.-Latin Relations,* edited by Lars Schoultz, William C. Smith, and Augusto Varas (Miami: University of Miami North-South Center, 1994), p. 123.

75. Cited in Peter Andreas et al., "Dead-End Drug Wars," *Foreign Policy,* no. 85 (Winter 1991–1992): 108. See also Raphael Perl, "The U.S. Congress, International Narcotics Policy, and the Anti-Drug Abuse Act of 1988," *Journal of Interamerican Studies and World Affairs* 30, nos. 2–3 (Summer–Fall 1988): 19–52.

76. Tokatlian, "Latin American Reaction," p. 123.

77. U.S. GAO, "The Drug War: Colombia Is Undertaking Anti-Drug Programs, but Impact Is Uncertain," GAO/NSIAD-93-158, Washington, D.C., August 10, 1993, p. 10.

78. Eva Bertram and Bill Spencer, "Democratic Dilemmas in the War on Drugs in Latin America" (case study for the Carnegie Council on Ethics and International Affairs, Georgetown University, Washington, D.C., 2000).

79. In October 1988, Thomas McNamara, a former director of antiterrorism and narcotics at the National Security Council, was named ambassador to Colombia in a move to bolster counternarcotics efforts in Colombia.

80. See U.S. House of Representatives, Select Committee on Narcotics Abuse and Control, "The Andean Summit Meeting, February 15, 1990," March 7, 1990.

81. See Michael Reid, "Bush, Latin Leaders Seek Drug Pact," *The Christian Science Monitor,* February 15, 1990; and Michael Isikoff, "Colombian President Complains to Bush About U.S. Policies," *The Washington Post,* February 13, 1990.

82. See Richard Benedetto, "Bush's Colombia Trip Still On," Gannett News Service, December 9, 1989; and Douglas Jehl, "Drug Strategy May Face Hard Road," *The Times,* February 12, 1990.

83. See Peter Grier, "No Carrier off Colombia—For Now," *The Christian Science Monitor,* January 16, 1990.

84. Spencer Reiss et al., "Adios to the Andean Strategy," *Newsweek,* September 10, 1990.

85. Cited in Joseph Treaster, "Seven Nations to Broaden Battle Against Drugs," *The New York Times,* February 26, 1992.

86. Chris McGreal and Tim Ross, "Drug War Loses Ground As America Turns Its Back," *The Independent,* February 10, 1991.

87. "Andean Governments Face Cut in U.S. Anti-Drug Aid," *Notimex* (Mexico), April 6, 1993.

88. Ibid.

89. "Enérgico rechazo de Samper y EEUU," *El Tiempo,* September 30, 1994. See also "Revisarán papel de DEA en Colombia," *El Tiempo,* October 6, 1994.

90. "Estamos solos contra narcos," *El Tiempo,* July 12, 1994. For more on Gaviria's tough stance on the antidrug issue, see "Las explicaciones de EEUU, insuficientes," *El Tiempo,* July 13, 1994.

91. See Douglas Farah, "U.S. Teamwork with Colombia Against Drugs Comes Unstuck," *The Washington Post,* June 12, 1994.

92. Robert T. Buckman, "The Cali Cartel: An Undefeated Enemy," *Low Intensity Conflict and Law Enforcement* 3, no. 3 (Winter 1994): 439.

93. John S. Kerry, "Law Enforcement a Kingpin Could Love," *The Washington Post,* April 6, 1994. See also Pamela Constable, "Charges Strain Ties Between U.S., Colombia," *The Boston Globe,* June 26, 1994.

94. Cited in Buckman, "The Cali Cartel," p. 441.

95. James Brook, "U.S. Halts Flights in Andes Drug War Despite Protests," *The New York Times,* June 4, 1994; and "U.S. Rethinking Radar Ruling," Associated Press, June 5, 1994.

96. Buckman, "The Cali Cartel," p. 441.

97. Cited in Farah, "U.S. Teamwork."

98. Buckman, "The Cali Cartel," p. 441.

99. Ibid., p. 442.

100. James M. Van Wert, "The State Department's Narcotics Control Policy in the Americas," *Journal of Interamerican Studies and World Affairs* 30, nos. 2–3 (Summer–Fall 1988): 8.

101. Ibid.

102. For more on the beginnings of the relationship between the U.S. government and the Colombian National Police, see U.S. GAO, "Drug Control." For more on the evolution of U.S. drug policy in Colombia, see U.S. GAO, "Drug War: Observations on Counternarcotics Aid to Colombia," GAO/NSIAD-91-296, Washington, D.C., September 30, 1991; U.S. GAO, "The Drug War: Colombia Is Undertaking Anti-Drug Problems"; and U.S. GAO, "The Drug War: Observations on the U.S. International Drug Control Strategy," GAO/NSIAD-95-182, Washington, D.C., June 27, 1995.

103. Cited in John Dillon, "Congress Drafts Military to Battle Drug Traffickers," *The Christian Science Monitor,* March 23, 1989. See also Morris Blachman and Kenneth E. Sharpe, "The War on Drugs: American Democracy Under Assault," *World Policy Journal* 7, no. 1 (Winter 1989–1990): 135–167.

104. Confidential author interview with U.S. State Department official, Bogotá, June 1999.

105. Confidential author interview with U.S. Department of Defense official, Washington, D.C., November 2000.

106. Confidential author interview with U.S. State Department official, Washington, D.C., April 2001.

107. For a discussion of the benefits and detriments of the certification process, see Coletta Youngers, "The Process Has Become an Annual Charade," *The Washington Post,* March 21, 1999. It is safe to say that most observers—especially those in Latin America—believe that the certification process is a counterproductive procedure that should be revised, if not abolished. There is current discussion—mostly at the OAS—regarding the adoption of a multilateral certification process.

108. See Perl, "The U.S. Congress."

109. U.S. Department of State, Bureau of International Narcotics and Law Enforcement Affairs, "The Certification Process," January 4, 1999.

110. Ibid.

111. Perl, "The U.S. Congress."

112. Ibid., p. 42.

3

The Roots of Violence
in Colombia

The traditional use of violent means to accomplish personal or political ends has evidently set an example which, unfortunately, some Colombians continue to follow to this day. It is a characteristic which has become embedded in Colombian society and political culture, and it poses some of the most difficult challenges to the country's democratic institutions.

—Jorge P. Osterling[1]

To understand contemporary U.S. policy toward Colombia one must first study the evolution of Colombia's decades-old armed conflict. We know that U.S. policy in Colombia in the last few decades has been overwhelmingly driven by counternarcotics concerns. Therefore, the fact that there are links—at times inextricable and at other times loose—between armed belligerents and drug traffickers means that U.S. drug policies in Colombia are almost invariably formulated with the armed conflict in mind. This reality has become increasingly germane to U.S. policy concerns, especially now that guerrilla and paramilitary groups have recently increased their involvement in the cultivation and production of illicit drugs.

To study the evolution of Colombia's current political dynamics is to study violence. Colombia shares many cultural, economic, social, and historical characteristics with its neighboring countries, which makes explaining its unprecedented legacy of violence all the more difficult. Nevertheless, most observers agree that, among other things, Colombia's heritage of family feuds and interparty rivalries, which first flared up following independence in the early nineteenth century, has much to do with the shocking level of bloodshed that has plagued Colombia throughout its history. Yet even as Colombia suffered through over a

century of protracted civil conflicts and disputes, its economic performance has been almost unequaled among Latin American nations. For
example, as any proud Colombian will readily tell a foreigner, Colombia
was the one major Latin American country not to experience negative
growth during the "lost decade" of the 1980s. Colombia represents an
interesting paradox where prolonged violence has been matched by
concomitant economic dynamism. Thus in many ways there are two
contemporary Colombias: one is characterized by indiscriminate violence that resembles past conflicts such as Kosovo in 1999 or Rwanda in
1994; the other is an economically diverse and forward-thinking country that has been the economic envy of many other countries throughout
the hemisphere.

THE HISTORY OF VIOLENCE

Most Colombian political analysts, or *violentólogos,* who study the
country's tumultuous identity trace the current armed conflict back to
the violence that erupted throughout rural Colombia in the 1930s and
1940s.[2] More often than not, the violence during this time was the continuation of age-old hereditary quarrels between members of the country's two dominant political parties—the Liberals and the Conservatives.
During the 1930s and 1940s the violence between these two factions
seemed senseless, at least to the untrained eye. Liberals would attack
Conservatives; Conservatives would attack Liberals.

Most of the serious disputes revolved around landownership, especially in the Andean regions and eastern plains (*llanos orientales*); the
conflicts often involved land invasions or the removal of squatters. What
distinguishes the violence during this era and earlier decades is that it became more "official" as the Liberal and Conservative parties began directly encouraging their members to become involved in the fighting.[3]
Since one of these two parties was always in power, violence increasingly
began to resemble a battle between the government and its opponents.[4]

Between 1930 and 1946 the Liberals controlled the presidency and,
by extension, the political spoils, which in turn fueled Conservative
resentment. Consequently, when the opposition Conservatives finally
regained the presidency in 1946 with the election of Mariano Ospina
Pérez, they vented their frustrations against Liberals in the traditional
violent Colombian manner. Not surprisingly, the Liberals responded to
these attacks with their own reprisals, and eventually went on to form

their own guerrilla groups, which remained active during the next eleven years of Conservative rule—and which would grow into the modern guerrilla insurgents.

Richard Sharpless's portrayal of a battle that broke out in the department of Boyacá is indicative of the type of violence that was erupting during this era. In this particular example, what began as a partisan conflict between Liberals and Conservatives soon became a battle of government and its opponents:

> The techniques of the Conservative reconquest [referring to the reconquest of the department from the Liberals following Ospina Pérez's 1946 victory] were direct, simple, and brutal. In swing-vote areas the National Police ranks filled with Conservative sympathizers willing to carry out the orders of Conservative officials. Liberal job holders were dismissed, holders of Liberal identity cards intimidated, Liberal peasants were dispossessed of their lands, saw their property destroyed, and often were killed. In this atmosphere, old feuds over water, land, and local interest flared up and took on a partisan character. . . . Naturally, Liberals resorted to self-defense and attacks upon Conservatives; thus the spiral of terror and counter-terror continued upward in intensity, with the political parties adding their quotient of hatred with heated rhetoric.[5]

The powder keg that was the escalating violence between Liberal and Conservative forces exploded following the assassination of populist Liberal Party leader Jorge Eliécer Gaitán on April 9, 1948.[6] For many Colombians, Gaitán was seen as a progressive, modernizing leader committed to ending Colombian society's gross inequalities and injustices. In 1946, Gaitán ran for president through a splinter group within the Liberal Party in which he promoted the concept of "Gaitanismo"—a brand of populist policies that received support from the working class. Unwilling to work within the Liberal Party machine, Gaitán instead claimed that both the Conservatives and the Liberals were only interested in serving the interests of the "oligarchy," a word that before this time had not been used much in Colombia. This split within the Liberal Party further served to polarize Colombia's already fractious and violent political arena.

But this dream of creating a "workers paradise" along the lines of Juan Perón in Argentina or Getulio Vargas in Brazil was put to an end with an assassin's bullet. The news of Gaitán's murder sparked violent clashes in Bogotá—known as the *Bogotazo*—as well as in other cities.

In Bogotá, Liberal mobs devastated the city center, and Conservative president Ospina barely escaped with his life. Sharpless describes well the atmosphere in Bogotá:

> Bogotá resembled a European city after a World War II bombing attack. The capital's army garrison did not appear in force until two hours after the initial shooting. But the tanks and automatic weapons of the soldiers soon proved to be murderously effective. Despite suicidal charges by the rioters against armored units and heavy street fighting in some sectors between troops and armed civilians, the military prevailed. By nightfall the rioting had peaked as a result of both the army's actions and a steadily falling freezing rain. Flare-ups continued throughout the night and into the following Saturday, and there was continued fighting between the snipers and soldiers, as well as a brief battle in front of the U.S. embassy at eleven o'clock, but the army gradually regained control of the city. The arrival of more troops on April 10 meant the final containment of the uprising in Bogotá.[7]

But even as the level of violence subsided in Bogotá, it increased in the countryside. Indeed, although the escalation in rural Liberal versus Conservative violence actually began in the mid-1940s, the *Bogotazo* proved to be the catalyst that sparked even more killing and destruction in rural Colombia. This era from the mid-1940s to the mid-1950s is known as *La Violencia*. One particularly gruesome example illustrates the brutality of this era. In the town of Puerto Tejada, on the Cauca River near the southern city of Cali, a Liberal mob captured some prominent Conservative political leaders, decapitated them, and then proceeded to play soccer in the main plaza using their severed heads as soccer balls.[8]

This prolonged era of ubiquitous violence lasted through the coup by General Gustavo Rojas Pinilla in 1953 and finally came to an end in 1957 with the advent of the National Front. While *La Violencia* undoubtedly stems from age-old Liberal versus Conservative antagonisms, there are additional, more specific motives that explain the carnage that was inflicted, including landowners' justification of violence as a means to increase their landholdings and right-wing publicity that an international communist conspiracy was at work in Colombia.

THE NATIONAL FRONT

Although a fair amount of the violence subsided after the 1953 coup by General Rojas Pinilla, *La Violencia* continued in rural Colombia, and elites in both parties increasingly began to realize that such violence was not in their interests.[9] Thus, in order to bring some semblance of stability and normality back to Colombia, they decided to enter into a power-sharing agreement—the National Front—in which they would alternate the presidency every four years, and equally divide the important political appointments.[10]

The National Front pact was ironed out between Conservative Laureano Gómez and Liberal Alberto Lleras Camargo in Sitges, Spain, in 1957, ultimately producing the Pact of Sitges on July 20. A plebiscite on the pact was held later that year in which voters' options were to accept or reject the proposition. Powerful factions within both parties urged their supporters to vote in favor of the agreement. The final tally was 4,169,294 votes in favor, with 206,864 votes against and 20,738 blank ballots.[11] The National Front was thus codified and served to shape the course of Colombian politics for more than twenty years. Robert Dix writes:

> The National Front was to venture beyond all previous agreements. In conception it was more than just an "agreement from above" as a convenient political tactic, more than a device to reestablish by constitutional fiat a role for both contending parties, more than an instrument of the elite to resist change and combat leftist ideas. The National Front was all these things, and a good deal more. In its extent and purpose it was a new departure without a real precedent, either in Colombia or elsewhere.[12]

The National Front established that, beginning in 1957 for a period of twelve years, all seats in the Senate and Chamber of Representatives, departmental assemblies, and municipal councils were to be divided equally between the Liberal and Conservative parties, and only those parties. Further, all cabinet positions (except military appointees) and positions on the Colombian Supreme Court were to be equally divided, and all government officials and employees in the branches of public administration were to be appointed on a system of parity between the two parties. Dix writes:

> With its adoption, and with the simultaneous extension of the term of the National Front to sixteen years, the constitutional basis for Colombia's experiment in institutionalized coalition government was essentially complete. Its three pillars, constituting a unique form of bipartisanship, were to be: *parity* in all public elective bodies and in all executive departments and administrative posts; *alternation* in the

presidency every four years; and the requirement that decisions made
by public corporation be by *two-thirds votes,* thus presumably forcing
bipartisan cooperation on all legislation.[13]

The National Front lasted until 1974, when the presidency once
again became more freely contested. This power-sharing agreement was
quite successful in its primary goal of putting an end to the rural violence. But while violence in the countryside dropped precipitously during the period of the National Front, guerrilla groups born during the era
of *La Violencia* (1946–1957) or the National Front (1957–1974) continued their struggle, which as of today shows few signs of letting up.

The next significant step in Colombia's political evolution came
in 1991, when a constituent assembly introduced a new constitution.
In what was seen as a critical step in moving Colombia away from the
qualified democracy of the National Front years and toward a consolidated democracy, the new constitution instituted a variety of channels
for democratic participation, a bill of rights, and a restructured judicial
system. Yet while the 1991 constitution did succeed in ushering in an
era of political and social reform in Colombia, it was unable to im-
munize Colombia against the effects from what turned out to be a
significant increase in narcotics-, guerrilla-, and paramilitary-related
violence.

EVOLUTION OF THE GUERRILLA GROUPS

The First Generation

Colombia's first modern guerrilla groups can trace their roots back to
the time of *La Violencia.* When the Conservatives took power in 1946,
many Liberals—as well as members of the Communist Party—decided
it was better to organize as types of rural self-defense groups to protect
against Conservative attacks than to remain in the traditional political
party system. These groups then evolved into "semi-autonomous rural
communities" intended to serve as self-contained "islands" free from
the coercion of the Colombian state. Of the two major parties, only the
Liberals formed guerrilla groups, as from 1946 to 1953 the Conservatives were in power.

In an attempt to quell the carnage of *La Violencia* and rein in these
incipient guerrilla groups, on June 19, 1953, General Rojas Pinilla,
who had taken power in a military coup, offered amnesty to any and all

guerrillas who would lay down their weapons. Nearly 6,500 guerrillas took advantage of this offer in the following three months alone. Shortly thereafter, the Rojas Pinilla regime passed the first of two amnesty laws that ultimately benefited close to 20,000 Colombians. But while the amnesty laws prompted the Liberal guerrillas to give up their arms, the guerrilla groups linked to the Communist Party were more re-luctant, and many of these groups evolved into the modern guerrilla insurgents who still exist today. Not surprisingly, these groups saw the National Front as nothing more than a political charade intended to pre-serve the privilege of the elites at the expense of the masses. Marc Chernick describes the changing characteristics and goals of the guer-rilla groups during the era of the National Front and afterward:

> Peace at the national level, as happened in 1957–58 with the found-ing of the National Front, did not fully bring peace at the local level or pacify the myriad of social actors who were at war with each other. Moreover, the fact that the onset of the National Front coincided with the first years of the Cuban revolution gave new life to the revolu-tionary option of armed opposition. Yet in Colombia, unlike in other South American nations, guerrillas were able to consolidate their pres-ence in several rural areas during the first decades of the National Front. Despite enormous obstacles and confrontations with the Colom-bian military, student rebels, dissident Liberal guerrillas, and longtime peasant communists found some of the most propitious soil for revo-lutionary activity . . . anywhere in the Americas. The new Colombian guerrilla movements—some consciously organized as Cuban-style *focos* modeled on the revolutionary ideas of Ché Guevara, others with roots deep in earlier periods of peasant organizing—were able to in-sert themselves into remote communities that had already experienced several decades of rebellion and armed social conflict.[14]

The first national conference of "Popular Liberation Movements" took place in 1952 in the department of Cundinamarca and served as a signal that these incipient guerrilla groups were serious about their com-mitment to armed struggle. But although they normally operated in re-mote, sparsely populated areas of the country far away from the reaches of the state, these guerrillas would not be able to operate with impunity from the Colombian government forever. Eventually the Colombian state attacked the guerrillas, prompting the consolidation and institu-tionalization of what would become the "first-generation guerrilla groups." As Daniel Premo has pointed out, the Colombian state's deci-sion to declare war on the autonomous zones dramatically altered the nature of the guerrilla insurgents. In the 1960s, after the attacks on the independent republics, autonomy was no longer the guerrillas' only goal: "Unlike the Liberal-Conservative banditry, the existence of self-contained 'independent republics' and the short-lived actions of the MOEC and FUAR [two small guerrilla groups] during the early years of the National Front, the ELN and FARC placed primary focus on the seizure of national power."[15]

Fuerzas Armadas Revolucionarias de Colombia (FARC; Revolutionary Armed Forces of Colombia). One of the major semi-autonomous communities, Marquetalia, was located in the southern department of Tolima, an isolated part of the country. Marquetalia was an area in which communist guerrillas (numbering about 200) worked side-by-side with farmers in order to build what they believed would be a better, more just society. The guerrillas considered Marquetalia to be an independent "republic" in which guerrilla leaders held cabinet positions determined by their military experience and Marxist education.

The Colombian state, however, saw the institutionalization of autonomous zones like Marquetalia as a direct threat to its legitimacy. In 1964, President Guillermo Leon Valencia, under pressure from a congress that mocked him for his inability to do something about these movements, ordered the Colombian military to attack Marquetalia, sparking a bloody battle.[16] The Colombian military utilized approximately 3,500 government soldiers, including 170 troops from the elite Batallón Colombia (which had specific orders to capture the guerrillas' leader, Manuel Marulanda (see Photo 3.1), who still controls the FARC today) as well as scores of Paez Indians, who served as guides for the troops.[17] The seemingly easily ensured victory proved much more difficult to achieve. While the government's troops prevailed, that they struggled to defeat a few hundred guerrillas was an embarrassment. The attack also galvanized the guerrillas, bolstering their belief that profound political, social, and economic change in Colombia could only come through armed struggle.[18]

Shortly after the incident, and despite the fact that virtually all of the "republics" had been recovered by the Colombian military, the guerrillas escaped to a nearby communist autonomous community called Rio Chiquito. A few days later the Fuerzas Armadas Revolucionarias de Colombia was formally organized.[19] In July 1964 the "First Convergence of the Nation's Southern Bloc" took place. Taken to be the FARC's first official conference, the FARC declared its identity by announcing: "Beginning

FARC leader Manuel "Sureshot" Marulanda. Photo by Marcelo Salinas.

today, July 20, we are a guerrilla movement." In 1965, Colombian army intelligence reported that the total number of guerrillas active in Colombia was between 700 and 800 persons.[20]

At that time, the FARC had much in its favor as it drew upon its organizational and logistical roots in the communist self-defense organizations active in the 1940s and 1950s. The FARC also maintained links with the Communist Party, although the ties between the two groups were never nearly as intimate as some in Colombia and the United States have suggested. Then, as is the case today, the FARC resorted to kidnapping, extortion, and war taxes to fund its insurgents, providing them with cash to keep themselves well-armed over the course of several decades. As Jorge Osterling makes clear, the FARC has utilized a variety of methods to generate revenue:

The system allegedly works as follows: the *Estado Mayor* (senior staff) of a *frente* budgets its economic needs and plans a series of fundraising operations using various tactics. One of the classic ones involves the temporary seizure of a small town for propaganda purposes, usually including the robbery of all local banks and credit unions, a tactic which is said to have decreased use since the signing of the 1984 agreements. A second tactic, allegedly still used, has been the kidnapping of the wealthy, both in urban and rural areas, demanding exorbitant amounts of ransom money in exchange for the victim's safe return, threatening his life if the national authorities intervene. [Another] fundraising tactic, known as *gramaje* (payment based on grams) has allegedly developed in the Eastern Plains in the form of protection services to the owners of cocaine plantations, laboratories, and narcotraffickers in exchange for a percentage of the grams of cocaine paste produced in the area.[21]

Knowing that it was not nearly powerful enough to overthrow the Colombian government, over the years the FARC decided to disperse its forces throughout the country, believing that more frequent attacks in a greater number of areas would be the best strategy to compensate for their numerical disadvantage vis-à-vis the Colombian military. These dispersed groups, called *frentes,* have operated in a semi-autonomous manner since their inception, and doubtless, at times, have little or no idea what type of operations—or even specific ideologies—other *frentes* are implementing. Moreover, there remains a great debate today in Colombia as to whether the central hierarchy of the FARC is always able to effectively control all of its *frentes,* which now number roughly 100. As will be discussed later in this chapter, in the fall of 1998 the Colombian government granted the FARC a 16,000-square-mile liberated zone in the department of Caquetá. The FARC continued to control this region through February 2002.[22]

Ejército de Liberación Nacional (ELN; National Liberation Army). Colombia's second major guerrilla group is the ELN. Unlike the FARC, with its pro-Moscow–oriented origins, the ELN began in 1964 more as a traditional Latin American revolutionary group, along the lines of Fidel Castro's movement in Cuba in the 1950s. The ELN believed that it could repeat the *foco* strategy—in which a group of committed, educated leaders over time wins the trust of the local, rural population and turns them into revolutionaries—that Fidel Castro had used so successfully in the Sierra Maestra in Cuba in the 1950s. In fact, during the early 1960s a number of the ELN's leaders traveled to Cuba to study methods of fomenting revolution. On November 11, 1962, from Havana, the ELN leadership formed the Brigada Pro Liberación Nacional de Colombia José Antonio Galán. This brigade soon dissolved, but its Cuban-influenced principles and tactics nevertheless became embedded in the ELN's ideology.

Upon returning from Cuba, the leadership of the ELN chose to establish itself in the department of Santander in the eastern Andes, mainly because this area had an incipient rural labor force that seemed conducive to political mobilization. The ELN was formally founded in Santander on July 4, 1964. The group gained notoriety when in 1966 a well-known Belgian-trained Catholic priest named Camilo Torres left the National University in Bogotá and joined the ELN. Torres was killed in combat soon thereafter, but his involvement with the group brought it greater recognition and legitimacy.

The 1970s was a period of military consolidation for the ELN, as the group was experiencing a relative degree of success in its operations in and around Santander. This growing strength prompted President Misael Pastrana (father of president Andrés Pastrana) to call for a total war against the ELN in 1972. In less than two months the Colombian military almost completely destroyed the ELN, exemplified by the deaths of several of their top military commanders. For the rest of the 1970s the ELN was mired in a deep crisis as it attempted to rebound from this defeat as well as deal with a myriad of internal disputes.

During the 1980s the ELN moved away from the *foco* strategy and more toward an ideology of economic nationalism, best seen by targeting foreign oil executives, bombing oil pipelines, and accusing the state-owned oil company—ECOPETROL—of selling the nation's patrimony. The ELN particularly targeted oil companies that were operating the Caño Limón-Coveñas pipeline, which runs between the department of Arauca and the Caribbean coast. It is estimated that between 1986 and 1997 there were 79 million barrels of crude oil spilled in pipeline attacks.[23] For most of the 1980s and well into the 1990s, the ELN did not go much beyond what had come to be routine pipeline bombings or the occasional kidnapping of a multinational company executive.

In recent years, however, the ELN has stepped up the frequency of its attacks, and increasingly these actions seem to have very little to do with economic nationalism. For example, in April 1999, ELN commandos hijacked an Avianca Airlines flight from Bucaramanga to Bogotá and took the passengers hostage. As of late 2001 three passengers from that flight were still being held captive.[24] A month later, the guerrilla organization kidnapped an entire church congregation while it was attending mass in a wealthy neighborhood in Cali; in 2000, the ELN also bombed the Caño Limón-Coveñas pipeline an estimated twenty-three times.[25] Some observers suspect that as the government has once again entered into peace negotiations with the FARC, the ELN has undertaken such brazen operations in order to reinforce the point that it too deserves a seat at the negotiating table. In 2001 the ELN continued to insist that successful negotiations would only occur after its receives a liberated zone along the lines of what the FARC received in 1998. Under the auspices of several European countries and Cuba, negotiations between the Colombian government and the ELN over the granting of a 1,000-square-mile liberated zone in north central Colombia continue.[26]

Ejército Popular de Liberación (EPL; Popular Liberation Army). Smaller than either the FARC or the ELN, the third major first-generation guerrilla group is the EPL. Founded in April 1967, it was originally a Maoist-oriented organization, although like the ELN it admired the success and tactics of the Cuban revolution. Over time the group turned away from this orientation and focused more on a combined urban-rural strategy. By the late 1970s and early 1980s, the EPL had broken completely from its links with China and instead attempted to diversify both its ideologies and its military strategies. The EPL signed a peace agreement with the Betancur administration in 1984, but this broke down a little over a year later. Today the EPL is an extremely small guerrilla group, although the exact number of members is difficult to estimate. Its activities are concentrated in the departments of Antioquia, Urabá, and Santander, and its ability to carry out military operations pale in comparison to that of either the FARC or the ELN.

The Second Generation

Movimiento 19 de Abril (M-19; April 19 Movement). Beginning in the 1970s, another series of guerrilla groups took up arms in Colombia, many of which were small, regionally focused groups emerging in the "narrow institutional space and rebellious greenhouse of Colombian politics."[27] Chief among these new movements was the M-19, founded after the 1970 presidential election, in which it was alleged that former coup leader and populist presidential candidate Gustavo Rojas Pinilla from the political party Alianza Nacional Popular (ANAPO; National

Popular Alliance) had victory stolen from him through fraud (April 19 was the day of the election). While it never seriously threatened to seize power from the Colombian government, the M-19 nonetheless did carry out a number of flamboyant operations that brought it a great deal of attention. These included:

- The January 17, 1974, theft of Simón Bolívar's sword. This operation had symbolic significance, for in committing it the M-19 laid claim as the legitimate heirs to Bolívar's legacy. The M-19 said that they would only return the sword once Bolívar's ideals had been introduced into the political system. They also painted revolutionary slogans on the walls of Bogotá's city hall.
- The New Year's Eve 1979 theft of approximately 5,000 weapons from a Bogotá army arsenal using a hand-hewn tunnel.
- The February 1980 seizure of the embassy of the Dominican Republic. The M-19 held the embassy with fifteen foreign ambassadors inside for two months. Fidel Castro became involved in the negotiations, and the M-19 received a U.S.$1 million cash payment and its commandos were given safe passage to Havana.
- The 1981 "invasion" of Colombia near the Atlantic Coast town of Tumaco. This operation was a military disaster and marked the M-19's shift from an urban to a more rural movement.
- The November 6, 1985, seizure of the Palace of Justice in Bogotá. The Colombian military stormed the palace and in the fighting eleven (out of twenty-four) supreme court justices were killed, along with several civilians and almost all of the commandos.

The raid on the Palace of Justice provoked widespread condemnation throughout Colombia, and was one of the catalysts that led to the M-19's decision to transform itself into a political movement. Americas Watch has written:

> Public reaction against the M-19 for attacking the Palace of Justice was massive. Moreover, the episode confirmed many Colombians' worst fears about the M-19. For the right, the attack was conclusive proof that the M-19 is no more than a group of assassins and terrorists to whom no quarter should be given. For those who were more neutral towards the group or even sympathetic, the attack was an enormously costly strategic error that indicates how isolated from political and military realities the M-19 has grown, and how far it has fallen from the group that once offered the possibility of a non-Marxist left-wing in Colombia.[28]

It has also been reported that the M-19 received U.S.$1 million from the Medellín cartel in order to carry out the palace attack. Since the supreme court justices had just declared their support for a U.S.-Colombian extradition treaty, some observers believe the objective of the attack was to destroy the documents that linked drug traffickers to several pending extradition efforts.[29] The attack was the last gasp for the M-19. In 1990 it became one of the few serious guerrilla groups to permanently lay down its arms and enter the mainstream political system.

Movimiento Armado Quintín Lame (MAQL; Quintín Lame Armed Movement). The other major second-generation guerrilla group was the MAQL. It was founded in March 1985 in the department of Cauca as an indigenous guerrilla force seeking to promote indigenous rights and provide defense against hostile landowners. During the two decades leading up to the formation of the MAQL, the Paez and Gambiano Indians, most of whom reside in the departments of Cauca, Tolima, and Huila, had established ties with the FARC. Yet as some of the Indian groups became more militant, they clashed with elements in the FARC who believed that any armed indigenous group should be subordinate to their own organization. This brewing tension culminated in February 1981 when FARC members in the department of Cauca murdered seven Paez leaders.

This growing competition with the FARC prompted the armed indigenous groups to form their own independent guerrilla group. In April 1985 the newly formed MAQL kidnapped a group of journalists in the southern city of Popayán and took them to a remote location, where they were told about the new guerrilla group. MAQL members described themselves as a self-defense group created "because the Indians had been left alone in a cross-fire between the landlords, the Colombian armed forces, and the FARC-guerrilla forces."[30] The MAQL remained a relatively small organization, and it eventually laid down its arms and participated in the 1991 Constituent Assembly.

Coordinadora Nacional Guerrillera (CNG; National Guerrilla Coordinating Group). With many guerrilla groups active in Colombia over the past few decades, it is not surprising that they eventually decided to unify themselves under a national coordinating body. Created in June 1985, the CNG consisted of those armed groups such as the ELN that never signed an agreement with the Betancur administration, as well as those such as the EPL and the M-19 that signed agreements only to soon afterward return to armed activity. The MAQL, as well as a few other even smaller guerrilla groups, were also members. The FARC did not participate, as at this time it was still observing the cease-fire it had signed with the Betancur administration.

The idea behind the creation of the CNG was that by increasing communication among the various guerrilla groups they would be able to improve the coordination—and in turn success—of their armed activities. The body was initially organized by the M-19, who thought that by uniting the guerrilla groups they would be in a strong position to defeat the Colombian military. Yet while the CNG was able to coordinate attacks (it averaged roughly one per week in the late 1980s), its lack of aggregate military power vis-à-vis the military prevented it from achieving its ultimate goal of a complete military victory. And as the following excerpt makes clear, like most of the individual guerrilla groups, the CNG had its share of internal problems. In August 1986 a CNG conference was held in northeastern Antioquia under the motto "Unity Is Part of Victory":

> The conference was attended by the commanders of the ELN, EPL, M-19, PL, and PRT [the PL and the PRT were two of the smaller guerrilla groups]. Absent was the delegation of the Commando Quintín Lame. Six reporters of the nation's most important newspapers and magazines were invited. According to Bogotá's *Semana,* the conference consisted of a disorderly discussion of a variety of issues which included ways of humanizing the war, attempts to justify personal threats, and condemnation of extortion, blackmail, ransom, but not of kidnapping. Media people who attended were impressed by the inability of the guerrilla commanders to discuss clearly and precisely and to justify their political goals, objectives, and actions. For example, when the guerrilla commanders were invited to discuss the 1985 attacks against General Samudio [then army commander, later minister of defense] or against Jaime Castro Castro [then minister of government, later temporarily compelled to leave Colombia], or the whole peace process, their answers were vague and evasive.[31]

In 1986 the CNG changed its name to Coordinadora Guerrillera Simón Bolívar (CGSB), bolstered by the recent inclusion of the FARC following the breakdown of its cease-fire agreement with the government. Quickly, however, the M-19, the MAQL, and a faction of the EPL entered into peace negotiations with the government. The FARC, the ELN, and parts of the EPL thus became the groups that now composed the CGSB. Since this time, the CGSB has been largely ineffective, exemplified by the guerrilla groups' intermittent battles with each other. The body has now virtually disappeared, leaving each guerrilla group to operate and negotiate on its own.[32]

ATTEMPTS AT PEACE

The Betancur Administration: 1982–1986

In what seemed to be a good omen for peace in Colombia, several guerrilla groups greeted the 1982 election victory of Conservative Party candidate Belisario Betancur with an undeclared suspension of armed activity. On August 7, 1982, the day of his inauguration, Betancur offered a "white flag of truce" to the guerrillas and established an all-party peace commission that quickly got the guerrillas talking with senior government officials. At his inauguration, Betancur declared: "I am extending my hand to the rebels in arms so that they may join in the full exercise of their rights. . . . I declare peace to my fellow citizens without any distinction . . . to this priority I am committed."[33] In a gesture signifying that the guerrillas were pleased with Betancur's seemingly open-ended offer for peace, FARC leader Manuel Marulanda personally praised Betancur's commitment to a negotiated settlement.

Betancur's first substantive overture to the guerrillas was a sweeping amnesty law that, in its most important effect, did not require disarmament as a prerequisite for qualification. As Jorge Osterling has pointed out, for Betancur "peace was to be obtained by any means, and amnesty was seen as an invitation for dialogue and for a cease-fire."[34] According to official Colombian government figures, this amnesty law benefited 1,089 guerrillas, of whom 818 were members of the M-19, 152 were of the FARC, and 75 were of the ELN.[35]

Betancur's efforts began to produce results a few years later when in 1984, after negotiations with the government in the FARC's stronghold of La Uribe, the FARC agreed to a one-year cease-fire and agreed to end any type of terrorist activity such as kidnapping or economic extortion. This did not, however, force the FARC to relinquish its arms.[36] Shortly after the accord was signed with the FARC, the M-19 and the EPL also reached agreements with the government; these also did not require them to give up their arms (the M-19 unilaterally withdrew eight months later). The refusal of splinter factions within these two groups (as well as within the FARC) to negotiate revealed the weaknesses of these agreements. The Betancur government secretly met with leaders of the M-19 in Spain (October 1983) and in Mexico (December 1984), but these meetings did not lead to a lasting peace agreement. The ELN participated in negotiations in the early 1980s, but never signed an agreement with the government.

Throughout the Betancur years, guerrilla disarmament was the major sticking point during most of the negotiations with the various guerrilla groups. According to Americas Watch: "By not requiring the guerrillas to disarm, the accords tacitly recognize the guerrillas as ongoing armed organizations. But the accords fail to clarify what should follow from this fact. . . . The ambiguity created by the accords' silence on arms has muddied—and bloodied—the peace process."[37]

A year later, on March 30, 1985, the FARC announced that it would reorganize itself as a political party, the Unión Patriótica (UP; Patriotic Union), marking the first time since its inception in the 1960s that this group would try its hand in the mainstream political system. Yet in the years following the creation of the UP, over 1,000 of its members were assassinated (mostly by drug traffickers and paramilitary groups), including its presidential candidates in 1986 (Jaime Pardo Leal) and 1990 (Bernardo Jaramillo Ossa). (On May 24, 1999, Chief Prosecutor Alfonso Gómez charged paramilitary leader Carlos Castaño for masterminding the murder of Bernardo Jaramillo Ossa, as well as the murder of 1990 M-19 candidate Carlos Pizarro.)[38] In light of growing attacks on the UP, the FARC gave up on the idea of political integration and instead renewed its effort to promote its armed struggle, leaving the orphaned UP to fend for itself. A 1986 letter that UP legislators sent to President Betancur describes the position that these political leaders found themselves in:

> Throughout the electoral campaign, detachments from the Armed Forces have attacked FARC camps, and, with the pretext of carrying out military campaigns, repress the peasant population in order to sow panic and threaten them if they vote for the Patriotic Union. Paramilitary groups, and even detachments from the Army and the police distribute propaganda, paint party slogans on walls, pass out bulletins and flyers, put up posters, and draw up false statements, among which they propagate the most infamous calumnies against the Patriotic Union. . . . These criminal actions are multiplied by the paramilitary groups that sow death and insecurity in the broad regions of influence of the Patriotic Union, including urban centers. . . . This is not a matter of occasional excesses on the part of the troops. These are truly plans prepared in advance and executed with care.[39]

In 1985 the truce brokered with the M-19 also broke down as the group accused the government of failing to implement the political reforms that it claimed had been promised as part of the peace agreement. Just three days before the M-19 signed its August 1984 accord with the government, former congressman and M-19 leader Carlos Toledo Plata was murdered in the provincial oil town of Barrancabermeja. To make matters worse, in November 1985 drug trafficker–financed paramilitary groups launched a grenade attack at a Cali restaurant, where along with several others, M-19 leader Antonio Navarro Wolff was seriously injured. These acts of violence made the M-19 rethink its agreement with the government, especially since the government never produced convincing answers as to who was responsible for these actions. It was in this same year that the M-19 launched its disastrous attack on the Palace of Justice in Bogotá.

The Barco, Gaviria, and Samper Administrations: 1986–1998

As exemplified by the failure of the UP, peace agreements brokered between the government and the FARC during the Betancur administration did not result in any lasting type of demobilization. Nevertheless, subsequent Colombian administrations would have greater success negotiating with the guerrillas, especially the second-generation groups. In 1990, for example, the M-19, led by their charismatic leader Carlos Pizarro, once again entered into negotiations with the Colombian government. This time it was the Barco administration that adopted a much less flexible negotiating strategy. Specifically, Barco pushed for the guerrillas' explicit disarmament and reincorporation into the orthodox political system in return for the government's willingness to negotiate with them. This strategy was markedly different from Betancur's broader-based, more flexible tactics, which included the negotiation of structural issues such as land reform.

Still reeling after their attack on the Palace of Justice five years earlier, in March of 1990 the M-19 signed an agreement that led to its demobilization and incorporation into the political process.[40] A month later Pizarro, now the leader of an M-19 that was recognized as a legal political party, Acción Democrática M-19, was assassinated while a passenger on an Avianca airliner, a gruesome reminder that peace in Colombia was far from consolidated even though "peace" had been negotiated.

Maintaining the narrower focus of the Barco administration, which above all refused to negotiate the sovereign right of the Colombian government to govern the country, the administration of César Gaviria (1990–1994) successfully negotiated peace agreements with the MAQL and the EPL. Both groups participated in the Constituent Assembly that ultimately produced a new constitution in 1991.[41] Gaviria used the assembly as a "carrot" to entice the guerrilla groups to lay down their arms and participate in this opportunity to construct a "new Colombia."

Gaviria also took the bold step of inviting M-19 presidential candidate Antonio Navarro Wolff (Wolff took over the presidential candidacy after the assassination of Pizarro and came in third in the 1990 election) to be his minister of health. But while Gaviria was able to broker a deal with the EPL, the MAQL, and the M-19, as well as with a few other small guerrilla groups who also took up his offer, the FARC and the ELN did not sign an agreement. Gaviria responded by stepping up military efforts to crush these "recalcitrant" guerrilla groups.

While progress was made during the Barco and Gaviria administrations to get the second-generation groups to lay down their arms, the two largest guerrilla groups—the FARC and the ELN—did not follow such a path. The Colombian government did in fact conduct negotiations with these groups in Caracas, Venezuela (1990), and Tlaxcala, Mexico (1991). Yet these negotiations did not get very far due partly to the government's demand that the guerrillas lay down their arms before the talks began. The guerrillas in turn insisted on security guarantees that the military found unacceptable.

The FARC and the ELN demanded a broad agenda (e.g., land reform, income distribution, regional autonomy) and the Gaviria administration, although it did consider this type of approach, began to swing back to a narrower focus first introduced by the Barco government. The willingness of the guerrillas to negotiate was further undermined by the dismal performance of the political parties formed by the erstwhile guerrillas in the current election. As Marc Chernick has pointed out, "the outcome of the peace initiatives of the Gaviria administration [were]: partial peace agreements, major constitutional reform, expanded guerrilla activity, higher levels of violence, and dirty war."[42] Amazingly, the Gaviria years are considered to be one of the high points of government-guerrilla negotiations over the past two decades. Gaviria eventually called off the talks in 1992 and more "normal" hostilities between the government and the guerrillas resumed and continue today.

President Ernesto Samper tried to revive the peace efforts that were started by Betancur and continued through the Barco and Gaviria years. Early into his term of office, he appointed former minister of education

Carlos Holmes Trujillo as High Commissioner for Peace and instructed him to open up discreet negotiations with the guerrillas. The ELN and the EPL responded positively to these feelers, but in May 1995 the FARC launched a countrywide offensive that made many in the Samper administration—and, more important, the military—believe that there was no use in pursuing negotiations.

The possibility of any further substantive peace talks died when the military vetoed Samper's plan to withdraw the Colombian military from the region of La Uribe, the site where the scheduled talks with the FARC were to take place. This is not to mention the fact that Samper's profound lack of credibility because of the drug issue made the guerrillas even more reluctant to negotiate. Instead, they preferred to wait until Samper's successor was firmly in power, as they knew he would most likely have the authority to actually implement any potential settlement.

During these stages of the peace negotiations the United States barely paid any attention to the conflict in Colombia. In the middle to late 1980s the United States was still beginning the Andean source-country component of its war on drugs. Thus guerrilla insurgents in Colombia were not seen as particularly important, especially since they were much weaker than they are today. Moreover, during these years, groups like the FARC were much less involved in the production and trafficking of cocaine and heroine and thus Washington did not see them as an enemy in the drug war.

This neglect, however, evaporated, as the U.S. government now views the Colombian guerrilla insurgents as one of the most important pieces of the counternarcotics struggle. And since these groups are currently involved in peace talks with the Pastrana administration, the United States has taken an unprecedented interest in these negotiations, which has included visits to FARC-controlled areas by congressional delegations and secret talks between State Department and FARC officials in Costa Rica in late 1998.

Andrés Pastrana's Peace Efforts

President-elect Andrés Pastrana's July 1998 visit to FARC-controlled territory to meet with Manuel Marulanda was received with great enthusiasm in Colombia.[43] After years of delay and frustration at the negotiating table, it was now widely believed that Pastrana was the person who could finally bring home a peace agreement with the FARC. A few months after this widely publicized visit, the Colombian government and the FARC entered into talks pertaining to the establishment of a liberated zone (or *despeje*) in a Switzerland-size area of south central Colombia that was one of the FARC's traditional strongholds (see Map 3.1).

On November 7, 1998, the Colombian government granted the FARC the *despeje* for a period of ninety days. This agreement extracted all Colombian military forces from the area, giving the FARC effective control; it has also allowed the FARC to set up a parallel local government, including its own judicial system and police force. Serious peace negotiations—the ostensible quid pro quo for the government's enormous concession—began with the FARC in the *despeje* in early January 1999. In what would turn out to be the first of countless insults and upstages, FARC leader Manuel Marulanda failed to show up to greet President Pastrana for the opening ceremony. Over the course of the next three years numerous peace dialogues were frozen and cease-fires were broken.

Adding insult to the Pastrana administration's already faltering peace strategies, reports started emanating from the *despeje* that the FARC was using the zone to cultivate coca and train troops, two things that were expressly forbidden when the deal was negotiated. But while the Colombian government and military were clearly furious about the FARC's apparent lack of faith at the peace talks, as time went by it became increasingly evident that the Colombian military could not take back the *despeje* even if it wanted to. Aware that its military could not defeat the FARC militarily, it is not surprising that the Colombian government has continuously extended the *despeje*'s deadline for over three years without an end in sight. One extension came in December 2000 fifteen minutes before the agreement was to expire, indicating that President Pastrana had profound difficulties in justifying another extension of the deadline with virtually no FARC concessions as compensation.[44] In early March 2001, some thirty ambassadors from around the world traveled to the *despeje* to meet with the FARC in hopes that the international presence would help to jump-start the peace talks. It is likely that no significant movement on the peace front will be made before Pastrana's successor is inaugurated in August 2002.

From the beginning of the government-FARC peace talks in 1998, the U.S. government made a point of maintaining distance from the process, stating that it was a Colombian issue and not one in which the United States should get involved. U.S. officials did discuss the peace process with FARC officials during secret talks in Costa Rica in December 1998, but any dialogue quickly ended after the FARC killed three U.S. environmental activists in early 1999.

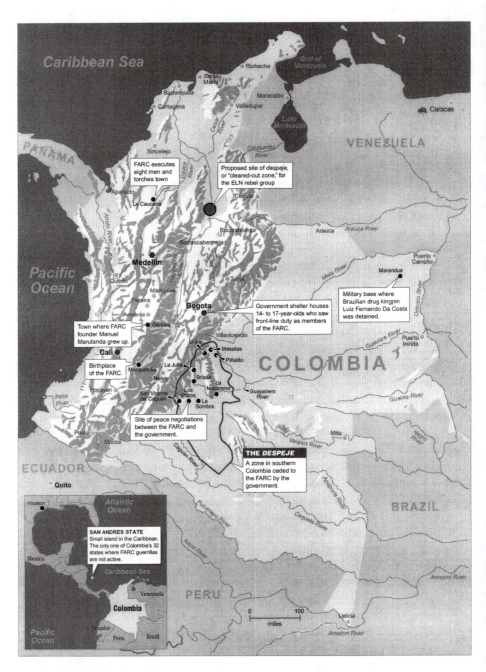

Caribbean Sea

Santa Marta
Riohacha
Gulf of Venezuela

Barranquilla
Maracaibo
Valledupar

Cartagena

VENEZUELA

Caracas

Sincelejo

FARC executes eight men and torches town

Proposed site of *despeje*, or "cleared-out zone," for the ELN rebel group

PANAMA

Apartadó

La Caucana

Cúcuta

Bucaramanga

Arauca

Arauca River

Puerto Carreño

Barrancabermeja

Medellín

Quibdó

Manizales

Tunja

Meta River

Marandua

Military base where Brazilian drug kingpin Luiz Fernando Da Costa was detained.

Pacific Ocean

Pereira

Armenia

Genova

Bogotá

Government shelter houses 14- to 17-year-olds who saw front-line duty as members of the FARC.

Guaviare River

Puerto Inírida

Town where FARC founder Manuel Marulanda grew up.

Villavicencio

Uribe

Mesetas

Piñalito

Cali

Birthplace of the FARC.

Marquetalia

La Julia

Neiva

Brisas

La Macarena

COLOMBIA

Guainía River

Popayán

San Vicente del Caguán

Los Pozos

La Sombra

Guayabero River

Patia River

Site of peace negotiations between the FARC and the government.

Pasto

Mocoa

Mitú

Vaupés River

Negro River

Caguán River

THE *DESPEJE*
A zone in southern Colombia ceded to the FARC by the government.

ECUADOR

Caquetá River

BRAZIL

Quito

Putumayo River

Atlantic Ocean

Houston

SAN ANDRES STATE
Small island in the Caribbean. The only one of Colombia's 32 states where FARC guerrillas are not active.

Mexico

Caribbean Sea

PERU

Leticia

Amazon River

Venezuela

Colombia

Ecuador

Peru

Brazil

0   100
miles

Amazon River

Pacific Ocean

Map 3.1 The FARC's *Despeje*

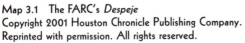

While the Colombian government's efforts to make headway with the FARC have gone nowhere, there have been interesting developments in the negotiations with the ELN.[45] This scenario is complicated, however, by the ELN's continued policy of economic terrorism and kidnapping as well as the gruesome reality that a peace deal between the government and the ELN will not necessarily prevent right-wing paramilitary groups from continuing their all-out assault on the ELN.

Over the past few years the ELN's pipeline bombings have resulted in an average loss of U.S.$3 million per day and a drop in total annual production from 2.2 to 1.9 million barrels. This is especially significant now that Colombia earns an estimated U.S.$3.7 billion from oil exports each year, replacing coffee as the country's leading source of foreign exchange. Colombia is also considered to be a prime location for increased oil exploration, as potential areas have not been analyzed for oil content due to the armed conflict. Not surprisingly, the U.S. government now considers Colombia's oil to be a "strategic resource" and issues such as the ELN's oil-related violence are receiving increased attention in Washington.

Many observers attribute the ELN's ongoing strategy of pipeline bombings to its long-standing policy of economic nationalism and anti-Americanism. Yet while the ELN's rhetoric has not noticeably changed from previous decades, there are growing indications that the group's actions might be as much about paving the way to a peace settlement with the government as they are a symbol of its hatred of foreign oil companies. This shift in strategy is due in part to the series of military defeats that the ELN has suffered at the hands of the military, paramilitaries, and even its current guerrilla rival the FARC. The ELN is desperate: it needs a peace deal with the government or it risks complete annihilation, most likely at the hands of paramilitary groups that have moved into the ELN's strongholds in recent years.

Thus the ELN's recent increase in attacks can be seen as a sort of saber-rattling exercise intended to demonstrate to the government that it is still a formidable force that, like the FARC, should be respected at the negotiating table. Bolstering this view is that in recent years the ELN has branched out from oil pipeline attacks into operations that are much more difficult to justify as promoting economic nationalism.

During the Pastrana years, negotiations between the Colombian government and the ELN have been centered around the idea that the ELN would be granted a *despeje* along the lines of that granted the FARC in 1998. In this case, the *despeje* negotiated was slated to be approximately 1,000 square kilometers, roughly the size of the U.S. state of Delaware. Colombian army and police forces were to be withdrawn, replaced with civic police forces organized by and under the control of local mayors. The ELN made repeated pledges that it would respect the jurisdiction of these civic forces during the initial nine-month period that the *despeje* would be in operation. The ELN has also stated that it would use the *despeje* period to conduct its National Convention, at which various sectors of Colombian society would join in a dialogue with the ELN about the peace process. The ELN's end game was most likely to use the National Convention and concomitant peace talks in order to insert itself into the orthodox political system, along the lines of the M-19's political incorporation in the early 1990s.

While it was clearly committed to going ahead with the agreement, in 2001 the Colombian government remained ambivalent about an ELN *despeje*. Most of this hesitation was fear that the area would become another "FARC-landia," the derisive term used to describe the reality in the FARC's *despeje* in south central Colombia. To ensure that there was no new "ELN-landia," the government has recruited a number of countries now named the "Group of Friends" (Spain, France, Norway, Switzerland, and Cuba) to be part of a verification commission that would monitor activities inside the ELN's zone. There has been a mixed response from local residents who live inside the proposed *despeje*. Some have voiced support for the initiative, as they believe that the *despeje* would provide the necessary jump-start to a long-delayed peace process. On the other hand, many residents have felt abandoned by Bogotá, as if their welfare is being negotiated away in a feeble attempt to broker peace with a terrorist organization.

Yet no matter how local sentiment leans, it is clear that the proposed *despeje* is still far from reality. For example, in March 2001 the ELN suspended talks with the government via an e-mail message to the government's High Commissioner for Peace; most believe this was due to the ELN's visceral dislike of U.S.-sponsored illicit crop fumigation efforts in areas where it operates. Further complicating this matter is that the paramilitary groups active in the region have responded to the potential ELN *despeje* with brutal force, stating that they would never recognize its "sovereignty." To the paramilitaries, the new *despeje* would be nothing more than a sanctuary that the guerrillas could use to bolster their fighting capability. Indeed, when the idea of another *despeje* was first announced in 2000, paramilitary forces responded by going on a drunken rampage, killing forty-five farmers—many were hacked to death and some were beheaded. In April 2001, in an area located just outside the proposed *despeje,* 800 paramilitary fighters attacked ELN positions, preventing some ELN commanders from attending peace talks with the government.

The ELN is engaged in a critical episode in its evolution. It is juggling its peace talks with the government with the threat of annihilation from the paramilitaries, all the while attempting to maintain its claim that it is fighting for Colombia's economic and social soul against imperialist foreign multinational companies and their domestic collaborators. There remains a distinct possibility that the ELN will not exist in a few years, either due to a successful peace agreement that promotes its insertion into civil society or due to military defeat by the paramilitaries. While at this point it is impossible to predict with any certainty the ELN's future, what is more certain is that the ELN's continued policy of economic nationalism of pipeline attacks, extortion, and kidnappings will ensure widespread economic disruption to Colombia's economy for the foreseeable future. On September 10, 2001, the ELN announced that it was pulling out of peace talks with the government and any potential for a liberated zone or peace agreement during Andrés Pastrana's term in office was effectively ended.[46]

THE ROOTS OF THE DRUG TRAFFICKERS

The cocaine-exporting business first began in any substantial form in Colombia in the 1970s.[47] But drug trafficking at this time was not the sophisticated, multinational entity that it has been characterized as since the mid-1980s. Rather, incipient cocaine trafficking consisted of only a few individuals with rudimentary technology, with many of the makeshift laboratories located in private homes. Rensselaer Lee and Patrick Clawson write:

> Human couriers—"mules"—smuggled small quantities of cocaine—a few grams or a few pounds in luggage as personal effects. Trafficking organizations typically were simple, comprised of a Colombian buyer, a smuggler-courier, and a point of contact in the United States who received the merchandise and sold it to a U.S. wholesaler. Trafficking entrepreneurs sometimes acted as their own mules. At one time most pioneers of the Colombian cocaine industry—Pablo Escobar, the Ochoa brothers, Carlos Lehder, the Rodríguez Orejuela brothers—personally carried small amounts of cocaine to the United States.[48]

As the profits from the cocaine trade continued to flow into their pockets, the drug cartels discarded the mule system and adopted a much more sophisticated strategy that utilized maritime fleets or aircraft that could carry loads of 400 to 1,000 kilograms of cocaine.[49] In 1976, former car thief Carlos Lehder became the first Colombian to implement such a strategy. He carried 550 pounds of cocaine on his first smuggling flight into the United States, earning him a U.S.$1 million profit.[50]

Amazingly, Lehder started using his drug profits to launch his own political movement, called the Movimiento Latino Nacional (MLN; National Latino Movement). It was anti-imperialist, anti-Zionist, and above all, anti-extradition. Interestingly, in the 1986 presidential election the MLN endorsed the leftist, former guerrilla UP party.[51] Lehder's ingenious drug-trafficking strategy caused U.S. attorney and chief prosecutor Robert Merkle to comment: "Lehder was to cocaine trafficking what Henry Ford was to automobiles."[52] Lehder was captured near Medellín in 1987 and extradited to the United States, where he is serving a life sentence plus 135 years.[53] Quickly, the two major organizations involved in the cocaine trade—the Cali and Medellín cartels—became household names in the United States, as these two groups were blamed for the rapidly growing and seemingly out-of-control cocaine (or "crack") epidemic in the United States.[54]

Such an extensive and large-scale "business" like the drug trade could never stay out of sight forever. A clash between the cartels and the Colombian government was inevitable, especially since it involved the issue of extradition to the United States. As the 1980s wore on, the Colombian government tired of the cartels' ability to act with virtual impunity and began to crack down on their illicit activities. The response from the Medellín cartel was predictable: violence.[55] During the 1980s and early 1990s, close to 500 policemen were killed by drug traffickers; between 1984 and 1990 a minister of justice, the director of the newspaper *El Espectador,* a supreme court justice, a leader of the UP, a governor of the department of Antioquia, an attorney general, and the leading Liberal Party presidential candidate in 1990 were all assassinated by the cartels.[56]

Violence took off beginning in 1989 when the Medellín "Extraditables"—a name they assumed to signal their opposition to extradition to the United States—declared "absolute and total war" against the government.[57] Now the cartels would enact violence throughout Colombia's urban areas, best seen by their indiscriminate car bomb operations (forty between 1989 and 1993) that left over 500 civilians dead.[58] The Medellín cartel's Pablo Escobar also went after some of Colombia's most prominent citizens, kidnapping Diana Turbay, a daughter of the former president, and Francisco Santos, news editor of the Bogotá daily *El Tiempo*.[59] The cartels and related paramilitary groups also targeted the leftist political groups, killing approximately 1,000 members of the UP.

The cartels' violence extended beyond the government and prominent civilians: the guerrillas also became targets of the traffickers. The traffickers' purchase of rural land with their profits put them into confrontation with the many insurgent groups who had roamed in these areas for decades. The drug cartels responded by forming paramilitary groups in order to combat the guerrillas and their civilian sympathizers. By mid-1989, approximately 11,000 paramilitary commandos were operating in Colombia, most under the control of the Medellín cartel.[60]

In an example of its bold tactics, the Medellín cartel also attempted to enter the political arena. In 1982, Pablo Escobar was elected to the Colombian Chamber of Deputies as the Liberal Party alternate from the department of Antioquia. In 1986, Carlos Lehder ran unsuccessfully for the Senate even though he was considered a fugitive. Furthermore, in his trademark Robin Hood fashion, Escobar courted Medellín's large disfranchised population by building them houses and soccer fields, as well as providing access to electricity and water.[61] Not surprisingly, this largess earned Escobar strong support within these poor communities.

Negotiations with the Medellín Cartel

At one point in the early 1980s it looked as though the Betancur administration was on the verge of striking a deal with the traffickers. Following the 1984 assassination of Justice Minister Lara Bonilla, the government declared a state of emergency and began to go after the cartel, seizing assets and declaring that military (not civilian) courts would try suspected traffickers. These moves frightened the Medellín cartel's leaders, who above all else feared extradition to the United States. They thus presented the Colombian government with a plan that, in return for their removal from the cocaine business, would have essentially granted them the same sort of amnesty that was being offered to the guerrillas.

While this quid pro quo might have been the one true opportunity to do something lasting about the drug-trafficking problem, it was firmly rejected by the Colombian political establishment, who viewed it as a thinly disguised form of capitulation to common criminals. On July 19, 1984, President Betancur issued a statement stating: "There has not

been, there is not now, nor will there be any kind of understanding between the government and signers of the memorandum—drug traffickers." The flirtation was over and the Medellín cartel continued its involvement in the drug-trafficking business.[62]

Several years later, following the August 18, 1989, assassination of
Liberal Party presidential candidate Luis Carlos Galán, one of three presidential candidates murdered before the 1990 presidential election, the
Barco administration declared its own war on the Medellín cartel. Negotiations with the cartels had been attempted throughout the 1980s without
any lasting result; the government felt it had no choice but to pursue a
more aggressive strategy. Spurred on by the United States, the Colombian
government approved an emergency law that now allowed Colombians to
be extradited to the United States, resulting in the extradition of more
than twenty drug traffickers.[63] The Barco administration set up a special
counternarcotics unit within the National Police headed by General Rosso
José Serrano and supported by British and U.S. intelligence services. Serrano's unit targeted the drug traffickers' pocketbooks by confiscating their
assets, such as property, weapons, and bank accounts.

After a while, however, with all of the violence that erupted following Barco's hard-line stance toward the cartels, the Colombian public
began to yearn for a return to negotiations, motivated mainly by the fear
and disgust of the levels of violence unleashed by the cartels against the
Colombian government and society. So even though newly elected president César Gaviria had ruled out negotiations during his campaign, once
in office he quickly reversed his stance and offered to talk with the cartels.[64] Gaviria initiated a "surrender policy" whereby those drug traffickers who surrendered to government officials were assured that they
would receive shortened sentences and not be extradited.[65]

This new policy at first proved effective, as it resulted in the surrender of many of the Medellín cartel's top leaders, including Pablo Escobar, who "surrendered" in June 1991.[66] Yet after revelations about the
plush conditions of the kingpins' imprisonment became public, there
was growing pressure to take a more militant line.[67] This view was
given even greater weight when in July 1992 Pablo Escobar and a dozen
other prisoners bribed their guards and walked out of their prison,
where the bathtubs were reportedly made of gold and Escobar was able
to handpick his guards, an act that no doubt embarrassed Gaviria, made
a mockery of his appeasement strategy, and infuriated the U.S. government. Gaviria responded by cracking down hard, creating an elite antidrug force called the Bloque de Búsqueda. After seventeen months of

searching, Colombian officials intercepted a cellular phone call on December 2, 1993, that Escobar had made to his son, enabling the security forces to track him to a Medellín rooftop, where he was then killed.[68]

While it achieved tangible results, Gaviria's strategy of appeasement had costs. In order to get at the Medellín cartel, Gaviria and his chief antidrug official, General Vargas Silva, relied upon the help of the Cali kingpins for information. And while this might have been vital for the efforts against the Medellín cartel, many believe that Gaviria in return did not seriously prosecute the Cali cartel.[69] Thus, once the Medellín cartel had been dismantled and the United States began to focus on the Cali cartel, Washington's relationship with the Gaviria administration quickly soured. Ironically, U.S. government officials initially greeted the election of Ernesto Samper with enthusiasm, as they thought he would be more effective than Gaviria in dealing with the Cali cartel's leaders.

Gaviria's negotiations did serve to eventually reduce the level of violence in Colombia, but they did little to mollify the U.S. government's concerns about overall drug production and exports to the United States. This discord clearly exemplifies how the interests of the Colombian government (reducing violence through negotiations with the cartels) were not the same as, and at times conflicted with, the interests of the United States (counternarcotics efforts). This issue will be discussed in detail, especially the case of the Colombian government's actions toward the Cali cartel, in Chapters 4 and 5.

The Cali Cartel

The vacuum in the drug trade created by the gradual dismantling of the Medellín cartel, which rapidly expanded following the death of Pablo Escobar at the hands of the Bloque de Búsqueda, was quickly filled by an increase in activity from drug traffickers operating in and around the southern provincial city of Cali. The decentralized business structure of the Cali cartel meant that their brand of drug trafficking was more dispersed and therefore more difficult for law enforcement officials to monitor. According to Robert Buckman, the Cali cartel can best been seen as a franchise operation that offers its services to the independent groups, providing logistical support and protection from the Medellín cartel in return for a share of the profits.[70]

This group of young criminals, led by drug kingpins such as Miguel and Gilberto Rodríguez Orejuela and José Rodríguez Londono, was not nearly as flamboyant or violent as its counterpart from Medellín and was generally known to prefer to influence politicians through bribes rather than bombs. It is estimated that one of the Cali cartel's leaders, Miguel Rodríguez Orejuela, spent several billions of the cartel's annual income bribing judges, police officers, politicians, and other government officials. One example in particular reveals the distinct approaches of the Medellín and Cali cartels. Medellín's Pablo Escobar offered a reward of U.S.$4,000 for each police officer slain; 400 officers were murdered while the reward was in effect. The Cali cartel, in contrast, apparently provided funds for police precinct stations to be built in the city in an effort to combat common crime.[71] The Cali cartel also utilized fewer people—about 5,000 personnel in 1991, compared to 70,000 for the Medellín cartel at its apex.[72]

The Cali cartel's kingpins—in particular the Rodríguez Orejuela brothers, José Santacruz Londoño, and "Pacho" Herrera—have been labeled the "world's most successful businessmen," collectively reaping higher annual profits than Boeing or Pepsi-Cola.[73] Through a very effective cocaine distribution network and widespread influence within the Colombian political system, the Cali cartel became, in the words of DEA chief Donnie Marshall, "the mob leaders of the '90s. However, they were far wealthier, far more dangerous, far more influential, and had a much more devastating impact on the day-to-day lives of the citizens of our country than either their domestic predecessors or the crime families from Medellín." On July 9, 1997, Marshall reflected:

> Miguel Orejuela and his confederates set up an extremely well disciplined system of compartmentalization that spanned and insulated every facet of their drug business. The organization's tentacles reached in to the cities and towns of the United States through their U.S.-based infrastructure or their surrogates who sold crack cocaine on the streets of locations as varied as Chicago, Illinois and Rocky Mount, North Carolina.[74]

Cocaine seizures linked to the Cali cartel increased significantly, and the manner in which the drugs were being smuggled reflected the cartel's "creative" characteristics (see Table 3.1).

The Cali cartel's rise to prominence—and subsequent persecution from the Colombian government—coincided with the administration of Ernesto Samper, who himself was accused of knowing that money from the cartel had entered his campaign. But even if the Cali cartel was less violent than its counterpart in Medellín, the United States still wanted it destroyed. To this end, the United States pressured the Samper administration to arrest the Cali kingpins and extradite them to the

Table 3.1　Major Worldwide Cocaine Seizures Linked to the Cali Cartel

Date	Location	Amount (metric tons)	Concealment Method
August 1991	United States	12.2	Concrete fence posts
April 1992	United States	6.7	Frozen broccoli
July 1992	Panama	5.4	Ceramic tiles
February 1993	Russia	1.1	Canned meat
October 1993	Mexico	8.0	False wall of vessel
November 1993	Mexico	6.8	Open marine cargo
March 1994	Italy	5.5	Shipment of shoes
June 1994	Mexico	4.0	False wall of vessel
August 1994	Colombia	5.6	Cocaine storage sites

Source: U.S. Department of Justice, "The Cali Cartel: The New Kings of Cocaine," DEA Drug Intelligence report, November 1994, p. 7.

United States for prosecution. Furthermore, the Cali cartel's less violent strategy had its limits, reflected in its brutal response to the notion that its members might be extradited to the United States.

Like the Medellín "Extraditables" from 1988 to 1991, the Cali cartel created its own brand of "Extraditables" and made it painfully clear that it too would resist extradition at all costs. In one potentially gruesome episode in November 4, 1996, a few days before the Colombian Senate was scheduled to debate the issue of extradition, a van loaded with 360 pounds of explosives was discovered in front of an industrial plant owned by a senator who was in favor of extradition. Many believe that the Rodríguez Orejuela brothers spearheaded this action from within their prison cells.

Unlike the drug war's current focus on crop eradication, U.S. antidrug policy in the late 1980s and early 1990s was formulated around the "kingpin strategy." As the name suggests, the strategy involved pursuing the leaders of the major drug-trafficking cartels: Medellín and Cali. The hope was that by capturing the kingpins, a leadership and logistical vacuum would form, forcing the cartels to implode.[75] This did not happen. Instead of reducing the amount of cocaine and heroine produced in Colombia, the kingpin strategy actually caused the production to shift to small- and medium-size traffickers. This in turn has "atomized" drug production and trafficking: drug-processing labs and shipments are now smaller, more dispersed, and much more difficult to locate and interdict.[76]

Another significant transformation in the nature of the drug war was the massive shift of coca cultivation from Bolivia and Peru to Colombia (see Figure 3.1). During the 1980s and through the mid-1990s, most of

Driven by Drugs

Figure 3.1   Coca Cultivation in the Andes

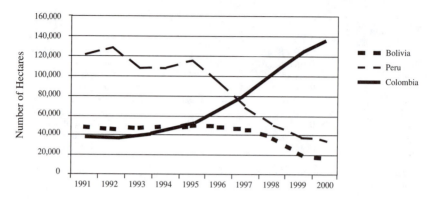

Source: U.S. Department of State, Bureau for International Narcotics and Law Enforcement, 2000.

the coca was cultivated in Bolivia and Peru and then transported into Colombia for processing. Under pressure from Washington, governments in Bolivia and Peru adopted rigorous programs of crop fumigation and substitution that drastically reduced the amount of coca under cultivation. Yet Colombian drug traffickers compensated for the drop in the supply of coca from Bolivia and Peru by increasing coca cultivation in Colombia (see Table 3.2). The explosion of coca cultivation in Colombia has served to fuel the armed conflict, as the main areas of cultivation—especially in the southern department of Putumayo—are located in traditional guerrilla areas. Moreover, paramilitary groups have increased their activity in these regions, such as taxing coca farmers, as they too are eager to capitalize on the tremendous revenues generated through direct involvement in the drug trade.

THE ROOTS OF THE PARAMILITARIES

As the FARC, the ELN, and other guerrilla groups gained strength in rural Colombia in the 1960s and 1970s, they began to demand "revolutionary taxes" from landowners who lived in these areas in order to continue funding their insurgents. This practice continued more or less unabated through the 1980s, but in some cases landowners or peasant organizations created self-defense groups in an attempt to counter the

**Table 3.2   Coca Cultivation and Eradication in Colombia
(1994–2000, hectares)**

	Total Coca Cultivated	Coca Sprayed	Coca Killed
1994	44,700	3,696	4,910
1995	50,900	24,046	8,750
1996	67,200	19,306	5,600
1997	79,500	41,847	19,265
1998	101,800	N/A	N/A
1999	122,500	42,000	N/A
2000	137,600	61,000	N/A

Source: U.S. Department of State, Bureau for International Narcotics and Law Enforcement, 2000.

influence of the guerrillas. This brand of paramilitary group was initially institutionalized by the Colombian state in the 1960s.[77] These militias received official government sanction and often military assistance.[78]

While these peasant self-defense forces compose one type of paramilitary group, the last decade has seen the rise of other types of paramilitary groups that are much more powerful and influential. These new forms of paramilitary groups were born out of drug traffickers' resistance to guerrilla harassment; today they are no longer directly related to the drug cartels, but instead consist of quasi-autonomous, drug revenue–supported groups committed to clearing the Colombian countryside of guerrilla influence.

As drug trafficking—especially in cocaine—brought immense profits to Colombia in the 1980s, many involved in the drug business began buying up land in rural areas. In fact, many legitimate landowners were more than happy to sell their land after so many years of harassment by the guerrillas. It is estimated that 5–6 million hectares of land changed hands between rural landowners and drug traffickers in the 1980s and early 1990s.[79] And since these new "narco-landowners" had the money to buy sophisticated weaponry, they were often reluctant to continue paying revolutionary taxes to the guerrillas. Consequently, wars erupted when landowners began recruiting, equipping, and training their own local armies (i.e., paramilitaries) and used them to rid the areas of guerrilla influence. Sewall Menzel writes:

> As fate would have it, the trafficker landowners, finding themselves to be
> the victims of exorbitant guerrilla tax increases, struck back. Fortified
> with considerable money, weapons and British and Israeli mercenaries to

train them, the traffickers formed self-defense groups, which, in time, were converted into the paramilitary death squads similar to those of MAS. These groups unmercifully hunted down the FARC guerrillas, sympathizers, and even campesino peasant organizations and union leaders lobbying for land reform and higher wages. . . . This left the majority of the population in the region in relative peace without having to pay any taxes at all. Again, what the army and police could not do, the narcotrafficker-sponsored, paramilitary *sicarios* [hired assassins] did.[80]

The most notorious of these first paramilitary groups was called Muerte a Secuestradores (MAS; Death to Kidnappers).[81] It was founded on December 2, 1981, by the Medellín cartel in response to the M-19's kidnapping of Martha Nieves Ochoa, whose brother Jorge Ochoa was a cartel member. In the weeks following the kidnapping, MAS conducted a brutal campaign against the M-19, which resulted in the deaths of several guerrillas and the release of Martha Nieves Ochoa. MAS quickly succeeded in decimating the M-19's entire Medellín-based urban unit, which not surprisingly resulted in the M-19's decision to no longer target drug traffickers or their families for kidnappings.

More relevant to contemporary issues in Colombia is that, even after it had exacted revenge against the M-19, MAS stayed in business and continued its campaign of terror, over the years expanding its influence and transforming itself into what are now called paramilitary groups. Americas Watch has written: "In the Middle Magdalena region, where people with land or businesses faced increased demands from so-called 'war taxes,' supplies, and food from the FARC, and were plagued by kidnapping for ransom, the MAS model represented a violent, yet effective means for fighting back."[82]

It has not always been just the narcotics traffickers who have utilized paramilitary groups in Colombia. The landowners who cultivate legitimate crops or herd cattle have also relied upon paramilitary groups for economic ends, expelling communities from areas where landowners would like to graze cattle or expand crop plantation, often causing incredible disruption to the targeted rural communities. It is estimated that over the past several years, close to 1 million Colombians have been displaced internally, with many of the more recent cases being directly linked to paramilitary activities.

These private paramilitary groups often enjoyed tacit or overt support from the Colombian military, since the latter preferred to have the paramilitaries conduct operations against the guerrillas (and their suspected civilian sympathizers) and thus take the blame for committing human rights abuses.[83] For example, in 1998 local residents in the oil-producing city of Barrancabermeja complained bitterly that the military never hindered the actions of the paramilitary groups, as evidenced by the fact that the paramilitaries were rarely stopped at military check-points.[84] At the time, many believed that without support from the Colombian military, the paramilitaries would not have been nearly so effective.[85] The result of the rise of this type of paramilitary group has meant that many previously guerrilla-ruled areas have become safe for ranching and other economic activities, but remain deadly for anyone suspected of having connections to or sympathies for the guerrillas.

CURRENT PARAMILITARY-GUERRILLA DYNAMICS

In recent years the paramilitaries have aggressively increased their presence in the armed conflict, seeking to eliminate the guerrillas' hegemony by terrorizing their social base within the civilian population. No longer content to sit idle while the guerrillas roam with impunity, the paramilitaries have enacted a brutal strategy of killing anyone who is even remotely linked—or purported to be linked—to guerrilla groups. Their strategy is that if the civilian population refuses to have any contact with the guerrillas for fear of retribution by the paramilitaries, then the guerrillas will eventually lose support and fade away.

Catholic Church workers and human rights activists, who used to be regarded as unbiased mediators between the military and guerrillas, have become targets of the paramilitaries, who view them as apologists for the guerrillas.[86] In February 1998, for example, in the southern state of Putumayo, paramilitary groups entered a town and listed the names of priests and other activists to signal that they had been marked for death. In July 2000, 300 armed paramilitary soldiers entered the town of El Salado and initiated a "trial" of suspected guerrilla sympathizers on the main square, an activity that resulted in a "rampage of torture, rape, and execution." According to one local resident, "They drank and they danced and cheered as they butchered us like hogs." Thirty-six residents were killed, including a six-year-old girl and an elderly woman.[87] One major consequence of the paramilitaries' methods has been to further weaken an already extremely fragile civil society in the Colombian countryside. This practice continues to be repeated throughout Colombia today.

In recent years the paramilitary groups have been gaining a life of their own, and their intermittent reliance on military support might not be as important as it was in previous years. Most of the paramilitary groups are now united under an umbrella group called the Autodefensas Unidas de Colombia (AUC; United Self-Defenses of Colombia). Led by former drug trafficker Carlos Castaño, the AUC has its headquarters in northwest Colombia. In recent years the AUC has acquired sophisticated weaponry, making it increasingly less reliant on the military. Most observers believe that drug trafficking provides the majority of the group's funding, a vital source of income for a war effort that reportedly requires U.S.$40 million per month to fund.[88]

Castaño's fighting force has been effective at confronting the guerrillas—or better said, at confronting putative civilian supporters of the guerrillas. The rise of the AUC—its numbers increased from 8,000 to 14,000 between 2000 and 2001—proves that the paramilitaries do not always work on behalf of the military.[89] Increasingly, the paramilitaries have their own agendas, using military support when it benefits them and fighting alone when it does not.[90]

Ironically, the frightening escalation of paramilitary violence might force the beginning of legitimate negotiations sooner rather than later. As manifested by the recent increase in raids, the FARC and the ELN have been able to withstand the Colombian military's counterinsurgency efforts. From 1995 to 2000 the guerrillas killed well over a thousand soldiers and took hundreds more hostage.[91] Yet only with the paramilitaries' recent successes at expelling the guerrillas from many areas (the paramilitaries call this practice *limpieza,* or "cleaning") have the guerrillas been put into any type of defensive. It is estimated that paramilitary groups exercise influence in roughly 40 percent of the country. In 2000 the AUC killed approximately 1,000 civilians in its campaign to cleanse areas under guerrilla control.

Compounding this problem is that many Colombian civilians, even if they personally abhor the violent methods, are increasingly coming to see the paramilitaries as the only effective counter to the guerrillas. The continued strength of the paramilitaries—and their growing political legitimacy—might encourage the guerrillas to seriously consider a negotiated settlement; yet this is far from certain given that the guerrillas' overall influence has increased in recent years despite the increased threat from the paramilitaries.

This scenario is complicated by the fact that the guerrillas are adamantly opposed to any legitimized political role for the paramilitaries.

AUC leader Carlos Castaño. Photo by Marcelo Salinas.

The FARC and the ELN see themselves as the rightful adversaries to the government and thus any "third party" only takes away from their ability to gain concessions. Yet continued success against the guerrillas could very well mean that the paramilitaries will have a seat at any eventual negotiating table whether the guerrillas like it or not.[92]

Another interesting development is that in 2001 Carlos Castaño stated that he would cease his involvement in military activities and instead focus on promoting the AUC's political agenda.[93] It is uncertain whether this was a sincere declaration. Yet even if Castaño moves into the political arena, there is little evidence to suggest that a successor leadership would alter its paramilitary tactics. In September 2001, U.S. Secretary of State Colin Powell announced that the United States had placed the AUC on its list of international terrorist groups, a list that already includes the FARC and the ELN.

GUERRILLA AND PARAMILITARY
INVOLVEMENT IN THE DRUG TRADE

Few observers dispute the claim that the past decade has witnessed a marked increase in guerrilla involvement in the cultivation and production of illicit drugs.[94] More often than not, guerrilla involvement in the drug trade consists of either taxing drug shipments or charging rural coca and poppy farmers protection money. The guerrillas charge an estimated 10–15 percent for each transaction between the crop farmers and the drug traffickers. This activity generates hundreds of millions of dollars in annual income for the guerrillas (mostly the FARC); when combined with the revenues from "revolutionary taxes," kidnappings, and other illicit activities, it is clear that the guerrillas possess a formidable "war chest," which is estimated at almost U.S.$500 million annually.[95]

This in turn has enabled the guerrillas to dramatically expand their influence throughout Colombia since the mid-1980s (see Table 3.3). In 1985 there was some type of guerrilla activity in 17.2 percent of all municipalities; in 1995 the figure had risen to 59.8 percent of all municipalities.[96] Today the figure is even higher. In one episode alone the FARC apparently received over 7,500 weapons that were purchased from Peru and air-dropped into FARC-controlled territory, something that was no doubt made possible by the FARC's sizable narcotics revenues.[97] In addition, FARC commander Jorge Briceño announced that all Colombians worth over U.S.$1 million should pay the FARC a "peace tax" or risk being taken hostage.

It is unclear to what extent the FARC's drug profits have influenced its military strategies. While the group had normally shied away from direct confrontations with the Colombian military, by 1998 this strategy had changed as more recruits and sophisticated weapons allowed the FARC to attack the military head on. Taken by surprise, the Colombian military was slow to react to these new tactics, but more recently the military has found its footing and has scored a number of victories against the guerrillas (see Photo 3.3). Due to the military's renewed ability to check these frontal assaults, the FARC has gradually moved back to its more traditional strategy of isolated attacks on army and police installations, often firing gas cylinders filled with explosives.[98] There is also evidence that the FARC might be considering increasing its urban terrorist activities such as car bombings. Most of this concern revolves around the August 2001 arrest of three Irish Republican Army (IRA) operatives who had apparently visited the

Table 3.3　The FARC's Growth (1986–1999)

	Number of Fronts	Number of Members
1986	32	3,600
1995	60	7,000
2000	85 (est.)	18,000

Source: Ricardo Vargas Meza, "The Revolutionary Armed Forces of Colombia (FARC) and the Illicit Drug Trade" (Cochabamba, Bolivia: Acción Andina, June 1999).

FARC's *despeje* and are suspected of being bomb experts. Colombian newspapers have also reported that twelve other alleged IRA members have visited the FARC's *despeje* since 1998.[99]

Although during the early 1980s the drug cartels and guerrillas were engaged in a fierce war with each other, in the 1990s the guerrillas became directly involved in the drug trade, providing them with tremendous financial profits. There is also no question that narcotics traffickers also benefit from the insurgents, as they view the guerrillas and paramilitaries as the muscle necessary to keep the Colombian state far away from their illicit operations. Alfredo Rangel writes: "Both illegal [guerrilla and drug trafficker] organizations need each other. The cash-short 35-year-old organization [FARC] protected narco-plantations, laboratories, aircraft, and airstrips from government incursion in exchange for a percentage of the profit generated by the drugs. This led to the coining of the term 'narco-terrorist.'"[100]

But guerrilla involvement in the drug trade does not—and did not—mean that all of the guerrillas are actually narco-guerrillas, in essence indistinguishable from the drug traffickers. In fact, while the guerrillas undoubtedly do participate in the drug trade, they maintain a distinct political and economic ideology, even if it does seem quite anachronistic now that the Cold War is over and Marxism-Leninism has been largely discredited worldwide. Some guerrillas are disgusted by the drug trade and view their involvement in it as a necessary but evil means in order to achieve a better end of social and political transformation.

This vision of the guerrilla-narcotics relationship might be changing, however, as more recent reports have directly linked the FARC to drug-trafficking operations. In the fall of 2000, for example, a joint U.S.-Colombian drug interdiction operation confiscated a cocaine-filled sea vessel containing a variety of FARC paraphernalia, suggesting that this was a FARC-controlled operation from start to finish.[101]

Colombian military displaying forty dead FARC troops,
Granada Military Base, Department of Meta. Photo by Marcelo Salinas.

While FARC involvement in the drug trade has received most of the attention, it is clear that the paramilitary groups are also financing their war efforts by drug profits. Critics of U.S. antidrug efforts have charged that Washington pressures the Colombian government to fumigate coca crops and destroy drug laboratories in guerrilla-held areas, but intentionally overlooks other areas where the paramilitaries are involved in drug activities. In response to these allegations the Colombian government has stepped up antidrug efforts in paramilitary strongholds, although the majority of these operations continue in areas where guerrillas are active.

It is within this uncertain and violent environment of protracted paramilitary and drug trafficker–sponsored violence, a flourishing drug trade, and a stronger, more aggressive guerrilla insurgency, that the United States has conducted its policies in Colombia since the 1990s. The paramilitaries and guerrillas—especially the FARC—are more involved in the drug trade today than ever before, an increasingly important concern for U.S. policymakers.

The next two chapters describe how the United States has conducted its policies in such an environment. We will see that it often formulated its policies not to address the complex and ever-changing dynamics of the civil conflict and related violence in Colombia, but rather to pursue its counternarcotics policy, often to the exclusion and minimization of other issues. The consequences of this narcotized policy for most of the 1990s were considerable and eventually drove a gradual but important shift in policy following Andrés Pastrana's inauguration in 1998.

NOTES

1. Jorge Osterling, *Democracy in Colombia: Clientalist Politics and Guerrilla Warfare* (New Brunswick, N.J.: Transaction, 1989), p. 261.

2. For an excellent overview of the Colombian political system, see Harvey F. Cline, "Colombia: Building Democracy Amidst Violence and Drugs," in *Constructing Democratic Governance: Latin America and the Caribbean in the 1990s,* edited by Jorge Domínguez and Abraham F. Lowenthal (Baltimore: Johns Hopkins University Press, 1996), pp. 20–41; and Alexander W. Wilde, "Conversations Among Gentlemen: Oligarchic Democracy in Colombia," in *The Breakdown of Democratic Regimes: Latin America,* edited by Juan J. Linz and Alfred Stepan (Baltimore: Johns Hopkins University Press, 1978), pp. 28–81.

3. Robert Dix, *Colombia: The Political Dimensions of Change* (New Haven: Yale University Press, 1967), p. 361.

4. Richard Sharpless, *Gaitán of Colombia: A Political Biography* (Pittsburgh: University of Pittsburgh Press, 1978), pp. 158–173.

5. Ibid., p. 161. The victory of Ospina in 1946 caused great alarm among the Liberals, with several Liberal mobs in Bogotá marching to demand that the election results be modified. Most of the violence before the *Bogotazo* in 1948 took place in areas of rural Colombia where Gaitán's support was the weakest.

6. Gaitán was shot while leaving his office in Bogotá by a man who was known to be mentally unstable.

7. Sharpless, *Gaitán of Colombia,* p. 178.

8. David Bushnell, *The Making of Modern Colombia: A Nation in Spite of Itself* (Berkeley: University of California Press, 1993), p. 202.

9. See Bruce Bagley, "Colombia: National Front and Economic Development," in *Politics, Policies, and Economic Development in Latin America,* edited by Robert Wesson (Stanford: Hoover Institution Press, 1984), pp. 124–160.

10. For an analysis of the National Front, see Jonathan Hartlyn, *The Politics of Coalition Rule in Colombia* (Cambridge: Cambridge University Press, 1988). See also Daniel L. Premo, "Coping with Insurgency: The Politics of Pacification in Colombia and Venezuela," in *Democracy in Latin America: Colombia and Venezuela,* edited by Donald L. Herman (New York: Praeger, 1988), pp. 228–230; and Robert Dix, "Consociational Democracy: The Case of Colombia," *Comparative Politics* 12, no. 3 (April 1980): 303–321.

11. Dix, *Colombia,* pp. 133–134.

12. Ibid., p. 130.

13. Ibid., p. 136.

14. Marc Chernick, "Negotiating Peace and Multiple Forms of Violence: The Protracted Search for a Settlement to the Armed Conflicts in Colombia," in *Comparative Peace Processes in Latin America,* edited by Cynthia J. Arnson (Washington, D.C.: Woodrow Wilson Center Press, 1999), pp. 163–164.

15. Premo, "Coping with Insurgency," p. 230.

16. See Americas Watch, *The Central-Americanization of Colombia? Human Rights and the Peace Process* (New York: Americas Watch, 1986), p. 19.

17. Dennis Rempe, "Guerrillas, Bandits, and Independent Republics: U.S. Counterinsurgency Efforts in Colombia, 1959–1965," *Small Wars and Insurgencies* 6, no. 3 (Winter 1995): 321.

18. For more on the government's attack on Marquetalia, see Eduardo Pizarro, "Revolutionary Groups in Colombia," in *Violence in Colombia: The Contemporary Crisis in Historical Perspective,* edited by Charles Bergquist, Ricardo Penaranda, and Gonzalo Sánchez (Wilmington, Del.: Scholarly Resources, 1992), pp. 169–193.

19. Osterling, *Democracy in Colombia,* p. 99.

20. Rempe, "Guerrillas, Bandits, and Independent Republics," p. 321.

21. Osterling, *Democracy in Colombia,* pp. 298–299.

22. Juan Forero, "Rebel Control of Large Zone in Colombia Is Extended," *The New York Times,* December 7, 2000.

23. Gabriel Marcella and Donald E. Schulz, "Colombia's Three Wars: U.S. Strategy at the Crossroads" (Washington, D.C.: Strategic Studies Institute, 1999), p. 11.

24. "Secuestro masivo en Cali," *El Tiempo,* September 18, 2000.

25. "Kidnapped in Colombia," *The Economist,* September 23, 2000.

26. Juan Tomayo, "Colombians Torn over Plan to Let Rebels Control a Region," *The Miami Herald,* January 14, 2001. The FARC's liberated zone consists of 16,000 square miles.

27. Chernick, "Negotiating Peace," p. 165.

28. Americas Watch, *The Central-Americanization of Colombia?* p. 72.

29. Sewall Menzel, *Cocaine Quagmire: Implementing the U.S. Anti-Drug Policy in the North Andes–Colombia* (New York: University Press of America, 1997), pp. 37–38.

30. Osterling, *Democracy in Colombia,* pp. 324–325.

31. Ibid., p. 319.

32. See Chernick, "Negotiating Peace," p. 199.

33. Americas Watch, *The Central-Americanization of Colombia?* p. 24.

34. Osterling, *Democracy in Colombia,* p. 285.

35. Ibid.

36. Americas Watch, *The Central-Americanization of Colombia?* pp. 32–33.

37. Ibid., p. 41.

38. *El Tiempo,* May 24, 1999.

39. Americas Watch, *Human Rights in Colombia as President Barco Begins* (New York: Americas Watch, 1986), p. 14.

40. See Chernick, "Negotiating Peace," pp. 196–199.

41. Ibid., pp. 180–182. A small group from the Atlantic Coast, the Partido Revolucionario de Trabajadores (PRT; Revolutionary Workers Party), also signed an agreement with the Gaviria administration.

42. Chernick, "Negotiating Peace," p. 182.

43. The incipient peace process begun by Pastrana provoked a tremendous amount of public enthusiasm and hence intense media coverage. See, for example, "Paras aceptan iniciar diálogos," *El Tiempo,* January 14, 1999; and "ELN, tema en Estados Unidos y Venezuela," *El Tiempo,* February 18, 1999.

44. Forero, "Rebel Control."

45. See Russell Crandall, "Bombs Litter Colombia's Road to Peace," *Jane's Defence Weekly Terrorism and Security Monitor,* June 2001.

46. "ELN definitivamente no dialoga con Gobierno de Andrés Pastrana," *El Tiempo,* September 11, 2001.

47. For an overview of the initial Colombian narcotics trade, see Bruce Bagley, "The Colombian Connection: The Impact of Drug Traffic in Colombia," in *Coca and Cocaine: Effects on People and Policy in Latin America,* edited by Deborah Pacini and Christine Franquemont (Ithaca, N.Y.: Cultural Survival, 1986), pp. 89–100; and Richard B. Craig, "Colombian Narcotics Control and United States–Colombian Relations," *Journal of Interamerican Studies and World Affairs* 23, no. 3 (August 1981): 243–270.

48. Rensselaer W. Lee III and Patrick L. Clawson, *The Andean Cocaine Industry* (New York: St. Martin's Press), p. 37.

49. Ibid., p. 38.

50. Robert Filippone, "The Medellín Cartel: Why We Can't Win the Drug War," *Studies in Conflict and Terrorism* 17, no. 4 (1994): 325.

51. Rensselaer W. Lee III, "Colombia's Cocaine Syndicates," *Crime, Law, and Social Change* 16, no. 1 (1991): 9.

52. Filippone, "The Medellín Cartel," p. 325.

53. Lee, "Colombia's Cocaine Syndicates," p. 10.

54. For a general analysis of the drug war—both inside and outside the United States—see Michael Massing, "The War on Cocaine," *The New York Review of Books,* December 22, 1988.

55. For more on the Medellín cartel, see Guy Gugliotta and Jeff Leen, *Kings of Cocaine* (New York: Simon and Schuster, 1989). See also Iván Orozco Abad, "La guerra del presidente," *Análisis Político* 8 (September–December 1989): 73–78.

56. For a chronicle of Pablo Escobar's kidnapping of several prominent Colombians, see Gabriel García Márquez, *News of a Kidnapping* (New York: Knopf, 1997).

57. See Iván Orozco Abad, "Los diálogos con el narcotráfico: Historia de la transformación fallida de un delincuente común en un delincuente político," *Análisis Político* 11 (September–December 1990): 44–48.

58. Lee and Clawson, *The Andean Cocaine Industry,* p. 51.

59. Santos was eventually released and Turbay was killed along with María Montoya, the daughter of Colombia's ambassador to Canada. See Lee, "Colombia's Cocaine Syndicates," p. 13.

60. Ibid., p. 53.

61. See Filippone, "The Medellín Cartel," pp. 336–337.

62. Lee, "Colombia's Cocaine Mafia," pp. 60–62.

63. In June 1987 the Colombian Supreme Court had struck down a 1979 extradition treaty with the United States, although exceptions were made due to government-declared "states of siege." Article 35 of the 1991 constitution banned extradition. The constitution was amended to allow extradition in November 1997.

64. See Rennselaer W. Lee III, "Making the Most of Colombia's Drug Negotiations," *Orbis* 35, no. 2 (Spring 1991): 235–252.

65. State-of-siege decrees 2047, 2147, 2372, 3030, of 1990, and 303 of 1991, "offered reduced sentences and immunity from extradition to those who turned themselves in and confessed to a crime." Americas Watch, *Political Murder and Reform in Colombia: The Violence Continues* (New York: Americas Watch, 1992), p. 11. The famous phrase "better a grave in Colombia than a prison in the United States" manifests their firm resistance to extradition. For a gripping account of the violence enacted by the Medellín cartel's "Extraditables," see Márquez, *News of a Kidnapping;* and "Los Extraditables prefieren tumba en Colombia," *Novedades,* November 16, 1996.

66. See Lee, "Making the Most of Colombia's Drug Negotiations," p. 237.

67. Rennselaer W. Lee III and Patrick Clawson write: "The conditions of Escobar's incarceration, established after marathon negotiations with the government, were quite favorable to him. Of course, the one condition was that the prison be located in a city where the trafficker enjoyed great influence. . . . Another condition was that Escobar and his representatives be allowed to screen the guard who would be responsible for internal security in the prison." Lee and Clawson, *The Andean Cocaine Industry,* p. 112. See also Douglas Farah, "To Colombian Drug Lords, There's No Place Like Prison," *The Washington Post,* September 26, 1993. Escobar was killed sixteen months later on a rooftop in Medellín, ending one of the most extensive manhunts in Colombian history. See James Brook, "Drug Lord Is Buried as Crowd Wails," *The New York Times,* December 4, 1983. For more on the Ochoa brothers' release from prison, see "Fabio Ochoa, último integrante del 'Clan Ochoa' del cartel de Medellín, recobrá su libertad," *Crónica,* September 17, 1996.

68. For more on the U.S. involvement and position toward the drug cartels, see Menzel, *Cocaine Quagmire,* pp. 79–103.

69. After leaving office Gaviria moved to Washington, D.C., in order to assume the position of secretary-general of the OAS.

70. Robert T. Buckman, "The Cali Cartel: An Undefeated Enemy," *Low Intensity Conflict and Law Enforcement* 3, no. 3 (Winter 1994): 434.

71. Ibid., p. 435.

72. Ibid., p. 434.

73. See U.S. Senate, Committee on Foreign Relations, "Corruption and Drugs in Colombia: Democracy at Risk," February 27, 1996.

74. Testimony by Donnie Marshall, DEA chief of operations, before the House Committee on Government Reform and Oversight, Subcommittee on National Security, International Affairs, and Criminal Justice, July 9, 1997.

75. Menzel, *Cocaine Quagmire*, p. 89.

76. For a look at the U.S. government's efforts to dismantle the Cali cartel, see U.S. Department of Justice, "The Cali Cartel: The New Kings of Cocaine," DEA Drug Intelligence report, November 1994.

77. In 1968 the Colombian Congress enacted Law 48, which allowed the government "to mobilize the population in activities and tasks" in order to promote normalcy. This legislation paved the way for what came to be known as self-defense groups.

78. These government-sponsored groups, the *convivirs*, were officially disbanded in 1997 after many were accused by human rights organizations of unjustified violence. A strong case can be made that the 1994 institutionalization of these groups contributed to the growth of the contemporary paramilitary groups. By providing government support for some types of paramilitary groups, the Colombian government left the impression that it was condoning all types of paramilitary activity.

79. Chernick, "Negotiating Peace," pp. 170–174.

80. Menzel, *Cocaine Quagmire,* p. 61; "El ejército desmiente vinculación con el mas," *El Tiempo,* January 12, 1983; and "El MAS: Tocando fondo?" *El Espectador,* January 13, 1983. For more on the roots of the paramilitaries, see Americas Watch, *The Drug War in Colombia: The Neglected Tragedy of Political Violence* (New York: Americas Watch, October 1990), pp. 11–30; "El Narco-Agro," *Semana,* November 29–December 5, 1988; and Laura Restrepo, *Historia de un entusiasmo* (Bogotá: Grupo Editorial Norma, 1998), pp. 55–58.

81. Cynthia Watson, "Political Violence in Colombia: Another Argentina?" *Third World Quarterly* 12, nos. 3–4 (1990–1991): 31.

82. Americas Watch, *Colombia's Killer Networks: The Military-Paramilitary Partnership and the United States* (New York: Americas Watch, 1996), p. 17.

83. For more on the Colombian military's links to paramilitary groups, see U.S. Department of State, *Annual Human Rights Report—Colombia,* 1998, 1999, 2000.

84. Confidential author interviews with a local human rights team in the city of Barrancabermeja, October 1997 and February 1998.

85. For more on the military-paramilitary link, see Americas Watch, *Colombia's Killer Networks.*

86. I first made these observations in "Colombia Needs a Stronger Military," *The Wall Street Journal,* June 12, 1998.

87. Larry Rohter, "Colombians Tell of Massacre as Army Stood By," *The New York Times,* July 14, 2000.

88. An exclusive interview with Carlos Castaño was conducted by María Cristina Caballero and published in "Esta Guerra no da mas," *Cambio 16* (Bogotá), December 15, 1997; Castaño gave another interview to *Washington Post* reporter Scott Wilson in March 2001. See "Colombia's Other Army," *The Washington Post,* March 12, 2001. For more on the rise of Carlos Castaño and the paramilitary groups, see "No Peace," *The Economist,* October 11, 1997; "Killing in Colombia," *The Economist,* November 29, 1997; and "Colombia's Other Armies," *The Economist,* November 29, 1997.

89. Scott Wilson, "Paramilitary Army Seeks Political Role in Colombia," *The Washington Post,* September 19, 2001.

90. Most Colombians are tired of this seemingly senseless violence (one leading magazine, *Cambio 16,* placed on its cover: "So What Are They All Fighting About?"—referring to interviews conducted with the paramilitaries and guerrillas revealing that both groups had similarly stated goals). Colombians also firmly believe that a negotiated solution is the best—and probably only—way that the conflict can be resolved. Underlying this view is a societal consensus that none of the belligerent groups will ever be able to gain a military victory.

91. "Cambio de frente en la guerra," *El Tiempo,* August 25, 1998. In January 2000 the Colombian military reported that 436 soldiers were killed by the guerrillas in 1998 and 330 in 1999. The military also reported that it had killed 1,019 guerrillas in 1999. "Farc no ha respetado la tregua: Mora," *El Tiempo,* January 7, 2000.

92. For a more in-depth analysis of the potential paths that the current Colombian peace process might take, see Chernick, "Negotiating Peace." In May 1999, Carlos Castaño's forces kidnapped Senator Piedad Córdoba and then released a statement declaring that the act was done in order to have the government accept the paramilitaries' political platform, which above all else demanded a seat at the negotiating table. See *El Espectador,* May 23–24, 1999.

93. Wilson, "Paramilitary Army."

94. For more on guerrilla involvement in the drug trade, see Alejandro Reyes Posada, "Drug Trafficking and the Guerrilla Movement in Colombia," in *Drug Trafficking in the Americas,* edited by Bruce Bagley and William Walker (Miami: University of Miami North-South Center, 1994), pp. 121–131.

95. The Colombian Department of National Planning has estimated that from 1990 to 1994 guerrilla groups raised U.S.$701 million from involvement in the drug trade, compared to U.S.$482 million from robbery and U.S.$328 million from kidnapping. See Lee and Clawson, *The Andean Cocaine Industry,* p. 93.

96. Chernick, "Negotiating Peace," p. 167. See also Daniel García-Peña Jaramillo, *Building Tomorrow's Peace: A Strategy for Reconciliation,* report by the Peace Exploration Committee, Bogotá, 1997.

97. "The Gringos Land in Colombia," *The Economist,* September 4, 2000.

98. Ibid.

99. Warren Hoge, "Sinn Fein Spurns U.S. over Arrests in Colombia," *The New York Times,* September 19, 2001.

100. Alfredo Rangel Suárez, *Colombia: Guerra en el fin de siglo* (Bogotá: Tercer Mundo, 1998), p. 125. Rangel also estimates that one in three guerrilla combatants is somehow linked to the drug trade. He also estimates that drug-related revenues make up half of the FARC's income. Author translation.

101. "EEUU acusa," *Cambio,* November 11–18, 2000.

4

U.S. Policy During the Samper Administration, 1994–1998

Washington hated the idea of Samper. Short of one of the Cali cartel leaders becoming president of Colombia, Samper's election was the worst scenario.
— *Myles Frechette, U.S. Ambassador to Colombia (1994–1997)[1]*

Samper was one of the most unscrupulous politicians I had ever met, and I've met a lot of people in a lot of countries. . . . U.S. policy toward Colombia during this time was a depressing performance.
— *Alexander Watson, Assistant Secretary of State for Inter-American Affairs (1992–1996)[2]*

The U.S. view of Ernesto Samper as a reliable ally in the war on drugs soured well before he took office in August of 1994. Beginning in 1982, when Samper was the campaign manager of Liberal Party presidential candidate Alfonso López Michelsen, the U.S. government had suspected Samper of taking bribes from drug traffickers.[3] This suspicion was compounded on November 14, 1984, when Cali cartel kingpin Gilberto Rodríguez Orejuela was arrested in Spain and officials found Samper's unlisted, unpublished phone number in Rodríguez Orejuela's address book.[4]

A decade later, when Samper was contending for the presidency himself, Washington wasted no time informing him that he was suspected of drug links. This came to a head on November 19, 1993, when Assistant Secretary of State Robert Gelbard met with Samper, who at that point was a contender for the Liberal Party's presidential nomination.[5] Gelbard, who as ambassador to Bolivia in the late 1980s took a controversial highly public stand against what he deemed to be Bolivian government involvement in the drug trade, squarely told Samper that there would be serious consequences if the drug funding continued:

"We have information, we believe it, and the money must stop if you want to have any kind of decent relationship with the United States."[6]

As this was one of the first reported meetings between U.S. officials and candidate Ernesto Samper, the logical conclusion is that the United States initially cooled to Samper, since U.S. officials were certain that drug money was funding—or had the potential to fund in the near future—his campaign. While this revelation altered the U.S. government's view of Samper, some U.S. officials had actually met with Samper a few months before Gelbard and, at that time, were completely unaware of any information that linked Samper to the Cali cartel. Instead, because of Samper's prior advocacy of drug legalization in the late 1970s and early 1980s, U.S. officials viewed him as potentially soft on the drug issue. Samper was known as "Mr. Legalization" by many in the U.S. government.[7]

This fact suggests that the negative view of Samper might have had as much to do with his ideological view of the drug issue as it did with the possibility that he received payments from the Cali cartel. Phil McLean, then deputy assistant secretary of state for inter-American affairs, met with Samper at the Washington Hotel in Washington, D.C., in July 1993.[8] He recounted:

> I said, "Ernesto, you have a major, major problem with the United States: you're perceived as being soft on narcotics. This is the problem and there's only one way to fix it—you've gotta show that you're serious about this issue and to do this you're gonna have to do something about this particular issue. . . ." At that time there was no specific information that I knew of, and I was supposedly in the center of all the "in" in intelligence on anything that implicated Samper.[9]

Regardless of the exact motivations for the U.S. government's decision to take a hard stance against Samper, the message that it wanted Samper to receive was that he would have to follow through on counternarcotics efforts as if he had never received funds from the Cali cartel. State Department official Michael Skol clarified this message when he stated, "Our point of view is that no matter what has happened in the past few months, the most important thing for our administration and for president-elect Samper is what begins to happen after he takes office on August 7th."[10]

If Samper complied, the U.S. government would in return act as though it knew very little about his links to the Cali cartel.[11] As we will see, starting first with the "narco-cassette" scandal and continuing through many other events that were seen as evidence of Samper's soft stance on drugs, the United States publicly targeted Samper's suspected drug links even though Samper's administration all but destroyed the Cali cartel in 1995.[12]

THE "NARCO-CASSETTES"

Whatever evidence the U.S. government had of Ernesto Samper's links to the Cali cartel was corroborated on June 16, 1994, when Conservative Party candidate Andrés Pastrana's campaign manager, Luis Alberto Moreno, walked into the U.S. embassy in Bogotá and delivered to Ambassador Morris Busby tapes of police intercepts that he had received on June 15.[13] On one of the tapes, Cali drug leader Miguel Rodríguez apparently tells journalist Alberto "Loco" Girardo that he has made arrangements to move U.S.$3.5 million into Samper's campaign.[14] Moreno, knowing that if the Conservatives released the tapes it would look like a ploy to steal the election, hoped that the U.S. embassy would make the tapes public. However, senior officials in the U.S. State Department thought that the issue was too delicate and instead directed Busby not to leak the tapes to the press.

A few days later, on June 19, Samper narrowly defeated Pastrana, with many observers believing in hindsight that the badly needed funds the Samper campaign received from the Cali cartel probably made the difference between victory and defeat. Fed up with what he believed was a whitewash of a candidate who was in the pocket of drug traffickers, Bogotá-based U.S. DEA agent Joe Toft leaked the narco-cassettes to the press.[15] Even though Toft resigned from the DEA only six weeks later, the firestorm that he created by leaking the tapes left an indelible legacy on the Colombian political system.[16] The narco-cassettes ignited a far-reaching investigation of those Colombian government officials believed to have ties to drug traffickers.[17] The investigation came to be called the "Proceso 8000" case, and before it was over, Samper's attorney general, defense minister, and campaign treasurer, along with several legislators, were convicted of drug money–related crimes.[18]

The controversy over the narco-cassettes continued not so much because of their content, but rather because of the accusations against Samper that the release of the tapes set off.[19] The *Miami Herald,* for example, wrote that unnamed sources in the U.S. government had more evidence than just the narco-cassettes regarding Samper's links to the

Cali cartel. Not surprisingly, Samper quickly denied the accusations, and since the cassettes only recorded drug traffickers discussing payments to Samper, he was correct to state that they did not directly implicate him.

Nevertheless, for most U.S. officials these tapes alone were more than enough evidence to convince them that Samper was corrupt. According to State Department official Michael Skol, "If you listen to the tapes it really doesn't say too much about Samper. Yet, I suspect that few people in the U.S. government actually ever listened to the tapes."[20] Samper quickly responded to the accusations by sending a letter to the *Miami Herald* in which he wrote: "I have never received money from any type of criminal organization in order to promote my political activities, and my campaign books can prove this, that I complied with a strict internal accounting of the origin of the funds."[21] Samper also sent a letter to members of the U.S. House of Representatives in which he promised that the Cali kingpins would go to jail and that his administration would create an elite police unit specifically to confront the cartel—something he indeed did.[22] Samper also promised to make the sentences against convicted drug traffickers more severe and proposed the creation of a binational commission with the United States in order to adopt joint antidrug strategies.[23]

While generally convinced that Samper was guilty, the U.S. government tried to play down the growing controversy in order not to taint relations with the new president before he had even taken office. In comments that almost seemed to excuse Samper even if he had committed illegal acts, Alexander Watson, assistant secretary of state for inter-American affairs, stated:

> I have known Samper for many years and consider him a friend, and for that these revelations have given me personal pain. But I believe that the important thing is to clarify these things as quickly as possible. . . . The Cali cartel is very powerful now, and they have been trying to use their money in these elections. It would not be the first time that these men have done this type of thing, and this is not the only country where they do these things. Remember that in the past Pablo Escobar of the Medellín cartel was doing these things and had a powerful influence.[24]

U.S. ambassador to Colombia–designate Myles Frechette also sounded conciliatory and not overly concerned with the growing narco-scandal: "My instructions are to work as hard as possible with the new president once he takes office on August 7 in order to increase cooperation and I will do this. These are the instructions that I like."[25]

President Bill Clinton took a similar position, manifested in a letter he wrote to president-elect Samper in which he promoted a strong bilateral relationship and made no mention of the narco-cassettes, although he did state that the drug war was the number-one priority.[26] In another political move suggesting that the Clinton administration was looking to smooth over the growing scandal, a State Department spokesman categorically denied the verity of a United Press International news article that claimed the White House had concluded that Samper had received U.S.$3 million from the Cali cartel: "[The article] is false, it's not official and it does not reflect President Clinton's policy toward Colombia."[27]

But while the executive branch might have decided not to make a big issue out of the accusations against Samper, there were some influential voices in Congress—especially Senator Jesse Helms (R–N.C.)—who were already claiming that the United States could not do business with the tainted Samper administration. On July 16, Helms introduced an amendment to the 1994 Foreign Assistance Act that would have only allowed U.S. assistance to Colombia if its government better complied with U.S.-led counternarcotics efforts, a move that signaled how some in the U.S. Congress were watching Samper very closely.[28] However, part of the motivation for Helms's amendment was a growing frustration not with Samper, but with César Gaviria's drug efforts.[29] This amendment was opposed by the White House and did not become law; the State Department was also unwilling to go along with Helms's tough stance. Robert Gelbard responded to the proposed amendment by stating: "Let there be no doubt what would occur as a consequence of the actions that we are taking in the legislature. We are going to deny, to one of our critical allies in the war on drugs, access to the equipment and information that they need to continue their war against drugs."[30] But Gelbard's statement would quickly cease to be State Department policy. In fact, by the time of Colombia's first decertification in 1996, Gelbard's congressional testimony essentially mimicked Helms's 1994 position, a point that reinforces the growing anti-Samper nature of U.S. policy toward Colombia during those years.

Leading up to Ernesto Samper's inauguration day, the State Department continued to feel out Samper in order to see if he would be an ally on the drug front.[31] The first pivotal meeting between the United States and then president-elect Ernesto Samper took place in early July 1994 in New York City and lasted for close to three hours.[32] Led by State Department officials Michael Skol and Crescenio Arcos, the U.S. delegation once again told Samper that if he would act as if he were not receiving money from the Cali traffickers—that is, if he would take a tough stance on drugs—the United States would act as if the links did not exist.[33]

Samper agreed to the U.S. demands, which included that he replace police commander General Octavio Vargas Silva, whose name was also mentioned on the narco-cassettes, with General Rosso José Serrano.[34] In Skol's words, "we made a gentlemen's agreement; he never accepted the charges, but agreed that he would go along with a tough antidrug policy."[35] Yet in return for ceding to U.S. wishes on the drug issue, Samper asked that the U.S. government issue a public statement noting that there was no basis for the claim that the Samper campaign had taken money from the cartels. The State Department team refused to grant his wish, and what might have been an agreement to let sleeping dogs lie regarding Samper's drug connections came to nothing.

Interestingly, while U.S. officials may have not been fully aware at that time of its eventual impact, their successful effort to bring in General Serrano to head the National Police would turn out to be a key move—and victory from the U.S. government's perspective—in that it allowed the United States to continue its counternarcotics efforts even while increasingly isolating the Samper administration.[36] Although General Serrano was still technically under the command of Samper, U.S. policy—which was essentially U.S. counternarcotics policy—gradually developed a bifurcated nature whereby the United States would support and cooperate with the "good guys" such as General Serrano and Chief Prosecutor Alfonso Valdivieso, while attacking the "bad guys" such as Samper and his interior minister, Horacio Serpa. It surprised few, therefore, when Interior Secretary Bruce Babbit, a relatively low-level official, led the U.S. delegation to Samper's inauguration while the presidents of eight Latin American countries were present.[37]

THE LEAHY AMENDMENT

At the same time that Jesse Helms was toughening his stance against Samper, Senator Patrick Leahy (D–Vt.) introduced legislation that would bar U.S. assistance to any elements within the Colombian Armed Forces suspected of committing human rights abuses, a move revealing that Congress was not in complete harmony regarding Colombia policy.[38] This concern over the nature of U.S. military assistance to Colombia was eventually addressed in the Leahy Amendment to the 1996 international affairs budget, which banned assistance to any military unit "if the Secretary of State has credible evidence to believe such unit has committed gross violations of human rights unless the Secretary determines and reports to the Committee on Appropriations that the Government of such country is taking steps to bring the responsible members of the security forces to justice."[39] The Leahy Amendment was intended to cover U.S. assistance to militaries anywhere in the world; one of its first true tests would come in Colombia.

The end result of the Leahy Amendment's application to the Colombia case was that beginning in fiscal year 1997, the U.S. government was forced to credibly certify that the Colombian military units receiving U.S. military assistance were not involved (or suspected of being involved) in human rights violations. While the impact this legislation had on U.S. policy toward Colombia should not be discounted, the Leahy Amendment never came close to even suggesting that U.S. antidrug assistance to Colombia should be stopped or reduced.[40] Rather, it just made clear that aid could not go to abusive military units. In fact, counternarcotics assistance actually increased during this time as the United States cultivated partners outside the Colombian military, above all the Colombian National Police.[41]

In March 1997 a Leahy Amendment–driven controversy erupted between members of Congress and the White House over the delivery of antidrug assistance to the Colombian National Police. The point of contention centered on the fact that the 1996 and 1997 decertification decisions meant that certain types of counternarcotics aid were being held up, thus necessitating a presidential waiver for these funds to be released.[42] The Clinton administration delayed issuing this waiver, arguing that it was better to delay the release of these funds in order to comply with the "spirit of the Leahy Amendment." This move infuriated congressional Republicans and countless hours and resources were spent in hearings quibbling over these issues.

This infighting notwithstanding, the crux of the debate between Congress and the Clinton administration was not over whether these funds should be released, but instead when they should be released: the State Department wanted to wait until the spirit of the Leahy Amendment had been assured, and the drug hawks wanted the materials delivered immediately. Assistant Secretary of State Jeffrey Davidow explained the administration's thinking:

The fact of the matter is, by a standard of common sense . . . if we're putting the same kinds of equipment into a country, under various authorities, that are going to be used by—perhaps by the same units, if that unit gets its left boot under one authority and its right boot under another authority, if we're going to maintain any sort of consistency in terms of end-use monitoring, then we ought to have a consistency in the standards that are applied.[43]

These disputes over the composition of U.S. assistance to Colombia came to characterize a large part of "U.S. policy" toward Colombia at this time. The attention of the U.S. State Department was focused as much on mollifying Congress as it was on implementing policy in Colombia. Yet the true level of disagreement between the State Department and Congress was relatively slim, a point reinforcing the idea that the bureaucratic battle that was "Colombia policy" at this time was one in which most of the major players basically agreed with each other. In this sense, the seemingly large divide on Colombia policy between Senators Leahy and Helms—or the more general debate in the House of Representatives between the Republican drug hawks and the liberal wing of the Democratic Party—was much narrower than first apparent. Patrick Leahy himself argued in a letter to the editor of the *New York Times*—in which he reiterated the importance of human rights in U.S. policy toward Colombia—that "[t]here should be no mistake that Congress and the Administration are committed to combating the drug trade."[44]

The Leahy Amendment served as a reminder that for some in Congress, issues such as human rights needed to be incorporated into the war on drugs. According to one Democratic staff member on the Senate Appropriations Committee, "Our intention [with the Leahy Amendment] was to ensure that if we were going to fight the 'war on drugs' that we wouldn't disregard human rights in the process."[45] Yet the thrust of the congressional focus over Colombia policy nonetheless remained with the drug hawks, who constantly put the Clinton administration on the defensive, even though there is little to suggest that the White House was in any way soft on Colombia policy.

1994 COMES TO AN END

The U.S. war on drugs increasingly became a war against Ernesto Samper. The transfer of the congressional majority from the Democrats to the Republicans in 1994 meant that Congress would press a hard line on the drug issue. Thus, compared to his predecessor, César Gaviria, who governed while the Democrats ruled the House of Representatives, Ernesto Samper would have to deal with a Republican Congress—and by extension with a brand of U.S. policy that was much more inclined to take a hard stand against any suspected lapses in fighting the war on drugs.

While Ernesto Samper was eventually forced to do more on the drug war issue than had any of his predecessors in order to have the semblance of good relations with the United States, for the rest of 1994 U.S.-Colombian relations were cordial. The U.S. government remained deeply suspicious of Samper, but it was generally pleased with the new administration, mostly because it seemed that Ernesto Samper was going to be tougher on drugs than had been César Gaviria. For example, in December 1994, Samper launched Operation Splendor, which consisted of fumigating illicit crops in the southern departments of Guaviare and Putumayo. The fumigation efforts infuriated the campesinos in these areas who made their livelihood from growing illicit crops. Soon after the operation started, thousands of campesinos marched demanding an end to the spraying, occupied seven oil pumping stations, and bombed 40,000 barrels of oil coming from Ecuador. Samper ordered the military to forcibly remove the protesters and also set up a U.S.$150 million fund for crop substitution.[46]

These types of sporadic yet unprecedented counternarcotics actions came to characterize Ernesto Samper's presidency, and often took place right before or after key U.S. decisions on Colombia policy such as drug certification or the revocation of Samper's visa, suggesting that U.S. arm-twisting on the drug issue was having the desired effect—at least for the United States. These actions also revealed Samper's profound lack of credibility on the drug issue in Washington. Knowing that critics both in Colombia and Washington were highly dubious about Samper's willingness to fight the war on drugs, Samper was forced to go further than either he or the United States had ever imagined. Thus we have the paradoxical situation whereby this supposedly narco-compromised president ended up, whether he liked it or not, being a reliable and predictable ally with Washington vis-à-vis the drug war.

Ernesto Samper's credibility gap, stemming from his earlier promotion of drug legalization and compounded by the narco-cassette revelations, forced him to govern Colombia with one eye focused on Washington. From the U.S. government's perspective, this concern with U.S. opinion served its interests: they knew that Samper had to prove himself, so they constantly put pressure on him to escalate his antidrug policies. As will be seen, while Samper did indeed take a stronger stance on the drug issue, it was still not enough to appease the U.S. government, especially some vocal members of Congress. This dissatisfaction arose despite the fact that the Colombian government went to great lengths in Washington to convince the U.S. government that Colombia should receive full certification.[47] In February 1995, for example, Samper sent yet another letter to the U.S. Congress that listed the Colombian government's counternarcotics achievements. The U.S. government knew that Samper was critically wounded on the drug issue and therefore saw no reason not to exact as many concessions out of his debilitated position as possible, no matter what damage it might do to the bilateral relationship.[48]

COLOMBIA PASSES 1995 DRUG CERTIFICATION

On March 1, 1995, the State Department declared Colombia—along with Peru, Bolivia, Paraguay, Pakistan, and Lebanon—"uncooperative" on the drug war, but it issued a national interest waiver to avoid full decertification. What is interesting about the State Department's move is not that it granted Colombia a national interest waiver, but rather its reasons for declaring Colombia uncooperative. In a characterization that would change dramatically the following year, when Ernesto Samper himself would be the reason for Colombia's decertification, U.S. officials cited inadequate efforts to crack down on the Cali cartel as the basis for their decision.[49] Robert Gelbard stated in congressional testimony:

> Three countries were given national interest waivers for the first time: Colombia, primarily for its failure to take actions promised against the Cali cartel. We applaud the positive steps Colombia took last year against narcotics trafficking, most notably the decision to eradicate coca cultivation through aerial spraying. Our concern with Colombia, however, is its failure to address the most serious challenge—the kingpins and their vertically integrated trafficking organizations. Police and other officials on the front lines showed considerable determination to bring drug traffickers to justice. . . . Nevertheless, the trafficking organizations and their leaders continue to operate with virtual impunity.[50]

In spite of the State Department's frustration with the lack of progress on the drug front, and the subsequent "uncooperative" label, Gelbard and

others believed that the pressure being applied by Washington was having the desired effect. As Gelbard testified, "This year's certification
message is already having an impact. Colombia has promised to make
significant progress incarcerating the leaders of the Cali cocaine networks and eradicating all of the country's coca and opium poppy cultivation."[51] This belief was also shared by Senator Jesse Helms's staff,
who wrote in a report: "Many Colombians in the public and private sec-
tor told the Senate Foreign Relations Committee that U.S. pressure,
specifically Senator Helms' July 1994 amendment and the 1995 Helms-
Mack-Hatch Colombia bill, acted as a catalyst for the Colombian government's actions against Cali kingpins last year."[52]

Based on the events that transpired over the next year—which included the arrest of six of the top seven Cali kingpins—a strong case
can be made that U.S. pressure did greatly help to bring down the Cali
cartel, especially the U.S. move to bring in General Serrano. But this
fact did not prevent Ernesto Samper from issuing a sharp response to
the certification decision, which he viewed as unacceptable and as a
"unilateral decision of a foreign country."[53]

Relations between the Samper government and Washington wors-
ened during a May 27, 1995, meeting in Colombia between Robert Gelbard and Foreign Minister Rodrigo Pardo. The meeting was apparently
going well until the issue of DEA agents operating in Colombia came
up. A couple weeks earlier, on May 15, Pardo had sent Myles Frechette
a letter that listed nine new conditions limiting DEA agents' conduct in
Colombia, including the specification that DEA agents inform Colombian officials of their activities.[54] The reaction from the U.S. government had been predictably negative. So when this issue surfaced in the
meeting between Gelbard and Pardo, it sparked a heated exchange in
which Gelbard stated that Pardo "could not talk to the United States that
way." Pardo replied that "in Colombia we can."[55]

The ill will generated from the disagreement over the DEA controversy escalated later in 1995 when independent Colombian congressman Carlos Alonso Lucio, whom the U.S. government suspected of having links to the Cali cartel, produced tapes of recorded conversations
between DEA agents in Colombia and agents in their headquarters in
Washington. These DEA agents apparently made disparaging comments
about the Colombian government and, according to Lucio, included
mention of a plot to undermine the Samper administration.[56]

These accusations in turn provoked a strong response from the U.S.
government, which viewed any secret recordings of conversations made

between U.S. government officials to be illegal. State Department spokesman Nicholas Burns stated: "We are not happy with the consistent litany of denunciations made by certain Colombian officials regarding the activities of the United States government."[57] But more than Robert Gelbard or anyone else in the State Department, it was the drug hawks in Congress who were demanding that the United States tighten the screws on Colombia, and this too would increasingly revolve around Ernesto Samper himself.

Pressure from Capitol Hill picked up in the spring and summer of 1995 as several influential congressmen, Senator Jesse Helms chief among them, saw the issuance of the national interest waiver as an appeasement on the drug war and an endorsement of a corrupt president. Helms stated that "the effect of this decision is to do nothing about Colombia's abysmal record, with our bilateral relationship continuing as if nothing is wrong. This is a grave moral and political mistake."[58]

Helms once again proposed that the United States cut off all antinarcotics aid and commercial concessions to Colombia if its government did not arrest and jail the Cali cartel's leaders.[59] Helms also announced that he would present the much anticipated witness "María," who supposedly worked with the Cali cartel and who would testify regarding the cartel's relationship with Ernesto Samper.[60] "María" eventually testified before the Senate Foreign Relations Committee on July 30, 1996, and stated that she was present at a meeting in 1989 when Ernesto Samper received payments from the Cali cartel in return for his expected commitment to oppose any possible return of extradition to the United States.[61]

THE CRACKDOWN ON THE CALI CARTEL

This combination of pressure from both the State Department and Congress no doubt had an influence on Samper's subsequent decision to crack down on the Cali cartel. Not long after Colombia received the stern warning in the form of a national interest waiver as well as the strong words from Gelbard and Helms, Samper announced that he was deploying 6,000 elite troops to Cali to search for drug leaders. He also vowed to make money-laundering a crime for the first time, a promise that became law on May 31, 1995.[62] Moreover, in July, Samper sent a letter directly to Helms stating that he was taking a strong role in the drug war.[63] But these actions did not prevent Colombia from being decertified the following year, further suggesting that U.S. policy in Colombia, beginning in the latter part of 1995 and continuing through 1996, had become overwhelmingly obsessed with Ernesto Samper himself.[64]

When General Serrano returned from his post in Washington to take over as head of the Colombian National Police, even his most loyal supporters could not have imagined how effective he would be in bringing down the Cali cartel. Upon assuming office, Serrano quickly fired scores of officers he believed to be corrupt, including three colonels, thirteen lieutenant colonels, twenty-five majors, and twenty-six other mid-level officers. He also fired several thousand rank-and-file police officers.[65] Equipped with up-to-the-minute intelligence information from the CIA and the DEA,[66] the Colombian security forces then set sight on the Cali cartel, most notably in early 1995 when they formed an elite Cali-based police squad modeled after the Bloque de Búsqueda, which had ultimately worked effectively against Pablo Escobar. The squad consisted of 6,000 special forces and conducted over 200 raids against the Cali cartel and related criminal organizations.

Six months later this elite squad—having moved its base to Bogotá and now flying into Cali unannounced to reduce the chances that corrupt officials in Cali would compromise its operations—began raiding the businesses and homes of the Cali drug leaders. They seized files, computer disks, and other evidence and used them to implicate the kingpins, as well as to uncover connections between the traffickers and politicians or other government officials.

General Serrano's results were unprecedented in the Colombian government's decades-long fight against drug traffickers. Serrano's unit had arrested the very kingpins whose jailing the United States had earlier demanded.[67] Washington's reaction to the arrests was predictably favorable (warrants were issued by the new chief prosecutor, Alfonso Valdivieso, who along with General Serrano was seen to be an ally to the United States).[68] President Clinton's drug policy adviser, Lee P. Brown, stated: "Colombia gets two thumbs up from me for this. . . . They have made a good start."[69] An emotional Myles Frechette commented that "this was a triumph of the Samper administration and one that without doubt is going to improve the relation between Colombia and the United States."[70] Nevertheless, much to his frustration, Ernesto Samper did not receive credit for the successful crackdown on the Cali cartel; rather, the resolve to do something against the traffickers quickly became personified in the form of General Serrano, whose success was seen in Washington to be taking place in spite of Ernesto Samper.

While there is little doubt that much of the credit for the crackdown lies in the efforts of General Serrano and his men, some Colombian officials who worked with Samper believe that he truly was committed to confronting the drug issue in order to demonstrate his resolve to the Colombian populace. As Samper's second High Commissioner for Peace, Daniel García-Peña Jaramillo was one of several high-level Colombian officials who shared this view. According to García-Peña, "Samper was tough on the drug issue because he wanted to prove his enemies wrong."[71] Not surprisingly, the view from the U.S. government was much different. One U.S. official remarked in an interview that Samper "took the credit for everything, but he had no input. It was Serrano backed up by us that did the trick with Cali."[72]

These competing conceptions of Samper's integrity on the drug war reveal how both sides saw the issue so differently: Washington viewed Samper as an obstacle (although an increasingly convenient one) to its counternarcotics efforts; the Samper administration saw itself as the champion of these strengthened antidrug operations. U.S. policy toward Colombia also became extraordinarily personalized. Led by Robert Gelbard, and to a lesser extent Myles Frechette, Washington was attempting to undermine Ernesto Samper—and traditionally one of its most reliable allies in Latin America—at all costs. This base, personal stance toward Samper continued for the remainder of his presidency.

1995 COMES TO AN END

By the middle of 1995 the state of the drug war suggested that the United States was getting what it wanted in Colombia, exemplified by the rapid dismantling of the Cali cartel. Moreover, that the DEA and the CIA were actively assisting in the apprehension of the cartel's leaders made many in Washington believe that the United States could work with the new Colombian administration. Even if most of the credit for this progress was going to General Serrano and not Ernesto Samper, it did seem as though any initial aversion that the U.S. government had to working with Samper was abating. But this incipient thaw in the U.S. government's position toward Samper was put on hold when in late 1995 new revelations emerged about his involvement with the Cali cartel during his 1993–1994 campaign for the presidency.[73]

Furthermore, the euphoria and optimism generated by the crackdown on the Cali cartel was more than offset by the smaller, seemingly tangential issues such as the controversies over the role of the DEA in Colombia or the phone conversations leaked in the Colombian Congress. This frustration continued into the 1996 certification process, in which, given the Colombian government's virtual dismantling of the Cali cartel, full certification should have been ensured. Yet rather than being rewarded for its efforts, Colombia was instead decertified. This suggests that, unlike the Gaviria years when Bogotá could disagree with Washington on counternarcotics issues and still enjoy warm relations (and receive certification), now Samper had to provide full and unconditional cooperation with the United States.

With a tainted president like Samper in office, dismantling the Cali cartel would not be enough. Even though it had accomplished what it wanted regarding the Cali cartel, the United States was willing to let the bilateral relationship deteriorate because there were issues on which Colombia was less than fully cooperative. The United States would not tolerate such affronts from a corrupt president, an act made easier given that there were few consequences for treating Colombia with such contempt. And unfortunately for the Colombian government, the remainder of 1995 saw a variety of new revelations that caused the U.S. government to sour on the Samper administration, no matter how successful it was in tearing down the Cali cartel.[74]

THE SAMPER SCANDAL ERUPTS

The Proceso 8000 scandal, which would ravage Colombia for the next few years, started in early 1995. New chief prosecutor Alfonso Valdivieso began to build a mountain of cases that revolved around the drug money–related investigations of nine prominent members of the Liberal Party. The investigation eventually involved accusations and indictments against more than twenty-five legislators and executive branch officials.[75] Valdivieso's investigative persistence began to pay off in April 1995 when his team revealed extensive lists, seized during the now increasing raids on drug traffickers' homes and businesses, that documented the names of politicians, police officers, and others who had supposedly received contributions from the Cali cartel.[76] True to form, seeing how violently the Medellín cartel had reacted to the issue of extradition in the late 1980s and early 1990s, in August 1995 the Colombian police found a bomb along Valdivieso's route to work.

Valdivieso's investigation, which over time publicly infiltrated the inner circles of Ernesto Samper's campaign team, received another big break on July 26, 1995, when Samper's campaign treasurer, Santiago Medina, was arrested on charges of illegal enrichment. During the arrest, prosecutors found a copy of a check from a cartel front company given to the Liberal Party and endorsed by Medina, further implicating the Samper campaign.[77] In September, Medina stated that not only did U.S.$6 million come into the campaign from the Cali cartel, but also that Samper knew about the transaction.[78] Ultimately, Medina provided prosecutors with approximately 400 documents that linked the Samper campaign to the Cali cartel. Medina received a sentence of sixty-four months in prison.[79]

Soon after Medina's arrest and confession, on August 15, Samper's former presidential campaign manager, Fernando Botero—then defense minister—was arrested for illegal enrichment. The impetus for the arrest came directly from Medina's confession, in which he stated that Botero had solicited drug funds. Botero followed Medina's example and agreed to cooperate with the Prosecutor's Office. His subsequent testimony was even more damaging to Samper than Medina's had been.[80] In two interviews from jail, Botero said that Samper knew about the contributions; he also revealed the existence of an October 1994 letter from the Cali cartel's Rodríguez brothers to Samper in which the brothers reminded Samper that they had "gladly joined the cause at an opportune moment, and had modestly tried to help without any type of guarantee."[81] That the U.S. Congress and other agencies in Washington had seen Botero as an ally gave even greater weight to the veracity of his testimony, even if he too was now being accused of receiving drug money.[82] Botero was sentenced to sixty-three months in jail and given a U.S.$2 million fine.

The revelations of both Medina and Botero once again focused Washington's attention on Ernesto Samper's links to the Cali cartel. The long-standing suspicions that Samper was receiving drug money, and even the infamous narco-cassettes, had not provided conclusive proof of his involvement. But now two of his top campaign officials were both revealing the extent to which drug money from the Cali cartel had infiltrated Samper's campaign. For many in the U.S. government, Medina's and Botero's testimony was proof positive that Samper's campaign was inextricably tied to drug money. This scandal, they believed, had compromised his ability to govern Colombia and, more important, to prosecute the drug war.

On December 14, 1995, the Colombian Congress's Committee of Investigations and Accusations—which has constitutional authority to investigate the president—decided in a 14–1 vote that there were insufficient grounds for pursuing allegations regarding Samper's drug connection.[83] This was decided despite Medina's testimony; most observers attributed the shocking decision to the fact that Samper's Liberal Party dominated the chamber. The committee's decision solidified U.S. aversion to Samper personally. In turn, this disgust dominated U.S. policy and the bilateral relationship for the remainder of his administration. Robert Gelbard responded to the committee's decision by stating: "It is evident that this was not a serious investigation. The committee's efforts show that there are still certain people in power linked to drug traffickers." Myles Frechette backed up Gelbard by commenting that Gelbard's statement "represented the American government's point of view . . . this is a fact, not a criticism."[84]

Along with the growing scandal surrounding the Cali cartel's contributions to Samper's election campaign, other events in the fall of 1995 served to worsen U.S.-Colombian relations.[85] At the same time that the Committee of Investigations and Accusations decided to halt its investigation into Samper's election finances, a law that would have decriminalized "illegal enrichment," apparently written with the help of lawyers representing the Cali cartel, passed in the Colombian Senate (56–32), making it the third time in two years that this "narco-rider" legislation had passed in at least one of the legislative houses. While this bill did not pass the lower chamber and thus did not become law, it infuriated U.S. officials, who were convinced that Samper was the driving force behind the amendment.

Samper also floated the idea that the Colombian government should attempt to reduce the role of "faceless judges," a judicial concept that many, including those in Washington, believed was crucial in the fight against the drug traffickers.[86] Ambassador Myles Frechette stated that "an end to the faceless justice system would have a terrible impact on drug trafficking and terrorism. . . . Without it, judges will begin to be slaughtered like before the law existed."[87] When the outcry from the United States reached Samper, he reversed his position and stated that he did not support such an idea, but the impression he made with his initial backing remained firm in the minds of U.S. officials in Washington and Bogotá.

Another major issue that caused great annoyance within the U.S. government was the realization that many of the recently arrested Cali kingpins were actually living quite well in prison and, at times, even continuing to run their drug-trafficking operations from within the prison compounds. U.S. officials were especially disgruntled by the fact that the Rodríguez brothers were having cellular phones smuggled to them in the La Picota prison, which presumably allowed them to continue running their drug empires. Moreover, several of the cartel leaders were now eligible to receive reduced sentences, due in part to legal technicalities codified in the Colombian penal system. DEA chief Thomas Constantine stated that "[t]he whole thing will be a sham if those guys [the Rodríguez brothers] do not stay locked up. . . . If they walk out or get little or no time, it is ridiculous."[88]

Contrary to the general perception that the newly available evidence of Samper's drug links caused the United States to virtually break off relations, it is clear that the Cali cartel's comfortable prison conditions fueled Washington's perception that the Samper administration was backtracking in its fight against the Cali cartel. Over the course of only a few months, the relative degree of cooperation between Washington and Bogotá was replaced by animosity, accusations, and mistrust on both sides. As one U.S. official commented, "There is no question that Serrano and Valdivieso are doing their best, and that is a lot. . . . The problem is, after them, who can you trust? It is fair to say things are at their worst level ever."[89] Samper, who himself was becoming fed up with U.S. arm-twisting, stated at a year-end news conference that Colombia would not be a docile partner with the United States, and that he certainly did not fear any threat of drug decertification. Yet it would indeed be the 1996 drug certification process, set to take place in only a few months, that would reflect how critically damaged the bilateral relationship had become.

THE 1996 DECERTIFICATION DECISION

If the 1996 drug decertification decision toward Colombia had been evaluated on the criteria laid out by the U.S. government during the 1995 certification process (i.e., gains against the Cali cartel), there is little doubt that from an objective standard Colombia should have received full certification. Yet there was little objectivity in the 1996 decertification of Colombia.[90] The criteria had shifted from an emphasis on the Cali cartel to the personal conduct of Ernesto Samper. Robert Gelbard's testimony on March 7, 1996, in which he justified the State

Department's decision to decertify Colombia, clearly shows the change in U.S. policy:

> The decision to deny Colombia certification was not made lightly. We work with some extremely dedicated Colombian officials who, in spite of tremendous odds, have continued to attack the drug syndicates. . . . During mid-1995, the situation appeared to be improving— the Colombian National Police arrested a number of the leading Cali kingpins and the country's top prosecutor launched a sweeping corruption investigation that left no branch of the government untouched. . . . [T]hese efforts have been undercut at every turn, however, by a government and a legislature not only plagued by corruption, but which are fostering corruption in order to protect themselves. The Cali traffickers have been running their operations from prison, and the Prosecutor General has been the target of a public campaign to undermine and discredit his efforts.[91]

Gelbard's position was similar to that of the drug hawks in the U.S. Congress, such as Jesse Helms. By the time of the 1996 certification process, U.S. policy toward Colombia was increasingly characterized by a sense of agreement that the United States should take a firm stance against the Samper administration, except for its trusted allies such as General Serrano and Valdivieso. In a letter to Senate Majority Leader Robert Dole a few days before the certification decision, Helms wrote:

> Based on the clear evidence presented by President Samper's closest personal confidants and collaborators, and the firsthand information obtained in this report, I recommend that the United States decertify Colombia this year with no national interest waiver. . . . No government can be completely committed to obliterating the drug cartels, drug corruption, and drug-related violence, nor effective in the achievement of these goals, if its senior officials owe fealty to drug kingpins. The Colombian government will never be dedicated to fighting drugs or drug corruption as long as Ernesto Samper is its leader, and its politicians, police, and judiciary are all guided by the money of drug kingpins.[92]

Echoing Gelbard, Marc Thiessen, a member of Helms's staff on the Foreign Relations Committee, made it clear that decertification was about Ernesto Samper: "This is a decertification not of Colombia, but of President Samper. This is a vote of no confidence for him, not the country."[93] Soon after the decertification decision, Helms announced that the

United States would be willing and able to work with Colombia (and possibly move toward certification) if Samper were not president.[94]

It is also clear that U.S. domestic political considerations were driving Colombia policy. The 1996 certification process took place during a U.S. election year, and few Congress members wanted to be portrayed as soft on drugs.[95] In an interview with National Public Radio, Myles Frechette made this point clearly: "I believe that the certification process for the behavior in 1995 is going to be much more difficult in Washington this year because, first of all, the counternarcotics policies of the United States now make up a part of the discussions of the presidential campaign."[96]

An additional factor that sealed the decision to decertify Colombia was that Robert Gelbard had in effect decided to "out-radicalize" the drug hawks in Congress. Up until this point Congress had used the certification process as a sort of saber-rattling exercise through which they appeared concerned about the war on drugs. Decertification decisions were almost always reserved for "rogue states" like Afghanistan and Nigeria and not for more "upstanding" countries like Mexico or Colombia. But now Gelbard, in what increasingly appeared a self-appointed role as "America's Number-One Drug Cop," was pushing even harder than Congress on the certification issue. This stance was compounded by the fact that Washington was going to certify drug-riddled Mexico, which put pressure on the State Department to decertify at least one major drug-producing country in order to soothe its critics in Congress. With Ernesto Samper in office, the easy choice was Colombia.[97]

SAMPER DEFENDS HIMSELF

The shared frustration stemming from both Congress and the State Department was not due solely to Medina's and Botero's confessions about Samper's drug links, but also to Samper's positions on faceless judges and the narco-rider bill. U.S. officials now were convinced that Samper had gone soft on drugs. According to one U.S. official, "Samper, on the one hand, was saying he was cooperating with us, but under the table he was cooperating with Colombia's congress to pass laws, so impunity is even more total. That was untenable."[98] This fact brings up a key characteristic of the U.S. view of Samper: the U.S. had become paranoid about Samper's credibility to the point that it almost automatically assumed that he was not doing enough on the drug war or that he was somehow subverting U.S.-led antidrug efforts. Now that Washington was unalterably convinced that Samper was a narco-president, there was nothing that Samper could do short of complete cooperation to change this perception.

But the Samper administration did not take these actions lying down. Armed with the knowledge that the Colombian government in 1995 spent U.S.$900 million on antidrug efforts and that 500 of its security agents were killed in the process, Samper responded quickly and forcefully to the U.S. decertification decision. In one nationally broadcast speech, for example, Samper lambasted the decision: "We put the money and the deaths in the drug war. And others reserved the right to sit and judge us." Earlier, at a year-end (1995) news conference, Samper had stated that he was "not losing any sleep over the possibility of decertification. . . . Colombia is too grown up to have to pass exams every year. . . . I am not going to allow this country to have to be passing exams set by any country in the world, but at the same time, we are not going to lower our guard in the fight against drug trafficking, because it is in our national interest to fight."[99]

On March 20, 1996, Samper continued his offensive during an interview with journalist Charles Krause on PBS's *News Hour with Jim Lehrer* in which he reiterated his commitment to fight drugs as well as his innocence in the campaign scandal. Samper's defiant stance reveals that on the domestic level he deftly stood up to what he believed were sanctimonious and counterproductive policies on the part of Washington. But no matter how much Samper stood up to the United States for domestic political reasons, he nonetheless had to cooperate with Washington's counternarcotics predilections or face complete isolation, something that he felt Colombia could not afford to do. To that end, Samper soon muted his defiant stance and instead gave a speech in which he hinted that he might resign if it would serve to improve relations with the United States, although his spokespersons quickly denied that this was the intended meaning.

THE COLOMBIAN PRESIDENT LOSES HIS VISA

Following the March 1996 decision to decertify Colombia, few observers would have imagined that U.S.-Colombian relations could possibly get any worse. They did. Following Botero's incriminating revelations against Samper, on February 14, 1996, the Prosecutor's Office formally accused Samper of illegal activities, paving the way for another vote in the Colombian Congress.[100] Several months later, on June 12, the Liberal Party–dominated lower chamber decided once again not to pursue the criminal charges against the Colombian president in a 111–43 vote.[101] The vote meant that the president could not be tried by the Colombian Senate or be investigated by the Colombian Supreme Court.

In a reaction that by this time had become routine, the United States railed against the decision. State Department spokesman Nicholas Burns said that the vote "was not based on an exhaustive review of the evidence."[102] Burns also made it quite clear to the Samper administration that it either do something about the drug issue or risk facing severe consequences: "[The Colombian government] has the next month or two or so to convince the United States that it is going to be a more serious, more effective, more committed partner in the fight against narcotics trafficking. . . . Colombia would, in effect, be a pariah state, should we choose to go down this road."[103] And while still defiant, in a change of tactics Samper cultivated a conciliatory response and once again announced new antidrug measures: "We are forced to work together. . . . None of these measures I announced can be carried out without the cooperation of the United States. We need each other to keep working, we have an unbreakable marriage, and I hope when this storm is past we can jointly evaluate where we are in the fight against drug trafficking."[104]

Also referring to the vote, President Bill Clinton said that "the United States judges its relationship between the two countries by one standard: whether they are cooperating with us in the fight against narcotics."[105] While it is certain that there was general agreement within the U.S. government that the lower house's vote was unacceptable, the driving force behind taking greater steps to isolate Samper came from Ambassador Myles Frechette.[106] A memorandum written by Frechette, first published on June 30 by the *Washington Post,* urged the U.S. government to "isolate and debilitate" Samper, including the revocation of his visa. The publication of Frechette's memo caused an uproar in Colombia, revealing how far the U.S. government was willing to go in order to punish Samper after the congressional vote.[107] This uproar started a highly personal feud between Frechette and Samper that lasted until Frechette left Colombia in the fall of 1997.[108]

On July 11, 1996, the United States followed Frechette's advice and stripped Colombia's democratically elected president of his visa to enter the United States.[109] While the United States intended this move to further isolate Samper and even bring him down, it actually had the effect of galvanizing public support in his favor. Samper was now seen, and able to portray himself, as a victim of U.S. bullying. There is no question that the decision to revoke his visa was provoked by the congressional vote absolving Samper of any illegal activities. With the strength of the evidence implicating Samper, the U.S. government believed only a corrupt congress could have possibly exonerated him. Since U.S. officials could not get the Colombian Congress to implicate Samper, they would do the next best thing.

Samper played this victim card deftly, responding to the U.S. slight by once again taking steps on the diplomatic front, manifested by his naming of the respected Liberal Party ally María Emma Mejía to be his foreign minister. Mejía immediately traveled to Washington with the stated intent to denarcotize the bilateral relationship. When Mejía was asked how she would deal with the United States, she replied, "We have to try to overcome the mistrust. Colombia has shown important gains in the fight against drugs, including opening the debate on extradition. We should say to the United States that we have a common enemy—narco-trafficking."[110]

Samper's appointment of Mejía sheds light on a fundamental aspect on the nature of the U.S.-Colombian relationship. While Samper could attack the visa issue at home, he still had to take a conciliatory stance on the international front, manifested in this instance by his selection of Mejía. By the time of the visa episode, Colombia had already been humiliated following the 1996 decertification decision; nevertheless, knowing that as a subordinate state Colombia could not further jeopardize its relationship with the United States, Samper was forced to adopt a conciliatory stance in order to hopefully mend fences with its dominant northern neighbor.

Samper continued to step up the Colombian government's counternarcotics efforts, including more vigorous efforts to fumigate illicit crops. This included the implementation of Operation Condor, which utilized thirty-eight helicopters and twenty-one aircraft. During the operation the Colombian government also experimented with the controversial herbicide Imazapyr.[111] As had been the case the year before with Operation Splendor, the government's antinarcotics efforts sparked violent protests from those campesinos who were being affected by the aerial fumigation. In August 1996, 30,000 farmers began protesting in the southern department of Putumayo in order to stop the planned fumigation of the area. The situation eventually calmed down after the government agreed to let the farmers destroy their own coca crops and handed out payments so that they could grow rubber, yuca, and other cash crops.[112]

While the revocation of Samper's visa continued to be the major issue of contention between the United States and Colombia for much of 1996, it was not the only controversial pressure exerted by the U.S. government on the Samper administration that year. Instead, the issue of extradition—and its retroactive application—came to dominate the bilateral relationship from the end of 1996 through most of 1997.

EXTRADITION

On June 26, 1996, shortly before the United States revoked President Samper's visa, and eleven days after Samper was absolved of wrongdoing by the Colombian Congress, U.S. Attorney General Janet Reno formally demanded the extradition of four principal leaders of the Cali cartel—the Rodríguez brothers, Juan Carlos Ramírez, and Helmer "Pacho" Herrera—asserting that the 1979 U.S.-Colombian extradition treaty still held.[113] Reno also hinted that the United States would consider applying sanctions against Colombia if the Samper administration rejected the petition.[114]

The Colombian government responded by asserting that its 1991 constitution negated the treaty and that extradition was thus illegal under Colombian law.[115] Nevertheless, Samper took the lead on this issue and began to actively push for an amendment to the 1991 constitution that would allow for extradition. He also presented before the Colombian Congress a law that would increase sentences against drug traffickers. The timing of Samper's tough antidrug stance suggests that the U.S. influence did play an important part in his decisions. Robert Gelbard responded to these moves by stating emphatically before the U.S. Congress what, along with the principal goal of obtaining retroactive extradition, the United States wanted to see done in Colombia:

> We have outlined for the Colombian government a set of specific, realistic objectives and actions we expect it to pursue, and upon which we will evaluate its cooperation. These include the enactment of tough asset forfeiture and sentencing laws; the strengthening of Colombia's inadequate 1995 money laundering statute; effective eradication of coca and opium poppy fields; reconsideration of Colombia's policy of not extraditing its nationals; support for investigations and prosecutions

targeting corrupt public officials; and the signing of a bilateral maritime interdiction agreement.[116]

First and foremost in the push for extradition of drug kingpins to the United States was the issue of its retroactive application.[117] Since many of the Cali leaders were arrested in 1995, any new extradition law that did not allow for retroactivity would not apply to them. Some have suggested that one central reason the United States wanted retroactivity was so that the Rodríguez brothers could be extradited and compelled to divulge their dealings with Samper.[118]

It is difficult to know if this was the underlying motivation for the push for extradition, but what is certain is that U.S. policy toward Colombia became almost singularly obsessed with this issue. Myles Frechette stated: "[T]he position of my government is clear—retroactivity is very important. The Rodríguez brothers are major criminals. If they approve the proposal [extradition without retroactivity] those men will end up safe and sound."[119] In October 1996, the Colombian Senate voted in committee to begin exploring the issue of redressing the constitution, which was eventually amended in December 1997 to allow for nonretroactive extradition.[120]

In many ways extradition was the new litmus test for the Samper administration. Weakened by the ongoing accusations of narco-related corruption, Samper knew that he had to look strong on the drug front. Washington also knew this and, given the fact that Samper was not easily going away anytime soon, sought to exploit Samper's credibility problem in order to extract as many concessions on the counternarcotics fronts as possible. As one U.S. government official stated, "The good thing about Samper was that we could do whatever we wanted on the drug front. The extradition issue was another instance when we moved the 'goal posts back' in order to see how far we could push Samper on the drug stuff."[121]

The Colombian government's push for extradition had consequences. As had been the case with Pablo Escobar and the Medellín cartel, the Cali cartel was terrified just by the prospect of being extradited to the United States to stand trial. In the fall of 1996 it looked as though the "Extraditables" were being revived, this time by the Cali drug lords instead of those from Medellín. In November, Colombian legislators received a note purportedly from drug traffickers—they called themselves the "New Extraditables"—that read: "We have 40 years to fulfill this promise—we condemn you to death and all of your families."[122] In

March 1997 a pro-extradition regional newspaper editor was killed and several months later a quarter-ton bomb killed noted Cali journalist Gerardo Bedoya, who also had supported extradition. In total, seven anti-cartel journalists were killed in 1997.[123]

In May 1997 the Colombian media reported that the narcotics leaders had targeted both Samper and Frechette for assassination, which suggests they believed that Samper was firmly committed to the antidrug effort. This issue notwithstanding, the media report reveals how committed the "New Extraditables" were to intimidating extradition supporters.[124] On September 16 the Colombian Senate voted to remove the clause that would have made the law of extradition apply retroactively. This vote came just ten days after a massive bomb was defused outside the offices of the Medellín newspaper *El Mundo,* a scare that served as a firm reminder of what might be the consequences if retroactivity were passed. Finally, when the Colombian Congress did pass a form of nonretroactive extradition in December 1997, Samper's chief press spokesman was kidnapped and once again most believed that the "New Extraditables" were responsible.

Some in the U.S. government, however, were not so sure that the "New Extraditables" were really as prevalent as some in the Colombian government and media made them out to be. One unnamed State Department official remarked, "I'm not convinced additional violence was kicked up by the retroactive extradition issue."[125] Yet it is also clear that U.S. officials did not want to attribute the new round of violence to their long fight for extradition policy.

In addition to the move toward extradition (although without the coveted retroactivity), there were other events that should have pleased the U.S. government. In December 1996, Samper successfully passed an asset forfeiture law through the Colombian Congress; he also worked to retroactively raise the sentences for drug traffickers, make them forfeit their profits, and punish those who collaborate with them.[126] In February 1997 the United States and Colombia signed a maritime ship-boarding agreement intended to combat drug running at sea, something that Robert Gelbard had made a priority in the bilateral relationship. During this same month, the Colombian National Police claimed to have captured and destroyed a cocaine laboratory of industrial-size proportions.[127]

But none of these achievements would be able to counterbalance the ill will and frustration on the part of the U.S. government when on

January 17, 1997, a Cali judge sentenced Miguel and Gilberto Rodríguez to twenty-one and eighteen years respectively, but then immediately halved the sentences because, among other legal particulars, they had confessed their crimes. U.S. Drug Czar Barry McCaffrey called the decision "totally unacceptable" and Myles Frechette accused the Colombian government of "backing drug trafficking."[128] President Samper also railed against the decision, but it was not enough to disabuse the newly kindled perceptions in Washington that the Samper administration was somehow responsible for the decision. For Colombia the timing could not have been worse as, once again, the annual drug certification decision date was only a few months away.

The debate in Colombia over extradition has changed substantially since the Samper years. On October 13, 1999, the Colombian government announced that it had arrested thirty-one suspected drug traffickers, including the Medellín cartel's Fabio Ochoa. Colombia's ambassador to the United States, Luis Alberto Moreno, stated: "They will be certainly extradited to the United States. . . . I think people came to recognize that extradition is a very useful tool in fighting the war on drugs."[129] In September 2001, Ochoa was indeed extradited and, at the time of this writing, was awaiting trial on charges of shipping thirty tons of cocaine a month into the United States.

THE 1997 DECERTIFICATION DECISION

The U.S. government fully decertified Colombia for a second straight year on March 1, 1997, this time joined by Nigeria, Afghanistan, Burma, Iran, and Syria.[130] The United States did, however, leave open the option that it would not apply economic sanctions, allowing for the possibility of reversing the ruling over the course of the year. But in order for the United States to reverse its decision, Colombia would have to reestablish extradition (at this point in 1997 it was still being debated), implement recently passed antidrug legislation, accept use of a more effective herbicide to fumigate illicit crops, tackle corruption, and crack down on the drug dealers who did business while in prison. According to Gelbard, "These steps, which are reasonable, can be achieved over the course of the next several months. Taking them, the government of Colombia can show the international community that it is committed to putting an end to the era of narco-domination."[131]

And as with the 1996 certification process, Gelbard was confident that Washington's heavy-handed tactics, whereby it would continue to support Serrano and Valdivieso while isolating Samper, were creating the desired outcome. As he testified in February 1997: "I believe that our strategy has produced results, and we have balanced our rejection of corruption in the Samper administration with increased support directly to the Colombian institutions that are combating the drug scourge."[132] Gelbard did not fail to mention that he believed Samper to be "a truly corrupt president who has a clear history of co-operating with the drug dealers."[133]

By this time, more than with any other Colombian administration, the United States had come to equate its success in Colombia with co-operation on the drug front. The annual certification process took on the character of an annual review of how well the Colombian government had fulfilled U.S. demands. And this evaluation process—based solely on the drug issue—drove the overall bilateral relationship. Certification meant relations were good; decertification signaled that relations were bad. Indeed, relations were at their most narcotized level, and the drug certification process was the glaring manifestation of this fact.

As 1997 came to an end, Ernesto Samper continued to tout his apparent tough stance on extradition, consistently urging that retroactivity be included. In December, conveniently after the Colombian Congress passed nonretroactive extradition, he announced: "[W]e would have preferred an extradition without condition, particularly with regard to the retroactivity. We're done with the 'taboo' of extradition. . . . [A]fter today no one in Colombia will be able to continue using this country to hide from acts committed in other countries."[134]

It is difficult to know whether Samper was taking this tough stance on retroactivity knowing that the Colombian Congress would never approve it. According to one U.S. embassy official, "Samper knew that retroactive extradition would never go anywhere. Thus, he could paint himself as the tough guy. In reality, he never wanted it."[135] Nevertheless, his stance did serve to deflect some of the pressure he had been receiving from Washington. But while Samper appeared committed to continuing his version of the war on drugs, by the end of 1997 and into 1998 it was the United States that had begun to tire of the combative, increasingly counterproductive policy of isolating Samper. Moreover, Samper was nearing the end of his presidency, and many U.S. officials believed that ties to the incoming administration could be preemptively ruptured unless they undertook to begin repairing relations with Colombia.

U.S. POLICY SOFTENS

In the fall of 1997, U.S.-Colombian relations began to improve somewhat, exemplified by Ernesto Samper's talk of a "new climate." This apparent thaw was driven by the fact that U.S. officials knew he was leaving office in less than a year.[136] From the U.S. side, a number of events signaled this change in policy. These included an October visit from ONDCP director Barry McCaffrey, who while still emphasizing the need for the Colombian Congress to pass unconditional extradition, spoke of cooperation and suggested that Washington was serious about adopting a more conciliatory tone.[137]

The departure of Myles Frechette in November was another sign that Washington was looking to defuse tensions, although this did not stop Frechette from boasting, "My job was to change Colombia. I have done that, and Colombia is better off for it."[138] In another signal that relations had become less narcotized, before Frechette left Bogotá he made an important speech in which he singled out the Colombian military's infamous Twentieth Brigade for human rights abuses.[139] The speech caused a sensation in Colombia, as heretofore the United States had not made many public statements regarding human rights. Ernesto Samper officially disbanded the brigade the following year.

Well before the next annual certification of drug efforts in March 1998, the tone of the State Department and the drug hawks in Congress had changed significantly. Interestingly, now there was a growing concern that the two-time decertification of Colombia had been counterproductive and was actually harming U.S. counternarcotics efforts. In particular, the U.S. government's concern focused on how the two decertification decisions, along with the Leahy Amendment, had slowed the delivery of antidrug assistance to the Colombian National Police. According to Benjamin Gilman, chair of the House International Relations Committee: "[T]he ill-advised decertification of Colombia two years in a row without a national interest waiver has cut the life line for our allies in the professional antidrug police. These real drug fighters are sorely in need of ammunition, of explosives, of helicopter spare parts, chopper upgrades along with armaments."[140] Myles Frechette, speaking on behalf of the State Department, shared a similar view: "While fully implementing the intent of the law, denial of certification for Colombia had the unfortunate effect of cutting off significant military financing funds—that's FMF [Foreign Military Finance] and IMET [International Military Education Training]—for counternarcotics purposes."[141]

Responding to the fact that U.S. firms had lost an estimated U.S.$875 million in potential business to the decertification decisions, Secretary of State Madeleine Albright wrote in a memorandum to President Clinton that the decision to decertify Colombia for two consecutive years "has demonstrated to be an unintentional disadvantage for the commercial interests of the United States. . . . [T]he continued interruption of this [some types of military] assistance would mean the continuation of serious damage to the vital interests of the national security of the people of the United States."[142]

A major unexpected consequence of the decertification decisions was the suspension of antidrug funding, even though the certification legislation was generally understood to provide for continued assistance in such cases. The controversy over whether antidrug aid should be suspended along with other forms of U.S. assistance stemmed from the vague language of the certification law. The suspension lasted for several months until a new ruling decided in favor of continuing antidrug aid to decertified countries. This dilatory process pleased virtually no one in either Congress or the State Department.

In its efforts to punish so-called bad guys like Samper, the United States realized that its policy of isolation had inadvertently hurt allies like General Serrano. And since the overwhelming priority of the U.S. government was to continue its war on drugs in Colombia, decertification became counterproductive if it meant impeding antidrug efforts. It is not surprising, therefore, that in March 1998 Colombia received a national interest waiver during the certification process so that the United States could continue to slap its hand but not have to endure the more complete cutoff of assistance, including some types of antidrug assistance, that full decertification required.[143]

Yet the decision not to fully decertify Colombia did not mean that the United States would now publicly condone Ernesto Samper for his efforts. There was even talk among U.S. officials that the United States should decertify Colombia and then reinstate certification on August 7, the day that Samper's successor would take office.[144] Secretary of State Madeleine Albright stated that Colombian government forces

> have conducted an effective eradication and interdiction effort. But the current government has not demonstrated full political support for counternarcotics efforts. . . . Coming on the eve of that country's congressional and presidential elections, the waiver decision is intended to lay the groundwork for increased cooperation and to support those

who are striving to strengthen the rule of law and buttress their embattled democracy.[145]

THE END OF SAMPER'S TERM

By the time Ernesto Samper was preparing to leave office it had become readily apparent to U.S. government officials that by isolating Samper the United States had helped to weaken the Colombian state at precisely the most inopportune time.[146] Indeed, while the discredited Samper administration was governing Colombia, the country's guerrilla groups were increasing their activity throughout the countryside. Ironically, a good part of the guerrillas' increased strength actually resulted from the U.S. government's successful efforts to better eradicate and interdict coca production and trafficking in Bolivia and Peru. This crackdown in Peru and Bolivia ended up encouraging greater coca cultivation in Colombia.[147] In light of these new realities, Washington realized that a diplomatically isolated Samper did not have the political capital or international legitimacy requisite for dealing with Colombia's rapidly escalating civil conflict. And with so much attention—both from the Samper administration and from the Colombian media—focused on the tumultuous relations with the United States, the growth of both guerrilla and paramilitary strength was at least initially overlooked.

The massive increase in coca production in Colombia in the mid-1990s provided the guerrilla groups—mainly the FARC—with substantially higher revenues as they began to tax cocaine production and demand protection money from coca farmers. When this revenue is combined with revenues from revolutionary taxes, kidnappings, and other illicit activities, the guerrillas now earn approximately U.S.$500 million annually from the illicit drug trade. This has enabled the guerrillas to dramatically expand their influence throughout Colombia in the last few years. A significant amount of this expansion occurred during Samper's tenure in office.

In several interviews with involved officials in both the Colombian and U.S. governments there was a general consensus that one effect of Samper's discredited presidency was the Colombian state's inability to adequately deal with the rapid increase in guerrilla strength. Nor was the Samper administration prepared to confront the rapidly escalating paramilitary problem, revealed by the increase in indiscriminate paramilitary attacks on civilian populations throughout Colombia. In fact, it was during Samper's tenure that former Medellín cartel member Carlos Castaño consolidated his paramilitary network, which is now claimed to have an armed force of approximately 12,000 men.

While the United States is clearly not responsible for this rapid escalation in paramilitary and guerrilla activity, U.S. officials nonetheless came to realize that a politically and diplomatically isolated Colombian government would not be able to effectively deal with the increasingly complex and violent situation in Colombia. This dynamic would compel a shift in Colombia policy as the U.S. government said goodbye to Ernesto Samper and awaited the upcoming presidential election.

CONCLUSION

What emerges from the analysis of the Samper era is that U.S. policy can be characterized as "overt narcotization." That is, since the United States decided to isolate Samper and instead cultivate ties with other government officials whom it better trusted, the U.S. demand that Colombia cooperate and obey on the drug front was quite explicit. As we will see in the next chapter, this comes in stark contrast to U.S. policy during the Pastrana administration, in which the United States, perceiving Pastrana to be more cooperative on the drug issue, has been more implicit about its antidrug requirements of the Colombian government. This in turn has allowed for a much broader bilateral agenda that better accommodates the pursuit of nondrug issues like the peace process, human rights, and economic ties. In other words, Colombian cooperation on the drug front has determined the nature of the broader bilateral relationship.

Because the current state of implicit narcotization means that relations are marked by a greater degree of cooperation than under the overt narcotization that characterized the Samper years, certain sectors of the U.S. government—especially the embassy in Bogotá—have greater flexibility to deal with complex issues such as the current peace process and the human rights crisis. It is during this time that we see the emergence of certain nondrug components of U.S. policy in Colombia. The U.S. State Department's forceful human rights reports between 1998 and 2000, as well as the several State Department–sponsored human rights conferences, are but a few of the signs that the U.S. government was making its policy toward Colombia more than drugs. Tacit support for Andrés Pastrana's peace efforts is another area where U.S. policy was softening. In many ways, following the Samper years, the war on drugs dominated U.S. policy, but it did not completely overwhelm any other component of the bilateral relationship.

While a fair amount of this change in policy was related to the change of presidents in Colombia, it also stemmed from Washington's realization that it could not focus on counternarcotics-related issues to the extent that other important issues were essentially forgotten or ignored. That said, all indicators confirmed that drugs remained the primary focus of U.S. policy in Colombia.

NOTES

1. Author interview with Myles Frechette, Washington, D.C., June 1999.
2. Author interview with Alexander Watson, Washington, D.C., October 1999.
3. Ibid.
4. See "Samper Scandal a History of Colombia's Drug History," *The Miami Herald,* November 5, 1995; and "Rodríguez tenía en 1984 número privado de Samper," *El Tiempo,* November 8, 1995.
5. For an insightful, if melodramatic, account of the initial U.S. overtures to Ernesto Samper, as well as the ensuing narco-cassette controversy, see Douglas Farah, "The Crackup," *The Washington Post,* July 21, 1996. See also "Advertimos sobre narcodineros," *El Tiempo,* June 6, 1996.
6. With concrete documents still classified, it is unclear exactly how much and when the United States knew about Samper's narco-connection to the Cali cartel. See "A menudo, el gobierno colombiano miente: Robert Gelbard," *El Tiempo,* August 21, 1996.
7. By the time he became president, Samper had backed away from his support of legalization, arguing that his view was directed solely toward marijuana and did not relate to either cocaine or heroine. For Samper's earlier involvement in the issue of drug legalization, see Iván Orozco Abad, "Los diálogos con el narcotráfico: Historia de la transformación fallida de un delincuente común en un delincuente político," *Análisis Político* 11 (September–December 1990): 28–58; and Ernesto Samper Pizano, *Legalización de la marihuana* (Bogotá: ANIF, Fondo Editorial, 1980).
8. McLean was deputy chief of mission in Colombia from 1987 to 1990.
9. Author interview with Phil McClean, deputy assistant secretary of state for inter-American affairs (1990–1993), Washington, D.C., May 10, 1999. There is purported to be a July 1994 CIA report stating that Samper not only received money from the Cali cartel, but also solicited it. McClean was unaware of this report at the time of his meeting with Samper.
10. "La descertificación era el final lógico," *El Tiempo,* March 3, 1996.
11. Author interview with Alexander Watson, former assistant secretary of state for inter-American affairs, Washington, D.C., October 6, 1999.

12. See "Ernesto Samper, sin visa para gobernar?" *El Tiempo,* July 14, 1996.

13. Moreno is the current Colombian ambassador to the United States.

14. For more on the events surrounding the beginning of the narco-cassette scandal, including a transcript of the taped conversations, see Luis M. Cañón, *La Crisis: Cuatro años a bordo del gobierno de Samper* (Bogotá: Planeta, 1998), pp. 23–55.

15. "Colombia, a desvirtuar acusación de EEUU," *El Tiempo,* July 11, 1994.

16. See "Drug Abuse," *The Economist,* July 2, 1994. At that point *The Economist* presciently argued that the disclosure of the narco-cassettes would force Samper to take a tough stance on the drug issue in order to bolster the belief that drug traffickers had not compromised him. On September 30, Toft appeared on national television in Colombia and denounced what he believed was a "narco-democracy." Interestingly, much of Toft's comments were directed toward the Gaviria administration and not Ernesto Samper. See "La descertificación era el final lógico," *El Tiempo,* March 3, 1996; and Sewall Menzel, *Cocaine Quagmire: Implementing U.S. Anti-Drug Policy in the North Andes–Colombia* (New York: University Press of America, 1997), pp. 148–150.

17. See "Fiscal promete juicio a jefes del narcotráfico," *El Tiempo,* July 27, 1994.

18. See "En qué va el Proceso 8000," *El Tiempo,* October 6, 1996.

19. See "Whose Fault?" *The Economist,* October 22, 1994.

20. Author interview with former U.S. State Department official Michael Skol, Washington, D.C., September 10, 1999.

21. See *The Miami Herald,* June 23, 1999; and "Samper pide rectificar," *El Tiempo,* June 24, 1994. For more on the narco-cassette controversy, see "Prensa mundial destaca caso de narco-cassette," *El Tiempo,* June 24, 1994.

22. "Guerra a fondo contra narcos," *El Tiempo,* July 22, 1994.

23. "Samper to Propose U.S.-Colombian Anti-Drugs Commission," Agence France-Presse, June 22, 1994.

24. "Watson pide acladar caso de narcocassete," *El Tiempo,* June 28, 1994. Author translation.

25. "El embajador Frechette," *El Tiempo,* August 8, 1994. Author translation.

26. See "Relaciones con EU," *El Tiempo,* July 14, 1994; "Clinton le desea exitos a Samper," *El Tiempo,* July 4, 1994.

27. "Es irresponsable, el informe sobre Samper," *El Tiempo,* July 15, 1994. Author translation.

28. See "Colombia rechazaría ayuda," *El Tiempo,* July 16, 1994; and "Jesse Helms, duro y radical," *El Tiempo,* July 17, 1994.

29. "Avanza distensión con EEUU," *El Tiempo,* July 28, 1994.

30. "Comienza distensión con EEUU?" *El Tiempo,* July 22, 1994. Author translation.

31. "Más condiciones para la ayuda de EEUU," *El Tiempo,* July 18, 1994.

32. Before he was inaugurated, Samper also met with Ambassador Busby for ninety minutes. Samper apparently told Busby that "there was no campaign with better and stricter controls than ours." See David Adams, "Colombia in

Gloom over Drugs Accusation," *The Times,* June 25, 1994. White House spokesman Mike McCurry stated at the time that the tapes were discussed and that Busby expressed concern over them. McCurry stated, "We expect that there should be a full and prompt investigation of those types of allegations that can lead to understanding of what the truth is." See "Colombia President-Elect Meets with U.S. Ambassador; Envoy Troubled by Drug Cartel Allegation," *The Washington Post,* June 25, 1994.

33. Author interview with Michael Skol, Washington, D.C., September 10, 1999.

34. Because many of the meetings between Samper and U.S. officials were confidential, it is hard to know exactly what was discussed. Shortly after the meeting, Samper announced to the press that the results were "very favorable" and that "my campaign was absolutely transparent, that I would respond to any evidence that they presented." See "Carta Bill Clinton a Ernesto Samper," *El Tiempo,* July 1, 1994. Author translation.

35. Author interview with Michael Skol, Washington, D.C., September 10, 1999.

36. Samper initially confirmed Vargas Silva as commander of the National Police and sent Serrano to Washington as an attaché. U.S. pressure quickly reversed this and brought Serrano back to Bogotá to head the National Police.

37. Robert T. Buckman, "The Cali Cartel: An Undefeated Enemy," *Low Intensity Conflict and Law Enforcement* 3, no. 3 (Winter 1994): 444. For a transcript of Samper's inauguration speech, see Ernesto Samper Pizano, "Tiempo de la gente," Imprenta Nacional de Colombia, Bogotá, August 7, 1994.

38. See "American Drug Aid Goes South," *The New York Times,* November 25, 1996.

39. See Gabriel Marcella and Donald E. Schulz, "Colombia's Three Wars: U.S. Strategy at the Crossroads" (Washington, D.C.: Strategic Studies Institute, 1999).

40. See "Bad Precedent on Arms Sales," *The Washington Post,* September 20, 1996.

41. The Colombian military and National Police are both components of the Colombian Armed Forces, whose civilian commander is the minister of defense. In reality, the National Police is a quasi-autonomous organization.

42. U.S. Senate, Committee on Government Reform and Oversight, Subcommittee on National Security, International Affairs, and Criminal Justice, "Drug Control Policy and Colombia," July 9, 1997.

43. Ibid., comments by Assistant Secretary of State Jeffrey Davidow.

44. Patrick Leahy, "Drug Aid to Colombia Must Carry the Rule of Law," letter to the editor, *The New York Times,* December 5, 1996.

45. Author interview with Tim Reiser, Democratic Staff member, Senate Committee on Appropriations, Washington, D.C., October 1999.

46. "Standing Guard for Uncle Sam," *The Economist,* January 14, 1995.

47. See "Difícil situación de Colombia en EU," *El Tiempo,* February 9, 1995; and "Canciller se reune con representante Torricelli," *El Tiempo,* February 10, 1995.

48. See "La certificación condicionada no existe," *El Tiempo,* February 16, 1995.

49. See "Captura de otro narco de Cali es fundamental," *El Tiempo,* March 22, 1995.

50. Testimony by Robert Gelbard, assistant secretary of state for international narcotics and law enforcement affairs, before the House Committee on International Relations, Subcommittee on the Western Hemisphere, July 29, 1995.

51. Ibid.

52. Letter to Senate Majority Leader Robert Dole from the Senate Committee on Foreign Relations, February 27, 1996.

53. "La certificación, una decisión unilateral," *El Tiempo,* March 8, 1995. Author translation.

54. "DEA está estudiando condiciones," *El Tiempo,* June 5, 1995.

55. The U.S. embassy released a statement regarding the DEA controversy; the Colombian government countered with its own statement.

56. Andrés Cavelier Castro, "Otra dura advertencia de EEUU," *El Tiempo,* October 6, 1995.

57. Ibid.

58. Thomas W. Lippman, "Colombian Warrants Suggest Drug Money Trail Leads to Prominent Officials," *The Washington Post,* April 28, 1995.

59. Thomas W. Lippman, "Colombia Eases U.S. Concern on Antidrug Drive; Cali Cartel Crackdown, Leader's Arrest Gets 'Two Thumbs Up' from White House Aid," *The Washington Post,* June 18, 1995.

60. D'Artagnan, "Por qué Helms es asi?" *El Tiempo,* April 21, 1995.

61. "Lo de 'María' es una verguenza—Serpa," *El Tiempo,* July 31, 1996.

62. See Douglas Farah, "Colombian Defends Efforts to Crimp Drug Trade; President Denies U.S. Charge of Cartel Link, Addresses DEA Dispute," *The Washington Post,* June 3, 1995; and "La extradición no es pecado," *El Tiempo,* April 8, 1995.

63. See *El Tiempo,* March 6, 1995.

64. See Farah, "Colombian Defends Efforts to Crimp Drug Trade."

65. For more on General Serrano's efforts to cleanse the ranks of the Colombian National Police, see Menzel, *Cocaine Quagmire,* pp. 146–149.

66. James Risen, "U.S. Played Key Role in Arrest of Drug Lord," *The Los Angeles Times,* June 13, 1995.

67. For more on the arrests of the Cali cartel's leaders, see "La primera entrega después de la captura," *El Tiempo,* June 13, 1995.

68. See Buckman, "The Cali Cartel," p. 444.

69. Lippman, "Colombia Eases U.S. Concern."

70. "El Valle brindó con Frechette," *El Tiempo,* June 10, 1995. Author translation.

71. Author interview with Daniel García-Peña Jaramillo, former High Commissioner for Peace, Washington, D.C., April 1999. Carlos Holmes Trujillo was Ernesto Samper's first High Commissioner for Peace.

72. Confidential author interview with U.S. State Department official, Bogotá, May 1999.

73. For more on the U.S. government's reaction to the arrests of the Cali cartel's leaders, see "Hay malas interpretaciones en relación con EU—Pardo," *El Tiempo,* October 7, 1995; and "Clinton está muy satisfecho," *El Tiempo,* August 8, 1995.

74. See "Categorico rechazo de EEUU," *El Tiempo,* September 29, 1995.

75. It is estimated that at the height of the 1994 electoral campaign several million dollars were given by the Cali cartel to political candidates in both parties. See "El Golpe," *Semana,* April 25, 1995; *El Tiempo,* May 22, 1995; and *El Espectador,* June 4, 1995. A plethora of analysis has been conducted on Ernesto Samper's putative links to the Cali cartel, the Proceso 8000 case, and other related issues. Most of these have been written by either journalists or individuals who were directly involved in these events.

76. Transcripts of interviews with the Rodríguez brothers regarding the Proceso 8000 case can be found in "Lo de Medina fue novela: Samper," *El Tiempo,* December 9, 1995; and Ana María Jaramillo, "Que los Rodríguez den la plata," *El Tiempo,* August 26, 1997.

77. For Medina's version of events, see Santiago Medina Serna, *La verdad sobre las mentiras* (Bogotá: Planeta, 1997). See Menzel, *Cocaine Quagmire,* p. 149.

78. "Till When?" *The Economist,* December 16, 1995. See also "Los últimos pasos del 8000," *El Tiempo,* December 29, 1996.

79. See "Tribunal nacional confirmó condena a Santiago Medina," *El Tiempo,* September 27, 1996; and Ingrid Betancourt Pulecio, *Si sabía: Viaje a través del expediente de Ernesto Samper* (Bogotá: Temas de Hoy, 1996), pp. 23–47.

80. The major difference between the testimonies of Medina and Botero is that Medina claimed Botero received money from the Cali cartel, while Botero maintained he knew nothing until a few days before the second round of the election. The growing scandal resulted in the protest resignations of Samper's health minister and two more Colombian ambassadors (two had already resigned). Botero was eventually released from jail for good behavior in early 1998 after serving three years. See "Former Colombian Minister Implicated in Drugs Money Scandal Set Free," *BBC News,* February 23, 1998. See also "Crisis en Colombia es un asunto interno—EU," *El Tiempo,* August 4, 1995; and "Gobierno confiscó documentos—Botero," *El Tiempo,* February 26, 1996.

81. Letter to Senate Majority Leader Robert Dole from the Senate Committee on Foreign Relations, February 27, 1996. For more on Botero's revelations about the Samper campaign's links to the Cali cartel, see Cañón, *La Crisis,* pp. 319–347.

82. Several U.S. government officials who were interviewed for this book stated that they held admiration and fondness for Botero while he was still minister of defense.

83. "Till When?" *The Economist,* December 16, 1995.

84. Douglas Farah, "U.S.-Colombia Ties Strained Over Drugs; Americans See Pervasive Cartel Influence," *The Washington Post,* January 7, 1996.

85. Other issues also served to worsen relations between Washington and Bogotá, including accusations made by Interior Minister Horacio Serpa that the U.S. DEA had formulated a plot to hurt the Colombian government.

86. In the faceless judges system, the accused do not see their accusers (or judges) so that the judges can be protected from any type of retribution should a defendant be found guilty. In 1999 the faceless judges system was modified to be used only in extreme cases. See *El Tiempo,* June 10, 1999.

87. Farah, "U.S.-Colombia Ties."

88. Douglas Farah, "Drug Lord's Escape Hurts U.S.-Colombian Relations," *The Houston Chronicle,* January 13, 1996.

89. Farah, "U.S.-Colombia Ties."

90. The 1996 decertification decision resulted in the cancellation or delay of U.S.$35 million in counternarcotics assistance to Colombia. It eventually took the State Department eight months to fully determine what aid could be provided under the decertification decision. The General Accounting Office (GAO) concluded in 1998 that the decertification decision had "unclear" operational impact on U.S.-sponsored antidrug efforts. The GAO also concluded that the decertification decision had little impact on the Colombian economy mainly because discretionary sanctions were not applied. See U.S. GAO, "Drug Control: Counternarcotics Efforts in Colombia Face Continuing Challenges," Washington, D.C., February 26, 1998.

91. Testimony by Robert Gelbard, assistant secretary of state for international narcotics and law enforcement affairs, before the House Committee on International Relations, Subcommittee on the Western Hemisphere, March 7, 1996.

92. Report to Senate Majority Leader Robert Dole from the Senate Committee on Foreign Relations, February 27, 1996.

93. Douglas Farah, "What Went Wrong? This Is a Certification Not of Colombia, but of President Samper," *The Washington Post,* March 3, 1996. For more on the 1996 certification of Colombia, see "Proceso de certificación de EEUU sería más severo en 1996," *El Tiempo,* November 6, 1995.

94. See "Motes, Beans, and Drugs," *The Economist,* February 17, 1996.

95. Andres Franco, "La certificación, el circo de 1996," *El Tiempo,* December 24, 1995. See also Juan Gabriel Tokatlian, "Descertificar le cuesta a EEUU," *El Tiempo,* December 24, 1995.

96. "Certificación no depende de Colombia," *El Tiempo,* December 14, 1995.

97. Confidential author interview with U.S. government official, Washington, D.C., October 6, 1999.

98. Farah, "What Went Wrong?"

99. Farah, "U.S.-Colombia Ties."

100. "Los últimos pasos del 8000," *El Tiempo,* December 29, 1996.

101. See "Colombia, the Escapers," *The Economist,* June 15, 1996. If the lower chamber had voted to pursue the charges, the issue would have gone to

the Senate and Samper would have had to resign while the Senate conducted the trial.

102. Douglas Farah, "U.S. Weighs Response to Clearing of Colombian Leader; Samper, Absolved of Drug Connection, Calls on Washington to Show 'Mutual Respect,'" *The Washington Post,* June 14, 1996.

103. Douglas Farah, "Colombian President Says U.S. Sanctions Would Aid Drug Traffickers," *The Washington Post,* June 16, 1996.

104. Ibid.

105. Mary Matheson, "Exoneration of Samper Draws Heat from U.S.," *The Houston Chronicle,* June 14, 1996.

106. Tim Brown, "Colombia Warns U.S. of Crisis in Ties," *The Washington Post,* July 3, 1996.

107. "EU plantea las bases de recertificación," *El Tiempo,* July 10, 1996.

108. Brown, "Colombia Warns U.S." In November, Interior Minister Horacio Serpa accused Frechette of seeing himself as the "viceroy" of Colombia. See "Action Man," *The Economist,* November 23, 1996.

109. "Los últimos pasos del 8000," *El Tiempo,* December 29, 1996. For more on the visa controversy, see "Relaciones con EEUU," *El Tiempo,* July 22, 1996.

110. "Al congreso colombiano, la enmienda para extraditar a capos," *La Jornada,* July 18, 1996. Author translation.

111. According to General Serrano, in 1996 the Colombian government seized over 55 tons of cocaine and 193 kilograms of opium paste, morphine, and heroin. In that same year the military and police arrested more than 2,500 persons on drug-trafficking charges. Thirty-six Colombian policemen were killed and sixty-one were injured. Prepared statement by General Rosso José Serrano, director of the Colombian National Police, before the House Committee on Government Reform and Oversight, Subcommittee on National Security, International Affairs, and Criminal Justice, February 14, 1997.

112. "Coca Clashes," *The Economist,* August 17, 1996. Coca yields three to four harvests a year. Farmers often begin the processing procedure that turns raw coca into cocaine by mixing the coca leaves with gasoline and chemicals to make a paste. It is estimated that farmers get one cent for each dollar of cocaine sold on the street.

113. For more on the U.S. request for extradition, see "EU examina ley de extinción," *El Tiempo,* December 14, 1996; and Ana María Jaramillo, "Gaviria: Valdría la pena revivir la extradición," *El Tiempo,* December 11, 1996.

114. "EEUU pide en extradición a los Rodríguez O.," *El Tiempo,* June 27, 1996.

115. In Colombia a simple majority in both houses, in two legislative periods, is needed to amend the constitution.

116. Testimony by Robert Gelbard before the House Committee on International Relations, September 11, 1996.

117. See Juan Gabriel Tokatlian, "Extradición: Derecho o política?" *El Tiempo,* September 1, 1996.

118. See "Unextraditable?" *The Economist,* September 20, 1997. In November 1997, Senator Ingrid Betancourt stated, "We need to be clear—the retroactivity is called the Rodríguez Orejuela brothers." See *El País,* November 27, 1997. Author translation.

119. *El País,* October 24, 1996. Shortly before the initial extradition vote, 3.7 kilograms of heroin were found in the plane that President Samper used to fly to a UN conference in New York. See *La Jornada,* September 24, 1996.

120. "Al congreso colombiano, la enmienda para extraditar a capos," *El País,* July 18, 1996.

121. Confidential author interview with U.S. State Department official, Bogotá, June 1999. For some insightful comments on the U.S. motives for pursuing the extradition treaty, see Juan Gabriel Tokatlian, "El mensaje de Frechette," *El Tiempo,* August 18, 1996.

122. "Bombazo en Colombia," *Novedades,* November 19, 1996. Author translation.

123. "The Mob Fights Back," *The Economist,* December 13, 1997.

124. *La Jornada,* May 20, 1997. On May 23, 1997, the Senate approved a bill to reintroduce retroactivity. On that same day the National Police intercepted a document from Cali kingpins that threatened to kill, in addition to Samper and Frechette, General Serrano and Justice Minister Carlos Medellín Forero. See "Colombia Contemplates Extraditing Its Drugsters," *The Economist,* May 31, 1997.

125. Author interview with unnamed U.S. government official, Bogotá, June 1999.

126. "The President Struggles On," *The Economist,* February 8, 1997. The law was passed on December 16, 1996.

127. "Colombia and the United States: Allies or Enemies?" *The Economist,* February 22, 1997. In an extraordinary session on February 14, 1997, Samper reiterated his call to increase penalties for drug trafficking, organized crime, and money-laundering.

128. "Latin America's Other Hostages," *The Economist,* January 25, 1997.

129. Barry Meier, "Pledges of Extradition Accompany Colombian Drug Arrests," *The New York Times,* October 14, 1999.

130. See Douglas Farah, "Colombia Suspends Anti–Drug Crop Effort; Actions Further Erode Relations with U.S.," *The Washington Post,* March 6, 1997. See also Juan Gabriel Tokatlian, "Hacia una nueva descertificación de Colombia," *El Tiempo,* September 15, 1996.

131. *Novedades,* March 1, 1997. Author translation.

132. Testimony by Robert Gelbard, assistant secretary of state for international narcotics and law enforcement affairs, before the House Committee on Government Reform and Oversight, Subcommittee on National Security, International Affairs, and Criminal Justice, February 14, 1997.

133. "Colombia and the United States: Allies or Enemies?" *The Economist,* February 22, 1997.

134. *Notimex* (Mexico), December 16, 1997. Author translation.

135. Confidential author interview with U.S. government official, Bogotá, June 1999.

136. See "EU estudia bajar presión a relaciones con Colombia," *El Tiempo,* September 23, 1997; and "La última visita al Tío Sam," *El Tiempo,* September 21, 1997.

137. See Andrés Cavelier Castro, "Serpa no es nuestro tipo—McCaffrey," *El Tiempo,* October 28, 1997.

138. "The Ambassador Says Good-bye," *The Economist,* November 15, 1997.

139. Author phone interview with Robin Kirk, Colombia Officer for Human Rights Watch, November 22, 1999.

140. U.S. House of Representatives, Committee on Government Reform and Oversight, hearings on counternarcotics efforts in Colombia, July 9, 1997.

141. Ibid. For more on the 1998 certification process, see "Sigue amenaza de descertificación," *El Tiempo,* November 28, 1997.

142. Andrés Cavelier Castro, "Descertifiación fue un bumeran para EU," *El Tiempo,* May 27, 1997.

143. See Serge F. Kovaleski, "Colombia Hails Lifting of Sanctions; Samper Government Continues to Assail U.S. Certification Process," *The Washington Post,* February 27, 1998.

144. See Andrés Cavelier Castro, "EU se inclina por descertificación III," *El Tiempo,* January 30, 1998.

145. Rudolf Hommes, "Certificación," *El Tiempo,* February 28, 1998; and Juan Gabriel Tokatlian, "Descertificación silenciosa," *El Tiempo,* January 11, 1998.

146. Confidential author interview with U.S. State Department official, Bogotá, May 1999.

147. The United States responded to the massive increase in coca cultivation in Colombia by escalating its fumigation efforts. So far, these increased efforts have been ineffective in slowing the growth in coca cultivation in Colombia. In 1998, for example, the U.S.-led efforts resulted in the fumigation of 135,000 hectares of coca plants, but total coca under cultivation still increased by 25 percent.

5

U.S. Policy During the Pastrana Administration, 1998–2002

By the summer of 1999 the U.S. government responded to the perceived deteriorating situation in Colombia, as well as to the recognition that its past policies had been failures, by reformulating its policies in Colombia. Almost overnight Colombia went from a mid-level concern to one of Washington's foremost foreign policy priorities; in 2000 it became the third largest recipient of U.S. foreign assistance. Yet most of the Clinton administration's new Colombia policies reflected many of the same considerations that drove policy during the 1990s: fighting the war on drugs remained the overriding U.S. priority; policy decisions were often formulated to please domestic constituents such as the U.S. Congress and defense contractors; and Washington continued to formulate its policies in a highly unilateral manner, without significant consultation with the Andean countries or European allies.

For the United States, the arrival of the Pastrana administration represented a convenient opportunity to implement a substantial change in its antidrug policies. First, the U.S. government now realized that the ostensibly successful kingpin strategy had done nothing to reduce the supply of cocaine leaving Colombia; a new approach was needed. Second, Washington admitted that its efforts to publicly undermine Ernesto Samper had resulted in an undermining of the Colombian state at the very time that guerrilla and paramilitary groups were becoming stronger than ever. Indeed, Washington considered the Pastrana government to be a reliable antidrug ally, a transition that allowed the United States to adjust its drug policy strategies without having to admit that its previous policies had been failures. While Washington knew that it needed to modify its policies, it was not sure what this new direction should be.

U.S. RELATIONS WITH THE PASTRANA ADMINISTRATION

Washington spent the first half of 1998 awaiting the arrival of a new president, with many U.S. officials hoping that it would be Conservative Party candidate Andrés Pastrana and not Samper ally Horacio Serpa of the Liberal Party. After the results of the June 21 election were tallied, it was announced that Pastrana had won with just over 50 percent of the vote; Serpa received 46.5 percent.[1] Before leaving office, President Samper acknowledged for the first time that drug money had entered his campaign, although he maintained that he did not know the source of the funds: "We have seen how drug money has financed violence and corrupted our institutions. . . . As is known, I was victim of the invasion [of drug money] in the campaign that won me the presidency, as has been confirmed by the confessions of those who administered the campaign."[2]

While the election of Andrés Pastrana would mean a new face in the Casa de Nariño (Presidential Office), there also was a substantive change of personnel among U.S. officials working on the Colombia issue. After Myles Frechette's departure in November 1997, in early 1998 Assistant Secretary of State Robert Gelbard was reassigned to work on the implementation of the U.S.-brokered peace accords in Bosnia. Frechette's replacement in Bogotá, Kurtis Kamman, while also a hard-liner on the drug issue, was much less abrasive (especially publicly) than his predecessor. In fact, a major reason Kamman was chosen was to ensure that Washington did not have "another Frechette" running the embassy.[3] Randy Beers took Gelbard's position and he too was noted for taking a more conciliatory approach in dealings with the Colombian government. In a sense, knowing that the arrival of a new president would provide an opportune time for a denarcotization of the bilateral relationship, the United States wisely removed its own reminders (mainly Frechette and Gelbard) of the prior era—an era that most were now eager to forget.

The U.S. government—whether it was Congress, the State Department, or even the Justice Department—did not want Liberal candidate and Samper ally Horacio Serpa to win the June 21, 1998, election.[4] Not only did the United States loathe Serpa for his combative remarks toward U.S. officials, which included statements about Myles Frechette being an "ugly gringo," but it also suspected him of having ties to the drug cartels. In that sense, the general feeling among U.S. officials was that a Serpa victory would imply another four years of Samper-like relations. Moreover, unlike Samper, Serpa had not been publicly linked to the drug cartels, which meant that he did not have nearly the credibility problem on the drug issue that Samper had. Thus the United States would not have been able to push Serpa on counternarcotics issues the way it had done with Samper. From the U.S. perspective, a Serpa administration would have had all the negative elements of the Samper years without any of the benefits to U.S. counternarcotics policy that came with the publicly discredited Samper administration. In this regard, Serpa might have been similar to César Gaviria—soft on drugs (at least softer than Samper had been), but not afraid and more able to stand up to the United States.

The U.S. government was eager to work with the Pastrana administration, reflected by high praise from the White House and State Department, as well as by an invitation for President Pastrana to visit Washington only a few months after he took office. This did not mean, however, that the United States failed to make it clear to Pastrana that he too would have to comply with U.S.-led counternarcotics efforts.[5] Not surprisingly, much of this pressure came from Capitol Hill, where many Congress members were concerned that Pastrana's moves to initiate peace negotiations with the FARC might undermine antidrug efforts.

To that end, the U.S. Congress passed a resolution that would cut off counternarcotics assistance to Colombia if Pastrana's peace initiatives—especially the proposed plan to grant the FARC a demilitarized zone—interfered with coca eradication efforts.[6] But these cries from Congress aside, there is no doubt that the U.S. government was committed to giving Andrés Pastrana much more room to maneuver on the issue of peace than it had ever considered granting to Ernesto Samper.

Taken at face value, U.S. policy during the Pastrana administration might seem less narcotized, and to a certain extent this is true. But a large part of this denarcotization evolved only because Pastrana agreed to implement and support the basic tenets of U.S. drug policy.[7] Ironically, though, Pastrana's cooperation did not translate into increased ease or success of policy implementation. In fact, many U.S. officials believed that the United States had been better able to pursue its counternarcotics strategy during the Samper era, as Samper had become so weakened and discredited that the United States could act virtually unimpeded. According to one U.S. embassy official: "Interestingly enough it was better to have Samper for the drug issue—we could totally ignore him and work directly with General Serrano. Now we've got to work through Pastrana's office. It was the same with Gaviria— George Bush loved him so we had to work with him even though we thought he was soft on drugs. We got so much out of Samper because he had to do what we wanted."[8]

This attitude suggests that if Andrés Pastrana were to suddenly reverse course on drug policy, there is a good chance that the U.S. would begin a renewed effort to force him to continue a tough antidrug stance. The continued uncertain and half-hearted U.S. support for the current Pastrana-led peace process would no doubt be affected. We can therefore characterize U.S. policy during the Pastrana administration as "implicit narcotization." Andrés Pastrana well understood the message from Washington: he must cooperate with the United States on drugs or he would become another Ernesto Samper.

THE UNITED STATES RESPONDS
TO PASTRANA'S PEACE EFFORTS

A number of events in late 1998 signaled that the Clinton administration was eager to work with the Colombian government. For example, in December 1998 working groups headed by U.S. Secretary of Defense William Cohen and Colombia's Defense Minister Rodrigo Lloreda signed an agreement that promoted greater cooperation between the two countries' militaries. The accord also called for the establishment of a new Colombian counternarcotics military battalion, which would soon become the cornerstone of U.S.-Colombian relations vis-à-vis the drug war.

In an even stronger indication that the United States was firmly behind the Pastrana administration, on December 13–14, 1998, State Department representative Phil Chicola secretly met with the FARC's Raul Reyes in Costa Rica.[9] During this meeting, which the FARC had requested via the Colombian government, Chicola pushed antidrug issues, the peace process, and the status of several Americans who had been missing in Colombia for years.[10] That the United States accepted the offer to meet was seen as evidence that it was considering doing business with the FARC. However, this notion was suddenly and tragically discarded only a few months later. On February 25, 1999, three U.S. indigenous rights activists working with the U'wa Indian tribe in the northeastern department of Arauca were abducted by the FARC. Their dead bodies were found two weeks later. While it initially denied any involvement, the FARC soon took responsibility for the killings, although there was continued uncertainty over exactly who within the FARC hier-archy had ordered the executions.[11] The FARC subsequently announced that it would conduct an internal investigation of the killings and punish those responsible, but this was not enough for the U.S. and Colombian governments, which demanded that the FARC hand over the perpetrators. The FARC never met this demand, and the case of the three murdered American activists served to usher in a harder U.S. line toward the FARC.

The murders also furthered the perception in Washington that the Pastrana-led peace strategy was turning out to be more naive and less credible than many had believed just a few months earlier. The event also fueled Washington's growing suspicions that the FARC was un-willing to cooperate and negotiate in good faith. The doubts about the guerrillas (both the FARC and the ELN) were compounded on April 12, 1999, when the ELN hijacked the Avianca Airlines flight en route from Bucaramanga to Bogotá. About six weeks later the ELN struck again, kidnapping 143 churchgoers in Cali. While many suspected that this was the ELN's way of getting enough attention to warrant a greater say at the negotiating table (especially regarding the possibility of its own liberated zone), in Washington it served to empower those who believed that more sticks and less carrots should be used in dealings with the guerrillas.

To make matters worse, the Colombian government's credibility on the negotiating front began to further erode in May 1999 when Defense Minister Rodrigo Lloreda abruptly resigned over what he deemed to be unacceptable concessions at the peace negotiations as well as unduly heavy-handed demands from the United States that certain military of-ficers be fired for suspected links to paramilitary groups.[12] Following Lloreda's lead, more than fifty high-ranking Colombian military offi-cers submitted their resignations to Commander Fernando Tapias of the Colombian Armed Forces. While Tapias quickly rejected these resigna-tions, the unrest within the military ranks affected the legitimacy of the Pastrana-led peace process.

COLOMBIA AS A CRISIS CASE

Due to the combination of American activist murders, stalls in the peace talks, seemingly daily guerrilla attacks and kidnappings, and an explo-sive increase in coca cultivation (especially in the southern department of Putumayo, where the FARC is extremely active and has used drug profits to further increase its control in that area), by the summer of 1999 Colombia had become a crisis case for the United States. Indeed, the Clinton administration now considered that Colombia's instability posed a serious risk to U.S. national security. As one might expect, this change in perception was matched by a greater focus by senior foreign policy officials in the executive branch.

In what came to be the first indication that the United States was considering a drastic adjustment to its policies toward Colombia, on July 13, 1999, the office of Drug Czar Barry McCaffrey leaked a State Department memo that called for a massive increase in assistance to Colombia of nearly U.S.$1 billion. The State Department had apparently prepared three memos listing varying levels of assistance to Colombia, the most ambitious of which was leaked by McCaffrey's office.[13]

Because Barry McCaffrey was well liked by President Clinton, he had the bureaucratic backing to force the issue in Washington, and the figure of U.S.$1 billion quickly became the benchmark in the Clinton administration's considerations for the upcoming year.[14] McCaffrey's call for such an unprecedented increase in aid also served to take the wind out of the sails of Republican critics in the House of Representatives who had been claiming that the Clinton White House had not been doing enough to fight the drug war. Indeed, the Clinton administration had outflanked the drug hawks, a maneuver that would become readily apparent by January of the following year.

In early August, Undersecretary of State Thomas Pickering became the highest-ranking U.S. government official to visit Colombia in several years. Pickering returned to Washington convinced that the United States needed to do more to stop the bleeding, a point of view that put him in agreement with Barry McCaffrey's earlier call for a massive increase in aid. Indeed, the Pickering-McCaffrey partnership would form the underpinnings of the Clinton administration's new policies toward Colombia.[15] Another signal that the White House was taking a greater interest in Colombia came on August 10, 1999, when Secretary of State Madeleine Albright published an op-ed in the *New York Times* titled "Colombia's Struggles, and How We Can Help." All these actions were intended to send a strong message not only to Colombia but also to the U.S. Congress that it was the State Department and the White House that would be coordinating Colombia policy.

PLAN COLOMBIA

The Clinton administration's desire to implement a new strategy toward Colombia was conveniently met by Andrés Pastrana's announcement of a U.S.$7.5 billion plan to revive the Colombian economy, promote social development, eradicate illicit crops, and jump-start the stalled peace talks.[16] Labeled "Plan Colombia," Pastrana's initiative called for the Colombian government to fund U.S.$4 billion, with the remaining U.S.$3.5 billion to be provided by the international community. Within the U.S.$3.5 billion from international sources, the plan specified that the United States would provide primarily military assistance, while the European Union would provide aid of a more humanitarian nature.

In strictly political terms, Plan Colombia was brilliant for the Clinton administration. The growing perception in Washington that Colombia was imploding led many officials to believe that something needed to be done. Yet because the overriding policy priority for the United States in Colombia remained antidrug efforts, Washington's solution for saving Colombia (i.e., the component of Plan Colombia provided by the United States) was composed overwhelmingly of counternarcotics measures. The United States could therefore justify a new and urgent need for its original antidrug policy.

Given the potential for congressional opposition, driven mainly by the concern that the assistance package would lead the United States into "another Vietnam," the Clinton administration wisely presented the plan as being primarily an antidrug effort. The White House knew that few members of Congress would be willing to oppose assistance to help fight the drug war, and therefore took painstaking efforts to distinguish between counterinsurgency and counternarcotics initiatives. As Assistant Secretary of Defense Brian Sheridan testified in September 2000:

> The targets are the narco-traffickers, those individuals and organizations that are involved in the cultivation of coca or opium poppy and the subsequent production and transportation of cocaine and heroin to the U.S. Only those armed elements that forcibly inhibit or confront counterdrug operations will be engaged, be they narco-traffickers, insurgent organizations, or illegal self-defense forces. I know that some are concerned that we are being drawn into a quagmire. Let me assure you, we are not.[17]

The administration's attempts to distance itself from Colombia's internal conflict by focusing solely on drugs helped to ensure a relatively quick and controversy-free approval through Congress.

The ostensibly comprehensive "Colombian" Plan Colombia was basically a Washington creation. In fact, many U.S. officials readily admitted that it was essentially devised by the United States and that a copy in Spanish did not exist until months after a copy in English was available.[18] Nonetheless, Pastrana's statement that this was truly a Colombian plan allowed the Clinton administration to act as if were selflessly filling the request of a reliable hemispheric ally. The Clinton White House attempted to sell the assistance not as a unilateral infusion of U.S. assistance, but rather as one component of a larger, Colombian-driven program. Yet as we will see, Washington's attempt to cloak its policy desires proved unsuccessful, as Plan Colombia increasingly came to be seen as a Washington creation.

On January 11, 2000, the Clinton administration announced a U.S.$1.6 billion package to fund Plan Colombia, with roughly U.S.$1 billion of the total slated for military and police aid.[19] The military component of the aid consisted principally of a combination of Huey and Black Hawk helicopters designated for antidrug operations. The proposal also called for the creation of two more military counternarcotics battalions to be used in the department of Putumayo, where drug cultivation had increased so greatly in the preceding years.

Secretary of State Madeleine Albright traveled to Colombia a few days after the announcement to sell the proposal to the Colombian government and people.[20] In order to create a sense of urgency that would enhance the prospects of the package being quickly approved by Congress, the Clinton administration sold the new proposal as if time were of the essence.[21] An example of this tone of urgency came from Senator Joseph Biden (D–Del.), who became a key supporter of the administration's policy:

> Never before in recent history has there been such an opportunity to strike at all aspects of the drug trade at the source. . . . The United States should seize this rare enforcement opportunity by providing assistance to Plan Colombia. . . . There are considerable costs associated with Congress' delay in approving the Colombia supplemental. . . . Helping Colombia is squarely in America's national interest. It is the source of many of the drugs poisoning our people. It is not some far-off land with which the United States shares little in common. It is an established democracy in America's backyard—just a few hours by air from Miami.[22]

While the White House's initial proposal did set aside a few hundred million dollars for human rights issues, the peace process, and judicial reform, the package could still be seen as an essentially antidrug plan.

THE DEBATE IN THE HOUSE AND SENATE
OVER PLAN COLOMBIA

The House of Representatives

Unlike the Senate version of the assistance package, which included relatively significant changes in the language of the assistance package regarding human rights, the House version closely resembled the plan submitted by the Clinton administration. There were some moves to drastically revamp the package, such as Representative Nancy Pelosi's (D–Calif.) unsuccessful amendment (by a 23–31 vote) in the Appropriations Committee calling for the proposed U.S.$1.3 billion to be shifted from Colombia to domestic drug treatment and rehabilitation programs.[23]

In the full House of Representatives, Nancy Pelosi once again attempted to reintroduce her domestic drug-treatment funding. While the Rules Committee denied this request, Pelosi's maneuver allowed her to open up the debate on the House floor, allowing twenty-two representatives to make speeches supporting the amendment.[24] Representative Jim Ramstad (R–Minn.) submitted an even more aggressive amendment that would have cut the entire U.S.$1.6 billion of counternarcotics aid. It failed by a 159–262 margin, but it too served to indicate that the Clinton administration's package would not emerge from Congress without at least a few bruises. Criticism from some of the liberal wing of the Democratic Party aside, the House package passed 263–146, a vote that signaled strong support for the Clinton proposal.[25]

The Senate

Discussion over the merits of the White House's plan to support Colombia moved to the Senate in May 2000. What became immediately apparent, and somewhat surprising to some administration officials, was that a sizable force within the Senate wanted to soften the assistance package to de-emphasize the military component and allow for more funding of human rights, alternative crop development, and judicial reform.[26] Senator Slade Gorton (R–Wash.) put forth an ultimately unsuccessful amendment (defeated in an 11–15 vote) that would have reduced U.S. aid to U.S.$100 million. The Senate Appropriations Committee reduced the military and police component of the aid to U.S.$450 million, U.S.$350 million less than the House version. The thirty UH-60 Black Hawk helicopters were scratched and replaced with seventy-five of the less expensive UH-1H Super Hueys.[27]

Human rights concerns also received significant attention in the deliberations of the Appropriations Committee. Longtime human rights proponent Senator Patrick Leahy successfully introduced a condition that the secretary of state would have to certify that Colombian military officers accused of committing human rights violations were being tried in civilian courts, and that the Colombian Armed Forces was terminating links between the military and paramilitary groups. If the secretary of state could not issue the certifications, aid to the military could not continue. While this certification was ultimately waived, and then proven not legally binding to certain components of the aid package, it sent an important signal that human rights concerns would not be overlooked.

While human rights aid was significantly increased and military aid was slightly decreased, there was a general consensus in the Senate that the White House package, with its strong focus on providing military assistance to bolster Colombian antidrug capacity, should be approved. Senator Paul Wellstone (D–Minn.), for example, introduced an amendment to eliminate the "push into southern Colombia" and instead invest the resources saved into domestic drug treatment.[28] The amendment was overwhelmingly defeated in an 11–89 vote, suggesting that while there might have been some movement within the Appropriations Committee for a softer version of the aid package, the full Senate was strongly behind a version similar to the original Clinton proposal.

The real tension in the Senate actually rested with the *type* of military assistance that Colombia should receive. Specifically, a debate erupted over whether to provide high-tech Black Hawk helicopters, manufactured by the Sikorsky Company in Connecticut, or the less sophisticated and less expensive Hueys, manufactured by Bell-Textron. The initial Senate Appropriations Committee version replaced all of the Black Hawks requested by the White House with Super Hueys. Interestingly, it was Senator Christopher Dodd (D–Conn.), a vocal opponent of the Reagan administration's support for the Nicaraguan contras in the 1980s, who proposed that the Black Hawks be included in the package.

Many believe that the fact that Black Hawks are manufactured in Dodd's home state of Connecticut influenced his stance. Knowing that the Colombian government coveted the high-tech Black Hawks, Dodd wisely suggested that the legislation should allow Colombia's military and national police to select the type of helicopters they wished to receive. While Dodd's proposal lost 47–51, it would not be long before the House version resurrected the Black Hawks, ensuring that they would be included in the final congressional version of the legislation. The final Senate version of the package passed 95–4.

After leaving the Senate, the bill went to the House-Senate Conference Committee for reconciliation of its two competing versions. Perhaps the committee's most important decision was to maintain the Senate's tough human rights conditions, but to give the president the ability to issue a "national security waiver" that could override a noncertification decision. The committee also resolved the Black Hawk versus Huey dispute, deciding that the Colombian military would receive forty-two Hueys and eighteen Black Hawks, with twelve of the Hueys and two of the Black Hawks set aside for the National Police.

CLINTON SIGNS PLAN COLOMBIA INTO LAW

On July 13, 2000, President Clinton signed H.R. 4425 into law.[29] This bill provided U.S.$860.3 million of aid to Colombia (see Table 5.1), in addition to the U.S.$329 million that had been approved in fiscal year 2000 (the total U.S.$1.3 billion also included antidrug assistance for Bolivia, Peru, and Ecuador), meaning that Colombia would receive roughly U.S.$1.2 billion over two years. In that the final congressional version closely resembled Clinton's initial proposal, Plan Colombia represented a clear victory for the his administration.

In fact, because the Republicans seemed to be even more enthusiastic about the package than the Democrats, the Clinton White House had preempted any criticism that it was not doing enough to fight the war on drugs. But at the same time, the tremendous emphasis that was and continues to be placed on Plan Colombia—especially the push into southern Colombia—means that there is now tremendous pressure on the U.S. government to show results of this extremely costly support package. And in the ever violent and uncertain context of Colombia, this will be very difficult to achieve.

The package signaled an important U.S. policy change in a number of areas. Dating back to the isolation of Ernesto Samper, the U.S. government had worked almost exclusively with the Colombian National Police on antidrug efforts; but now the package signaled that the Colombian Armed Forces would be brought into the antidrug arena, especially with the creation of the counternarcotics battalions. This move ran into trouble in the fall of 2000 as longtime National Police supporter

Table 5.1   Total Aid for Plan Colombia (U.S.$ millions)

Upgrades to overseas "Forward-Operating Locations" (Ecuador, Aruba, Curaçao)	116.5
Defense Department Andean-ridge intelligence gathering	62.3
Antidrug radar upgrades	68.0
"Drug Kingpin" program	2.0
Defense Department aircraft	30.0
Aid for Peru	32.0
Aid for Bolivia	110.0
Aid for Ecuador	20.0
Aid for other countries	18.0
Aid for Colombia	860.3
Total	1,319.1

Source: Office of Management and Budget, 2000.

Congressman Benjamin Gilman began to voice his concern that the National Police had been marginalized by Clinton's plan.

Second, the package revealed that Washington had grown weary of the Pastrana peace process. Only U.S.$3 million was approved to support the Colombian peace process (see Table 5.2), an almost insignificant sum compared to the hundreds of millions of dollars that the United States was spending for the push into southern Colombia. Washington's thinking behind this meager sum was that Plan Colombia should be associated solely with antidrug efforts and not with either the civil conflict or the peace process, as both were considered too close to the counterinsurgency question.

Third, the significant increases in human rights and alternative development assistance enabled the White House to deflect criticisms that the assistance consisted of strictly military components. While helicopters and the push into southern Colombia clearly dominated the assistance package, there were nevertheless substantial increases in nonmilitary aid to Colombia. The bill provided U.S.$51 million for a broad range of human rights issues, including programs to protect human rights workers and establish human rights units within the Colombian military. Although Senator Leahy's human rights certification language was loosened to include a national security waiver, it nonetheless still required the State Department to issue a certification decision before the aid could be delivered.

The issue of human rights certification arose almost immediately, as the State Department was required to issue its first certification decision in August 2000. Of the six conditions that were listed for certification, the State Department did not certify the Colombian military on five of

Table 5.2   Plan Colombia–Assistance for Colombia (U.S.$ millions)

Military assistance	519.2[a]
Police assistance	123.1
Alternative development	68.5
Aid to the displaced	37.5
Human rights	51.0
Judicial reform	13.0
Law enforcement/rule of law	45.0
Peace process	3.0
Total	860.3

Sources: Center for International Policy, 2000; Office of Management and Budget, 2000.
Note: a. U.S.$ 416.9 million will fund the "push into southern Colombia."

them. Not surprisingly, President Clinton quickly signed the waiver so that aid could begin to flow to Colombia. According to President Clinton, "I signed the waiver because I think that President Pastrana is committed to the issue of human rights, something that we are very worried about."[30]

Alternative development assistance for Colombia, resources aimed at balancing the disruptive effects of what would be the newly aggressive fumigation efforts, was surprisingly low at U.S.$68.5 million, less than the U.S.$106.5 million requested by the Clinton administration and the U.S.$108 million requested by the House. In fact, the legislation provided more alternative development assistance to Bolivia (U.S.$85 million) than to Colombia.[31]

The soft side of Plan Colombia initially composed approximately 18 percent of the administration's total request. This included resources earmarked for alternative economic development to provide basic social infrastructure; credit and technical assistance to communities committing to voluntary eradication; the provision of social services to internally displaced persons; and human rights strengthening, judicial reform, and other justice-related projects. The final bill that was signed into law actually increased the amount of soft programs to approximately 20 percent of the package, namely due to the quadrupling of alternative development aid to Bolivia.

The nondrug aspects of the plan were never the focus of the administration's request for supplemental funds. One need only look at the inception of the plan—Barry McCaffrey's declaration of a "drug emergency"—to realize that the essence of the plan was to reduce drug cultivation and traffic. Further, even if the soft side had been regarded

President Clinton during his August 2000 trip to Cartagena, Colombia.
Daughter Chelsea is to his right. Photo by Marcelo Salinas.

with the same priority as counternarcotics, democracy and human rights
are not big-ticket items. In that policy attention naturally centers on where
the money is, helicopters and interdiction by definition received more attention in the creation of the administration's supplemental request. In
full, funding for soft issues was an inexpensive, secondary component of
the proposal, and viewed as a necessary element to appease U.S. nongovernmental organizations and congressional Democrats.

This strategy worked. While some Democrats demanded that more funds be allocated toward the soft side, Congress ended up passing the bill with minimal change to the administration's request. Interestingly enough, however, the United States is only now seeing the full importance of the soft side of Plan Colombia. The ability of the United States to point to substantive democracy and economic growth programs has been imperative in selling the plan to both the international community and the Colombian people. Indeed, in light of growing criticism of the plan's military and drug focus, the United States has highlighted the importance of democracy and justice at the expense of the counternarcotics element. While the United States has not avoided severe criticism for the military dominance of the package, the existence of soft issues has clearly diffused greater condemnation. The United States can accurately highlight that USAID's program in Colombia has been increased more than tenfold.[32] Hence, in terms of placating opponents, nonmilitary programs have ironically become the linchpin of the U.S. contribution to Plan Colombia.

Soon after President Clinton signed the U.S. component of Plan Colombia into law, he led a bipartisan delegation to visit Colombia. There is little doubt that Clinton's deft political abilities put a strong face on the assistance package, serving to reinforce to the Colombian people that this was a Colombian initiative to which the United States and many other countries were just contributing.[33] He also chose to hold a press conference from one of Colombia's USAID-funded *casas de justicia* in the attempt to de-emphasize the controversial narcotics focus of the plan. In a press conference in the Caribbean port city of Cartagena (Clinton only spent eight hours in Colombia and did not visit Bogotá for security reasons), Clinton stated:

> [A] condition of this aid is that we are not going to get into a shooting war. This is not Vietnam; neither is it Yankee imperialism. Those are the two false charges that have been hurled against Plan Colombia. You have a perfect right to question whether you think it will work or whether we've properly distributed the resources. But I can assure you that a lot of the opposition to this plan is coming from people who are afraid that it will work.[34]

CRACKS APPEAR IN PLAN COLOMBIA

Almost before the first U.S. contribution to Plan Colombia had been even dispersed there were already signs that the package was running into difficulties. A U.S. GAO report issued in October 2000 stated that Plan Colombia's efficacy was being hindered by delays in the manufacturing and delivery of the helicopters as well as by the overall lack of coordination among the involved U.S. government agencies. Indeed, the full delivery of the helicopters would not occur until late 2002 or even into 2003, which was not the type of delivery schedule that would bolster the Clinton administration's claim that time was of the essence in Colombia. According to the report:

> U.S. agencies, including the Departments of State and Defense and USAID, are still developing comprehensive implementation plans for eradication and interdiction operations and alternative development projects. However, negotiating for the manufacture and delivery of major equipment, such as the helicopters, is ongoing, and staffing new programs in Colombia will take time. As a result, agencies do not expect to have many of the programs to support Plan Colombia in place until late 2001. . . . In addition, although State expects to initiate pilot projects such as alternative and economic development and judicial reform in September or October 2000, State and the U.S. Embassy cautioned that it will take years to show measurable results.[35]

The executive branch's admission that delivery of the helicopters would take significantly longer than expected served to provoke some of the drug hawks in Congress who had supported the package but still held out reservations as to whether the Clinton administration would be able to adequately implement it. Representative Dan Burton (R–Ind.) stated that "this is a war that's going to be lost if we wait two or three years."[36] Sonny Callahan (R–Ala.), chairman of the House Foreign Operations Committee, issued this statement through his chief of staff: "Just a few months ago they were blaming us for dragging our feet. Now we'd like to know why the president and the administration are dragging their feet."[37]

But the most damaging dissent came from Representative Gilman when he sent a letter to Barry McCaffrey stating that the United States should redirect its aid (at least forty Black Hawks) away from Colombia's military and toward its national police.[38] The principal catalyst to Gilman's assertion was the delay in the delivery schedule, but it was also motivated by the Colombian military's major defeat at the hands of the FARC. The casualties of this battle included the loss of a Black Hawk—the very symbol of U.S. support for Colombia—and the twenty-two Colombian soldiers aboard it.[39] In many ways, the bipartisan consensus over

Plan Colombia that had seemed so strong over the summer of 2000 was quickly eroding, with many former supporters now looking to blame the Clinton administration for the mistakes it was making in carrying out the new Colombia policy.

The Clinton administration's discouraging news on the domestic political front was matched by growing reports out of southern Colombia that the FARC had stepped up its military operations in order to prepare itself for the Colombian military's U.S.-backed push into southern Colombia. In November 2000 the FARC blocked roads in and around the commercial center of Puerto Asís in Putumayo, provoking the beginnings of a humanitarian crisis as the region was cut off from food and medical supplies.[40] The blockade lasted for nearly six weeks and ultimately forced the Colombian military to airlift 1,300 tons of supplies into the area.[41] It was estimated that 2,000 FARC soldiers were in the region.[42] Paramilitary groups have also been active in the region since 1998; recently they have become more active and have carried out a number of attacks against suspected guerrilla sympathizers.[43] There have also been accusations that the paramilitary groups active in Putumayo have been receiving assistance from the Colombian military. The BBC's Jeremy McDermott, for example, reported in August 2000 that the paramilitaries were operating just a few miles from a major military base:

> I was looking to contact the paramilitaries who control the town itself and some of the neighboring hamlets. . . . Finding them was not as hard as I had thought. Despite the fact that the Colombian state denies that there are any links between them and the right-wing death squads, their headquarters in Puerto Asís is five minutes drive past the local army base, in a luxurious villa. To get there I just hailed a taxi and asked the driver to take me to the paramilitary headquarters, as if I knew where it was and something I did every day of the week. He did not even blink, simply put the car in gear and sped down the potholed streets, passing the army checkpoint and into the countryside outside the town.[44]

Colombia's Neighbors Respond

Colombia's neighbors have been on edge ever since the United States announced that the main goal of its new assistance package to the Colombian government would revolve around pushing increased fumigation and military activities into the southern part of the country. With the real and ongoing threat that increased antidrug and counterinsurgency efforts in

Colombia's southern departments will provoke both civilians and belligerents to spill over into neighboring countries, the governments of Ecuador, Peru, and Brazil expressed concern and took measures to deal with this potential problem. According to Ecuador's Foreign Minister Heinz Moeller, "Our worry is that the removal of this cancerous tumor will cause it to metastasize into Ecuador."[45]

The Brazilian military decided to increase its presence along its border with Colombia; it also decided to purchase four Cougar AS-532 helicopters from France to increase its air mobility in the region. The Peruvian government moved a fleet of its helicopters from its border with Ecuador to its border with Colombia. Even the U.S. government began to publicly admit that the push into southern Colombia might provoke a regional crisis. According to Thomas Pickering during a November 2000 visit to Colombia: "The issue of spillover is real. . . . I have talked of the balloon effect, and others have; that is, if you push in one end, it is bound to bulge out on others. . . . So, in fact, there is already a balloon effect, and it is having its impact in Colombia."[46]

Administration officials went to the extent of promoting a new "Andean Regional Initiative" in fiscal year 2002. This regional strategy includes both hard and soft programs aimed to ensure that the spillover of antinarcotics activities is minimized and that drug cultivation doesn't spring up in Colombia's neighboring countries. It is unlikely that the roughly U.S.$800 million Andean Initiative will represent a dramatic change of course in U.S. policy; rather, it will serve as an extension of preexisting U.S. antidrug programs, enhanced by USAID contributions. But at the minimum, the priority the State Department now places on this initiative reflects the acknowledgment that the United States cannot have a policy toward one country without considering external effects, and that both its drug policies and its foreign policies must be regional in scope.

The International Community Responds

In order to reinforce the idea of Plan Colombia as a comprehensive, multilateral plan, both the Pastrana and Clinton administrations wasted no opportunity in reminding observers that a significant portion of the funding was scheduled to come from the European Union and Japan. But they refrained from publicly acknowledging the strong perception in Europe that Plan Colombia was a thinly veiled U.S. antidrug plan and that European support would send the wrong message to the Colombian people. The European Union did decide to provide approximately U.S.$321 million in direct assistance to Colombia; however, this amount was far below what Bogotá and Washington were hoping for.[47] A significant portion of the aid is in the form of concessional loans, making the assistance less valuable than the U.S.-style grants, and approximately U.S.$200 million is earmarked exclusively for non–Plan Colombia programs, reflecting the European ambivalence to the program.[48] This lower contribution from the European Union served to provoke a public perception in both Colombia and the United States that the international community was not on board with Plan Colombia. Many posed a legitimate question: If Plan Colombia is indeed a nationwide initiative that addresses social-, economic-, and justice-related needs, why is related international aid not included? The fact that hundreds of millions of dollars of international grants and loans existed outside Plan Colombia confirmed for many critics that Plan Colombia was indeed just a U.S.-imposed antinarcotics plan.

The Pastrana administration also holds part of the responsibility for Plan Colombia's current public relations crisis. While the plan was touted as a comprehensive nationwide initiative to move the country forward, no one in Colombia, aside from a small circle of Pastrana's advisers, was ever consulted. Neither mayors nor heads of nongovernmental organizations were asked their opinion on how they envisioned a country development strategy, despite the fact that both the soft and hard aspects of the plan rely on the active cooperation of municipal governments. Plan Colombia was not created as a cohesive Colombian vision; it is therefore quite difficult to present it as such, despite the efforts on behalf of both the Colombian and U.S. governments.

NOTES

1. "U.S. Sees New Era in Relations with Colombia," *BBC News,* June 23, 1998.

2. "Samper Admits Drug Money Used for Polls," *BBC News,* July 21, 1998.

3. See Cesar A. Sabogal, "Kamman, adios al tunel negro?" *El Tiempo,* March 22, 1998.

4. This point was made in several interviews with U.S. government officials. See also Thomas Vogel, "Cuanto mejorarán sus relaciones con EEUU?" *El Tiempo,* June 19, 1998.

5. For more on the arrival of Andrés Pastrana and the seemingly positive relationship with the United States, see Enrique Santos Calderon, "Andrés—A

lidiar una vez," *El Tiempo,* August 6, 1998; Juan Gabriel Tokatlian, "Pastrana y Washington," *El Tiempo,* July 5, 1998; and "Esperamos dar vuelta a la página— EU," *El Tiempo,* June 23, 1998.

6. "Colombia's Drug-Bedevilled Hopes of Peace," *The Economist,* October 3, 1998.

7. For U.S. government comments on the Pastrana administration's efforts on antidrug issues, see U.S. House of Representatives, record briefing on the release of the annual International Narcotics Strategy report, Washington, D.C., February 26, 1999; and "Perspectives on the Politics of Peace in Colombia," distributed notes from a seminar hosted by the Inter-American Dialogue, Washington, D.C., January 26, 1999.

8. Confidential author interview with U.S. government official, Bogotá, 1999.

9. Confidential author interview with U.S. State Department official, Bogotá, December 2000.

10. "EU cierra la puerta a futuros contactos con Farc," *El Tiempo,* March 26, 1999.

11. Ibid.

12. Confidential author interview with U.S. State Department officials, Bogotá, May 1999.

13. Confidential author interview with U.S. State Department official, Washington, D.C., November 2000. See also Tim Golden and Steven Lee Meyers, "U.S. Plans Big Aid Package to Rally a Reeling Colombia," *The New York Times,* September 15, 1999.

14. Confidential author interview with U.S. State Department official, Washington, D.C., November 2000.

15. Ibid.

16. A copy of Plan Colombia can be found in "Plan Colombia: Plan for Peace, Prosperity, and the Strengthening of the State," attached as an appendix to the Senate Committee on Foreign Relations hearing, October 6, 1999. See also Larry Rohter, "Plan to Strengthen Colombia Nudges U.S. for $3.5 Billion," *The New York Times,* September 18, 1999.

17. Testimony by Brian Sheridan, assistant secretary of defense for special operations and low-intensity conflict, before the House Committee on International Relations, September 21, 2000.

18. Confidential author interview with U.S. State Department official, Washington, D.C., November 2000.

19. Statement by the President of the United States, Office of the Press Secretary, January 11, 2000.

20. Steven Dudley, "Albright Discusses Anti-Drug Aid in Colombia," *The Washington Post,* January 15, 2000.

21. "Clinton le apuesta a Colombia," *El Tiempo,* January 24, 2000.

22. "Aid to 'Plan Colombia': The Time for U.S. Assistance Is Now," report to the House Committee on Foreign Relations from Senator Joseph Biden, May 2000.

23. For an excellent summary of the congressional deliberations over Plan Colombia, see Adam Isacson and Ingrid Vaicius, "Plan Colombia: The Debate in Congress," Center for International Policy, Washington, D.C., December 2000.

24. Ibid.

25. For more on this point, see Russell Crandall, "Deeper Into the Anti-Drug Mire," *The Christian Science Monitor,* June 29, 2000.

26. "El Plan Colombia: El debate en los Estados Unidos," Center for International Policy, Washington, D.C., August 2000.

27. Isacson and Vaicius, "Plan Colombia."

28. Later in 2000, Senator Wellstone published an op-ed in the *New York Times* urging the incoming Bush administration to rethink U.S. policy toward Colombia. See Paul Wellstone, "Bush Should Start Over in Colombia," *The New York Times,* December 26, 2000.

29. Statement by the President of the United States, Office of the Press Secretary, the White House, July 13, 2000.

30. "Colombia, certificada por excepción," *El Tiempo,* August 24, 2000. Author translation.

31. The alternative development assistance included U.S.$30 million for voluntary crop eradication, U.S.$12 million in assistance to local governments, and U.S.$2.5 million for environmental programs to protect frail lands and watersheds.

32. USAID is the agency that funds and manages all the soft elements of Plan Colombia. Its annual allocation for Colombia increased from $6.3 million in fiscal year 1999 (not including disaster earthquake assistance) to $119.5 million for fiscal years 2000 and 2001.

33. Remarks by the President of the United States in Video Address to the People of Colombia, the White House, August 29, 2000.

34. Press Conference by President Clinton in Cartagena, Colombia, the White House, August 30, 2000.

35. U.S. General Accounting Office, "Drug Control: Challenges in Implementing Plan Colombia," GAO-01-76T, Washington, D.C., October 12, 2000.

36. "U.S. Black Hawks for Colombia May Be Delayed Until 2002," Associated Press, September 22, 2000.

37. Juan Tamayo, "Colombia Drug Aid Runs Into Delays," *The Miami Herald,* October 10, 2000.

38. Juan Forero and Christopher Marquis, "Key House Leader Withdraws Support for Colombia Aid Plan," *The New York Times,* November 17, 2000. Barry McCaffrey replied to Benjamin Gilman in the *Washington Post* on December 15, 2000.

39. "Colombia's Military Suffers Heavy Blows in Three Days of Fighting Against Rebels," Associated Press, October 23, 2000.

40. Juan Forero, "To Make a Point, the Rebels Are Strangling a Town," *The New York Times,* November 3, 2000.

41. Juan Forero, "Key Roads Taken from Rebels, Colombia Says," *The New York Times,* November 14, 2000.

42. Adam Isacson and Abbey Steele, "U.S. Aid to Colombia," Center for International Policy. Washington, D.C., December 14, 2000.

43. "Parálisis total en la zona de Putumayo," *El Tiempo,* November 11, 2000; "Cruz roja suspende evacuación de combatientes heridos," *El Tiempo,* October 4, 2000.

44. Isacson and Steele, "U.S. Aid to Colombia."

45. Clifford Krauss, "Neighbors Worry About Colombian Aid," *The New York Times,* August 25, 2000.

46. U.S. Department of State, record briefing of Thomas Pickering, under-secretary of state, November 27, 2000.

47. Spanish president José María Aznar is the only European leader who openly backed Plan Colombia. He organized a donors meeting in Madrid in July 2000 in order to promote support for the assistance package. At this meeting the Spanish government pledged U.S.$100 million for Plan Colombia; other contributions totaling over U.S.$1 billion were announced, but most of this assistance was not actually going to Plan Colombia. See "Is Plan Colombia Dead?" Center for International Policy, Washington, D.C., October 27, 2000.

48. Juan Forero, "Europe's Aid Plan for Colombia Falls Short of Drug War's Goals," *The New York Times,* October 25, 2000.

6

Afterword

One of the greatest ironies of the Clinton administration's massive increase in support for the Colombian government is that most of the actual delivery and implementation of the assistance is scheduled to occur during President George W. Bush's term in office. Indeed, the very hallmarks of the U.S. component of Plan Colombia—the two counternarcotics battalions and the sixty helicopters—will all be put into use well into President Bush's first term. For that reason, while Plan Colombia might be Bill Clinton's baby, it has now become President Bush's adolescent and for that reason the new Republican administration needs to look long and hard before it signs off on its predecessors' plan to "save" Colombia.

Leading up to George W. Bush's inauguration in early 2001 were hints that the incoming Republican administration might take a different tack on Colombia policy. Above all, this entailed making the case that the United States should no longer couch its strategic objectives within the broader framework of the war on drugs; rather, it should more overtly support the Colombian government in its efforts to establish the rule of law throughout the nation's territory, even if this means more direct counterinsurgency assistance. According to Robert Zoellick, a top campaign foreign policy adviser to George W. Bush and subsequent U.S. trade representative:

> We cannot continue to make false distinctions between counterinsurgency and counter-narcotics efforts. . . . The narcotraffickers and guerrillas compose one dangerous network. . . . If the legitimately elected

leaders of Colombia demonstrate the political will to take their country back from killers and drug lords, and if the Colombian people are
willing to fight for their own country, then the U.S. should offer serious, sustained and timely financial, material and intelligence support.[1]

But while the Bush campaign made overtures that it would shift policy
objectives in Colombia, so far most indicators suggest that the Bush
administration has endorsed the Clinton-era Andean Regional Initiative.

Thus the Colombia policy of more regional support and soft-side
assistance that is currently being attributed to the Bush administration is
actually one inherited from the Clinton presidency. Therefore the
biggest development to date regarding President Bush's Colombia policy is that there is really no new policy. It is still too soon to tell whether
this is a result of bureaucratic inertia or the Bush team's genuine support
for Bill Clinton's policies. Nevertheless, the Bush administration's decision to effectively continue these policies ensures that the Plan Colombia model of U.S. assistance will continue well into the future.

One clear indication that the Bush team was strongly considering a
continuation of the Plan Colombia model occurred in late August 2001
when a high-level U.S. delegation led by Undersecretary of State Marc
Grossman visited Colombia to get a firsthand idea of the situation in the
country and the policy decisions that the Bush administration would
need to consider. Grossman commented: "We spent two hours reviewing what we are giving to Colombia and what our plans are for the future. We will support all of the efforts that contribute to Plan Colombia
and nothing is going to change."[2] The most likely path is that future
U.S. policy in Colombia will tend to remain narcotized, resembling
the policy initiatives introduced by the Clinton administration. The war
on drugs will remain the overriding priority; the state of the bilateral
relationship will largely depend on Bogotá's cooperation on antidrug
efforts.

The Bush administration will still have the opportunity to modify
the Clinton-era strategy; the difficulty, however, is that there is tremendous institutional pressure within the U.S. government to keep Colombia policy overwhelmingly focused on what it has been for the past
decade: fighting the war on drugs. This policy inertia that is the war on
drugs threatens to overwhelm the Bush team as it attempts to disaggre-
gate the war on drugs from the myriad of other pressing security issues
in Colombia, such as the growing threat from guerrilla insurgents and
illegal paramilitary groups.

It is also clear that the devastating terrorist attack on the United States on September 11, 2001, will influence how policymakers in Washington view events in Colombia. There is no doubt that Washington will view the FARC and the ELN with a much more critical eye, constantly looking to see if these groups' actions constitute terrorist behavior. This change of stance could have serious repercussions for U.S. policy and events in Colombia more broadly. For example, the United States could become increasingly less willing to support a peace process that it views as legitimizing a terrorist organization. This could in turn lead Washington to pressure the Colombian government to take a harder line in the talks or escalate its military efforts. A tougher government negotiatory or military stance vis-à-vis the FARC is a likely scenario with or without a change of U.S. policy, but strong words from Washington would undoubtedly influence decisions being made in Bogotá.

No matter what future scenarios play out in Colombia, let us hope that policymakers in Washington have learned from past mistakes and bad habits. For example, the U.S. policy to isolate Ernesto Samper had unintended but severe consequences for the bilateral relationship: it served to antagonize one of Washington's closest regional allies as well as to weaken the Colombian state at a critical time in its fight against armed belligerents. Relations have improved significantly since Andrés Pastrana took office, but this does not mean that narcotization has ended. In fact, there could easily be a return to a hypernarcotized state of relations if Washington once again perceives that a Colombian government is not cooperating on the drug war. This scenario is unlikely, as both sides realize how counterproductive this route is, but it remains in the realm of possibilities as long as the United States continues to make the drug war the overriding focus of its policies toward Colombia.

NOTES

1. "Bush Mulls Activist Colombia Stance," Associated Press, December 27, 2001.

2. "EU asegura que no cambiará frente al Plan Colombia," *El Tiempo,* August 30, 2001. See also Alan Sipress, "U.S. Reassesses Colombia Aid," *The Washington Post,* September 10, 2001.

Bibliography

Abel, Christopher. "Colombia and the Drug Barons: Conflict and Containment." *The World Today* 49, no. 5 (May 1993): 96–100.

Abernathy, David. "Dominant-Subordinate Relationships: How Shall We Define Them? How Do We Compare Them?" In *Dominant Powers and Subordinate States,* edited by Jan F. Triska, pp. 105–107. Durham: Duke University Press, 1986.

Abrams, Elliot. "Looking South: The U.S. and Latin America in the 1990s." Remarks to the Hudson Institute National Policy Forum, Washington, D.C., September 1998.

Allison, Graham. *The Essence of Decision: Explaining the Cuban Missile Crisis.* Boston: Little, Brown, 1971.

Allison, Graham, and Philip Zelikow. *The Essence of Decision: Explaining the Cuban Missile Crisis.* 2nd ed. New York: Addison Wesley Longman, 1999.

Americas Watch. *The Central-Americanization of Colombia? Human Rights and the Peace Process.* New York: Americas Watch, 1986.

———. *Colombia's Killer Networks: The Military-Paramilitary Partnership and the United States.* New York: Americas Watch, 1996.

———. *The Drug War in Colombia: The Neglected Tragedy of Political Violence.* New York: Americas Watch, 1990.

———. *Human Rights in Colombia as President Barco Begins.* New York: Americas Watch, 1986.

———. *The Killings in Colombia.* New York: Americas Watch, 1989.

———. *Political Murder and Reform in Colombia: The Violence Continues.* New York: Americas Watch, 1992.

———. *State of War: Political Violence and Counterinsurgency in Colombia.* New York: Americas Watch, 1993.

Andean Commission of Jurists. *Colombia: The Right to Justice.* New York: Lawyers Committee for Human Rights, 1991.

Andreas, Peter, Eva Bertram, Morris Blackman, and Kenneth Sharpe. "Dead-End Drug Wars." *Foreign Policy*, no. 85 (Winter 1991–1992): 106–128.

Arbena, Joseph L. "The Image of an American Imperialist: Colombian Views of Theodore Roosevelt." *West Georgia College, Studies in the Social Sciences* 6, no. 1 (June 1967): 3–27.

Arnson, Cynthia, ed. *Comparative Peace Processes in Latin America.* Palo Alto: Stanford University Press and Woodrow Wilson Center Press, 1999.

———. *Crossroads: Congress, the President, and Central America, 1976–1993.* University Park: Pennsylvania State University Press, 1993.

Bagley, Bruce. *Assessing America's War on Drugs.* Special Issue, *Journal of Interamerican Studies and World Affairs* 30, nos. 2–3 (Summer–Fall 1988).

———. "Colombia: National Front and Economic Development." In *Politics, Policies, and Economic Development in Latin America,* edited by Robert Wesson, pp. 124–160. Stanford: Hoover Institution Press, 1984.

———. "Colombia and the War on Drugs." *Foreign Affairs* 67, no. 1 (Fall 1988): 70–92.

———. "The Colombian Connection: The Impact of Drug Traffic in Colombia." In *Coca and Cocaine: Effects on People and Policy in Latin America,* edited by Deborah Pacini and Christine Franquemont, pp. 89–100. Ithaca: Cultural Survival, 1986.

———. "Dateline Drug Wars: Colombia: The Wrong Strategy." *Foreign Policy,* no. 77 (Winter 1989–1990): 154–171.

———. *Myths of Militarization: The Role of the Military in the War on Drugs in the Americas.* Miami: University of Miami North-South Center, 1991.

Bagley, Bruce, and Juan Gabriel Tokatlian. "Dope and Dogma: Explaining the Failure of U.S.–Latin American Drug Policies." In *The United States and Latin America in the 1990s: Beyond the Cold War,* edited by Jonathyn Hartlyn, Lars Schoultz, and Augusto Varas, pp. 214–234. Chapel Hill: University of North Carolina Press, 1992.

———, eds. *Economía y política del narcotráfico.* Bogotá: Ediciones Uniandes, 1990.

Bagley, Bruce, and William Walker III. *Drug Trafficking in the Americas.* Miami: University of Miami North-South Center, 1994.

Bejarano, Ana María. "La paz en la administración de Barco: De la rehabilitación social a la negociación política." *Análisis Político* 9 (1990): 7–29.

Beltran, Miguel. "Guerra y política en Colombia." *Estudios Latinoamericanos* 4, no. 7 (January–June 1997): 127–141.

Bergquist, Charles, Ricardo Penaranda, and Gonzalo Sánchez, eds. *Violence in Colombia: The Contemporary Crisis in Historical Perspective.* Wilmington, Del.: Scholarly Resources, 1992.

Bertram, Eva, and Bill Spencer. "Democratic Dilemmas in the War on Drugs in Latin America." Case study for the Carnegie Council on Ethics and International Affairs, Georgetown University, Washington, D.C., 2000.

Betancourt Pulecio, Ingrid. *Sí sabía: Viaje a través del expediente de Ernesto Samper.* Bogotá: Temas de Hoy, 1996.

Blachman, Morris, and Kenneth E. Sharpe. "The War on Drugs: American Democracy Under Assault." *World Policy Journal* 7, no. 1 (Winter 1989–1990): 135–167.

Block, Alan, ed. "The Politics of Cocaine." *Crime, Law, and Social Change* 16, no. 1 (1991): 1–133.

Bowden, Mark. *Killing Pablo: The Hunt for the World's Greatest Outlaw.* New York: Atlantic Monthly Press, 2001.

Buchanan, Paul. "Chameleon, Tortoise, or Toad? The Changing U.S. Security Role in Contemporary Latin America." In *International Security and Democracy: Latin America and the Caribbean in the Post–Cold War Era,* edited by Jorge Domínguez, pp. 266–288. Pittsburgh: University of Pittsburgh Press, 1998.

Buckman, Robert T. "The Cali Cartel: An Undefeated Enemy." *Low Intensity Conflict and Law Enforcement* 3, no. 3 (Winter 1994): 430–452.

Buenaventura, Manuel. "Human Rights Violations in Colombia: Colombian Governments and Military Perspectives." *Low Intensity Conflict and Law Enforcement* 4, no. 2 (Autumn 1995): 71–290.

Bushnell, David. *Eduardo Santos and the Good Neighbor Policy, 1938–1942.* Gainesville: University of Florida Press, 1967.

———. "The Independence of Spanish South America." In *The Cambridge History of Latin America,* vol. 3, edited by Leslie Bethell, pp. 140–151. Cambridge: Cambridge University Press, 1985.

———. *The Making of Modern Colombia: A Nation in Spite of Itself.* Berkeley: University of California Press, 1993.

Bustamante, Fernando. "The Armed Forces of Colombia and Ecuador in Comparative Perspective." In *Democracy Under Siege,* edited by Augusto Varas, pp. 17–34. New York: Greenwood Press, 1989.

Caffrey, Dennis. "The Inter-American Military System: Rhetoric vs. Reality." In *Security in the Americas,* edited by Georges Fauriol, pp. 39–59. Washington, D.C.: National Defense University Press, 1989.

Cañón, Luis M. *La Crisis: Cuatro años a bordo del gobierno de Samper.* Bogotá: Planeta, 1998.

Castañeda, Jorge. "Latin America and the End of the Cold War." *World Policy Journal* 7, no. 3 (Summer 1990): 469–492.

Chernick, Marc. "Colombia's 'War on Drugs' vs. the United States' 'War on Drugs.'" WOLA Briefing Series no. 3, Washington Office on Latin America, Washington, D.C., May 30, 1991.

———. "Legal and Illegal Export Booms: The Latin American Drug Trade, the Failure of Development, and the Formation of a New Entrepreneurial and Social Elite." Paper presented at Princeton University, 1993.

———. "Negotiating Peace Amid Multiple Forms of Violence: The Protracted Search for a Settlement to the Armed Conflicts in Colombia." In *Comparative*

Peace Processes in Latin America, edited by Cynthia J. Arnson, pp. 159–200. Washington, D.C.: Woodrow Wilson Center Press, 1999.

———. "Negotiations and Armed Conflict: The Colombian Peace Process (1982–1986)." Columbia University Papers on Latin America no. 1, August 1988.

Child, Jack. "Geopolitical Thinking in Latin America." *Latin American Research Review* 14, no. 2 (1979): 89–111.

Claudio, Arnaldo. "United States–Colombia Extradition Treaty: Failure of a Security Strategy." *Military Review* 71, no. 12 (December 1991): 69–77.

Cline, Harvey F. "Colombia: Building Democracy Amidst Violence and Drugs." In *Constructing Democratic Governance: Latin America and the Caribbean in the 1990s,* edited by Jorge Domínguez and Abraham F. Lowenthal, pp. 20–41. Baltimore: Johns Hopkins University Press, 1996.

Coletta, Paolo E. "William Jennings Bryan and the United States–Colombian Impasse, 1903–1921." *Hispanic American Historical Review* 47, no. 4 (November 1967): 486–501.

Collett, Merill. "The Myth of the Narco-Guerrilla." *The Nation,* August 13, 1988.

Collin, Richard H. *Theodore Roosevelt's Caribbean: The Panama Canal, the Monroe Doctrine, and the Latin American Context.* Baton Rouge: Louisiana State University Press, 1990.

Council on Foreign Relations. *Rethinking International Drug Control: New Directions for U.S. Policy.* New York: Council on Foreign Relations, 1997.

Crahan, Margaret. "National Security Ideology and Human Rights." In *Human Rights and Basic Needs in Latin America,* edited by Margaret Crahan, pp. 100–127. Washington, D.C.: Georgetown University Press, 1982.

Craig, Richard B. "Colombian Narcotics Control and United States–Colombian Relations." *Journal of Interamerican Studies and World Affairs* 23, no. 3 (August 1981): 243–270.

———. "Illicit Drug Traffic: Implications for South American Source Countries." *Journal of Interamerican Studies and World Affairs* 29, no. 2 (Summer 1987): 1–35.

Crandall, Russell. "Bombs Litter Colombia's Road to Peace." *Jane's Defence Weekly Terrorism and Security Monitor,* June 2001.

———. "Clinton, Bush, and Plan Colombia." *Survival* 43, no. 4 (Winter 2001–2002): 21–48

———. "Colombia Needs a Stronger Military." *The Wall Street Journal,* June 12, 1998.

———. "Colombia's Military Prospects Are Not Getting Any Brighter." *The Wall Street Journal,* October 27, 2000.

———. "Ecuador Experiences Its Own 'Balloon Effect.'" *Jane's Defence Weekly Terrorism and Security Monitor,* April 2001.

———. "The End of Civil Conflict in Colombia: The Military, Paramilitaries, and a New Role for the United States." *SAIS Review* 19, no. 1 (Winter–Spring 1999): 223–237.

———. "Explicit Narcotization: U.S. Policy Toward Colombia During the Presidential Administration of Ernesto Samper." *Latin American Politics and Society* 43, no. 3 (Fall 2001): 95–120.

———. "In the War on Drugs, Colombians Die, Americans Are Pardoned." *The Wall Street Journal,* April 20, 2001.

———. "New U.S. Aid to Colombia: Deeper Into the Anti-Drug Mire." *The Christian Science Monitor,* June 29, 2000.

———. Testimony submitted to the U.S. Congress, House of Representatives, Committee on Hemispheric Affairs, August 3, 1998.

———. "United States Policy in Colombia." Presentation at the "El Ejército y Paz en Colombia" conference, sponsored by *El Tiempo,* Bogotá, September 26–28, 1998.

Dangerfield, George. *The Era of Good Feelings.* New York: Harcourt Brace, 1952.

Desch, Michael C. "Why Latin America May Miss the Cold War." In *International Security and Democracy: Latin America and the Caribbean in the Post–Cold War Era,* edited by Jorge Domínguez, pp. 245–265. Pittsburgh: University of Pittsburgh Press, 1998.

Dix, Robert. *Colombia: The Political Dimensions of Change.* New Haven: Yale University Press, 1967.

———. "Consociational Democracy: The Case of Colombia." *Comparative Politics* 12, no. 3 (April 1980): 303–321.

———. *The Politics of Colombia.* New York: Praeger, 1987.

———. "Social Change and Party System Stability in Colombia." *Government and Opposition* 25, no. 1 (Winter 1990): 98–114.

Domínguez, Jorge. "The Americas: Found, and Then Lost Again." *Foreign Policy,* no. 112 (Fall 1998): 125–137.

———. "The Future of Inter-American Relations." Inter-American Dialogue working paper, Washington, D.C., June 1999.

———, ed. *International Security and Democracy: Latin America and the Caribbean in the Post–Cold War Era.* Pittsburgh: University of Pittsburgh Press, 1998.

Downes, Richard. "Landpower and Ambiguous Warfare: The Challenges of Colombia in the Twenty-first Century." Washington, D.C: Strategic Studies Institute, 1999.

Drexler, Robert. *Colombia and the United States: A Failed Foreign Policy.* London: McFarland, 1997.

Duzan, María Jimena. "Colombia's Bloody War of Words." *Journal of Democracy* 2, no. 1 (Winter 1991): 99–106.

Falco, Mathea. "Passing Grades." *Foreign Affairs* 74, no. 5 (September–October 1996): 15–20.

———. "U.S. Drug Policy: Addicted to Failure." *Foreign Policy,* no. 102 (Spring 1996): 120–133.

Falcoff, Mark. "A Look at Latin America." In *Sea Changes: American Foreign Policy in a World Transformed,* edited by Nicholas X. Rizopoulos, pp. 71–83. New York: Council on Foreign Relations Press, 1990.

Farer, Tom, ed. *Beyond Sovereignty: Collectively Defending Democracy in the Americas.* Baltimore: Johns Hopkins University Press, 1996.

Fauriol, Georges. "The Shadow of Latin American Affairs." *Foreign Affairs* 69, no. 1 (America and the World, 1989–1990): 116–134.

———. *The Third Century: U.S. Latin American Policy Choices for the 1990s.* Washington, D.C.: Center for Strategic and International Studies, 1988.

Filippone, Robert. "The Medellín Cartel: Why We Can't Win the Drug War." *Studies in Conflict and Terrorism* 17, no. 4 (1994): 323–344.

Fishel, John T. "Developing a Drug War Strategy: Lessons from Operation Blast Furnace." *Military Review* 71, no. 6 (June 1991): 61–69.

Fishlow, Albert. "The Foreign Policy Challenge for the United States." In *The United States and the Americas: A Twenty-First-Century View,* edited by Albert Fishlow and James Jones, pp. 197–206. New York: W. W. Norton, 1999.

García Márquez, Gabriel. *News of a Kidnapping.* New York: Knopf, 1997.

García-Peña Jaramillo, Daniel. *Building Tomorrow's Peace: A Strategy for Reconciliation.* Report by the Peace Exploration Committee, Bogotá, 1997.

Girardo, Javier. *Colombia: The Genocidal Democracy.* Maine: Common Courage Press, 1996.

Gleijeses, Piero. *Shattered Hope: The Guatemalan Revolution and the United States.* Princeton: Princeton University Press, 1991.

Goodman, Louis, and Johanna Mendelson. "The Threat of New Missions: Latin American Militaries and the Drug War." In *Military and Democracy: The Future of Civil-Military Relations in Latin America,* edited by Louis Goodman, Johanna Mendelson, and Juan Rial, pp. 189–195. Lexington, Mass.: Lexington Books, 1990.

Gugliotta, Guy, and Jeff Leen. *Kings of Cocaine.* New York: Simon and Schuster, 1989.

Haglund, David G. "De-Lousing SCADTA: The Role of Pan American Airways in U.S. Aviation Diplomacy in Colombia, 1939–1940." *Aerospace Historian* 30, no. 3 (September 1983): 177–190.

Hartlyn, Jonathan. *The Politics of Coalition Rule in Colombia.* Cambridge: Cambridge University Press, 1988.

Henderson, James. *When Colombia Bled: A History of Violencia in Tolima.* University: University of Alabama Press, 1985.

Herman, Donald, ed. *Democracy in Latin America: Colombia and Venezuela.* New York: Praeger, 1988.

Hill, Howard C. *Roosevelt and the Caribbean.* Chicago: University of Chicago Press, 1927.

Lael, Richard L. *Arrogant Diplomacy: U.S. Policy Toward Colombia, 1903–1922.* Wilmington, Del.: Scholarly Resources, 1987.

Langley, Lester. *The United States and the Caribbean in the Twentieth Century.* Athens: University of Georgia Press, 1982.

Leal Buitrago, Francisco, ed. *Tras las huellas de la crisis política.* Bogotá: IEPRI, 1996.

Lee, Rensselaer W., III. "Cocaine Mafia." *Social Science and Modern Society* 27, no. 2 (January–February 1990): 53–62.

. "Colombia's Cocaine Syndicates." *Crime, Law, and Social Change* 16, no. 1 (1991): 3–39.

. "Making the Most of Colombia's Drug Negotiations." *Orbis* 35, no. 2 (Spring 1991): 235–252.

. *The White Labyrinth: Cocaine and Political Power.* New Brunswick, N.J.: Transaction Press, 1989.

Lee, Rensselaer W., III, and Patrick L. Clawson. *The Andean Cocaine Industry.* New York: St. Martin's Press, 1998.

Lowenthal, Abraham F. "Changing U.S. Interests and Policies in a New World." In *The United States and Latin America in the 1990s: Beyond the Cold War,* edited by Jonathan Hartlyn, Lars Schoultz, and Augusto Varas, pp. 64–85. Chapel Hill: University of North Carolina Press, 1992.

. "Ending the Hegemonic Presumption: The United States and Latin America." *Foreign Affairs* 55, no. 1 (Autumn 1976): 199–213.

. "Learning from History." In *Exporting Democracy: The United States and Latin America, Themes and Issues,* edited by Abraham F. Lowenthal, pp. 385–405. Baltimore: Johns Hopkins University Press, 1991.

. *Partners in Conflict: The United States and Latin America in the 1990s.* Baltimore: Johns Hopkins University Press, 1991.

. "Rediscovering Latin America." *Foreign Affairs* (Fall 1990): 27–41.

. "The United States and South America." *Current History* 87, no. 525 (January 1988): 1–4.

. "United States–Latin American Relations at the Century's Turn: Managing the Intermestic Agenda." In *The United States and the Americas: A Twenty-First-Century View,* edited by Albert Fishlow and James Jones, pp. 109–136. New York: W. W. Norton, 1999.

Lozano, Pilar. "Los grandes 'capos' colombianos del narcotráfico escapan a la extradición pretendida por EEUU: La reforma constitucional adoptada el martes no tendrá caracter retroactivo." *El País,* November 27, 1997.

Mabry, Donald, ed. *The Latin American Narcotics Trade and U.S. National Security.* New York: Greenwood Press, 1988.

MacDonald, Scott. *Dancing on a Volcano: The Latin American Drug Trade.* New York: Praeger, 1988.

. *Mountain High, White Avalanche: Cocaine and Power in the Andean States and Panama.* New York: Praeger, 1989.

Manning, Bayless. "The Congress, the Executive, and Intermestic Affairs: Three Proposals." *Foreign Affairs* 55, no. 2 (1977): 306–324.

Marcella, Gabriel, and Donald E. Schulz. "Colombia's Three Wars: U.S. Strategy at the Crossroads." Washington, D.C.: Strategic Studies Institute, 1999.

. "War and Peace in Colombia." Washington, D.C.: Center for Strategic and International Studies, 1999.

Martz, John. *Colombia: A Contemporary Political Survey.* Chapel Hill: University of North Carolina Press, 1962.

. "National Security and Politics: The Colombian-Venezuelan Border." *Journal of Interamerican Studies and World Affairs* 30, no. 4 (Winter 1988–1989): 117–138.

————. "Party Elites and Leadership in Colombia and Venezuela." *Journal of Latin American Studies* 24, no. 1 (February 1992): 87–121.

Maullin, Richard. *Soldiers, Guerrillas, and Politics in Colombia*. Lexington: D. C. Heath, 1973.

McCollough, David. *The Path Between the Seas: The Creation of the Panama Canal, 1870–1914*. New York: Simon and Schuster, 1977.

Medina Serna, Santiago. *La verdad sobre las mentiras*. Bogotá: Planeta, 1997.

Menzel, Sewall. *Cocaine Quagmire: Implementing U.S. Anti-Drug Policy in the North Andes–Colombia*. New York: University Press of America, 1997.

Miner, Dwight C. *The Fight for the Panama Route: The Story of the Spooner Act and the Hay-Herrán Treaty*. New York: Octagon, 1966.

Mitchell, Nancy. "The Height of the German Challenge: The Venezuela Blockade, 1902–1903." *Diplomatic History* 20, no. 2 (Spring 1996): 185–209.

Morales, Edmundo. *Cocaine: White Gold Rush in Peru*. Tucson: University of Arizona Press, 1989.

Musto, David. *The American Disease: Origins of Narcotics Control*. New York: Oxford University Press, 1987.

Office of National Drug Control Strategy. Barry McCaffrey, director of the Office of National Drug Control Policy. "Hemisferio Reclama Compromiso Pleno Para Detener Drogas." May 4, 1998.

————. Barry McCaffrey, director of the Office of National Drug Control Policy. "Illegal Drugs: A Common Threat to the Global Community." June 9, 1988.

————. "FY 2000 Drug Control Budget Builds on Success: Budget Provides $17.8 Billion for Demand and Supply Reduction." 1999.

————. *National Drug Control Strategy*. 1990–1998.

Orozco Abad, Iván. "La guerra del presidente." *Análisis Político* 8 (September–December 1989): 73–78.

————. "Los diálogos con el narcotráfico: Historia de la transformación fallida de un delincuente común en un delincuente político." *Análisis Político* 11 (September–December 1990): 28–58.

Osterling, Jorge. *Democracy in Colombia: Clientelist Politics and Guerrilla Warfare*. New Brunswick, N.J.: Transaction Press, 1989.

Pardo, Rodrigo, and Juan Gabriel Tokatlian. "Teoría y práctica de las relaciones internacionales: El caso de Colombia." *Estudios Internacionales* (January–March 1988): 94–135.

Parejo Gonzalez, Enrique. *Radiografía de un prevaricato*. Bogotá: Panamericana, 1999.

Parks, E. Taylor. *Colombia and the United States, 1765–1934*. Durham: Duke University Press, 1935.

Pastor, Robert. "The Bush Administration and Latin America: The Pragmatic Style and the Regionalist Option." *Journal of Interamerican Studies and World Affairs* 33, no. 3 (Fall 1991): 1–34.

————. "The Clinton Administration and the Americas: The Postwar Rhythm and Blues." *Journal of Interamerican Studies and World Affairs* 38, no. 4 (Winter 1996–1997): 99–123.

————. "George Bush and Latin America: The Pragmatic Style and the Regionalist Option." In *Eagle in a New World: American Grand Strategy in the Post–Cold War World,* edited by Kenneth A. Oye, Robert J. Lieber, and Donald Rothchild, pp. 361–387. New York: HarperCollins, 1992.

————. *Whirlpool: U.S. Foreign Policy Toward Latin America and the Caribbean.* Princeton: Princeton University Press, 1992.

Peeler, John. *Latin American Democracies: Colombia, Costa Rica, Venezuela.* Chapel Hill: University of North Carolina Press, 1985.

Perl, Raphael. "United States Andean Drug Policy: Background and Issues for Decision Makers." *Journal of Interamerican Studies and World Affairs* 34, no. 3 (Fall 1992): 13–33.

————. "The U.S. Congress, International Narcotics Policy, and the Anti–Drug Abuse Act of 1988." *Journal of Interamerican Studies and World Affairs* 30, nos. 2–3 (Summer–Fall 1988): 19–52.

Perry, William. "In Search of a Latin American Policy: The Elusive Quest." *Washington Quarterly* 13, no. 2 (Spring 1990): 125–134.

Pizarro, Eduardo. "Colombia, hacia una salida democratica a la crisis social?" *Análisis Político* 17 (September–December 1992): 83–98.

————. "Revolutionary Groups in Colombia." In *Violence in Colombia: The Contemporary Crisis in Historical Perspective,* edited by Charles Bergquist, Ricardo Penaranda, and Gonzalo Sánchez, pp. 169–193. Wilmington, Del.: Scholarly Resources, 1992.

Premo, Daniel L. "Coping with Insurgency: The Politics of Pacification in Colombia and Venezuela." In *Democracy in Latin America: Colombia and Venezuela,* edited by Donald L. Herman, pp. 228–230. New York: Praeger, 1988.

Randall, Stephen. *Colombia and the United States: Hegemony and Interdependence.* Athens: University of Georgia Press, 1992.

————. *The Diplomacy of Modernization: Colombian-American Relations, 1920–1940.* Toronto: University of Toronto Press, 1977.

Rangel Suárez, Alfredo. *Colombia: Guerra en el fin de siglo.* Bogotá: Tercer Mundo, 1998.

Rempe, Dennis. "Guerrillas, Bandits, and Independent Republics: U.S. Counterinsurgency Efforts in Colombia, 1959–1965." *Small Wars and Insurgencies* 6, no. 3 (Winter 1995): 304–327.

Restrepo, Laura. *Historia de un entusiasmo.* Bogotá: Grupo Editorial Norma, 1998.

Reyes Posada, Alejandro. "La coyuntura de las guerras y la nueva estrategia de seguridad." *Análisis Político* 18 (January–April 1993): 55–65.

————. "Drug Trafficking and the Guerrilla Movement in Colombia." In *Drug Trafficking in the Americas,* edited by Bruce Bagley and William Walker, pp. 121–131. Miami: University of Miami North-South Center, 1994.

————. "Paramilitares en Colombia: Contexto, aliados, y consecuencias." *Análisis Político* 12 (January–April 1991): 35–41.

Richani, Nazih. "The Political Economy of Violence: The War-System in Colombia." *Journal of Interamerican Studies and World Affairs* 39, no. 2 (Summer 1997): 37–81.

Root, Elihu. "The Real Monroe Doctrine." *North American Review* (June 1914): 841–856.

Safford, Frank. "Politics, Ideology, and Society in Post-Independence Latin America." In *The Cambridge History of Latin America,* vol. 3, edited by Leslie Bethell, pp. 347–422. Cambridge: Cambridge University Press, 1985.

Samper Pizano, Ernesto. *Legalización de la marihuana.* Bogotá: ANIF, Fondo Editorial, 1980.

Schoultz, Lars. *Beneath the United States: A History of U.S. Policy Toward Latin America.* Cambridge: Harvard University Press, 1998.

———. *Human Rights and United States Policy Toward Latin America.* Princeton: Princeton University Press, 1981.

———. *National Security and United States Policy Toward Latin America.* Princeton: Princeton University Press, 1987.

———. "U.S. Values and Approaches to Hemispheric Security Issues." In *Security, Democracy, and Development in U.S.-Latin Relations,* edited by Lars Schoultz, William C. Smith, and Augusto Varas, pp. 33–56. Miami: University of Miami North-South Center, 1994.

Shafer, D. Michael. *Deadly Paradigms: The Failure of U.S. Counterinsurgency Policy.* Princeton: Princeton University Press, 1988.

Sharpe, Kenneth. "The Drug War: Going After Supply." *Journal of Interamerican Studies and World Affairs* 30, nos. 2–3 (Summer–Fall 1988): 77–85.

Sharpless, Richard. *Gaitán of Colombia: A Political Biography.* Pittsburgh: University of Pittsburgh Press, 1978.

Shifter, Michael. "Colombia at War." *Current History* 98, no. 626 (March 1999): 116–121.

———. "Colombia on the Brink." *Foreign Affairs* 78, no. 4 (July–August 1999): 14–20.

———. "Colombia's Security Predicament and Opportunities for Peace: Guidelines for U.S. Policy." Inter-American Dialogue policy brief, Washington, D.C., 1998.

Siino, Denise Marie. *Guerrilla Hostage.* Grand Rapids, Mich.: Fleming H. Revel, 1999.

Singer, Marshall R. *Weak States in a World of Powers: The Dynamics of International Relationships.* New York: Free Press, 1972.

Smith, Gaddis. *The Last Years of the Monroe Doctrine: 1945–1993.* New York: Hill & Wang, 1994.

Smith, Peter. *Talons of the Eagle: Dynamics of U.S.–Latin American Relations.* Oxford: Oxford University Press, 1996.

Snyder, Jack. *Myths of Empire: Domestic Politics and International Ambition.* Ithaca: Cornell University Press, 1991.

Spanier, John, and Eric Uslaner. *How Foreign Policy Is Made.* New York: Praeger, 1978.

Strong, Simon. *Whitewash: Pablo Escobar and the Cocaine Wars.* London: Macmillan, 1995.

Tambs, Lewis A. "International Cooperation in Illicit Narcotics and Illegal Immigration." *Comparative Strategy* 8, no. 1 (1989): 11–19.

Thoumi, Francisco. *Political Economy of Illegal Drugs in Colombia.* Boulder: Lynne Rienner, 1995.

Tokatlian, Juan Gabriel. "Colombia y EEUU." *Política Exterior* 60 (November–December 1997): 55–66.

———. "Drogas y relaciones América Latina–Estados Unidos: Reflexiones críticas." *Colombia Internacional,* no. 7 (July–September 1989).

———. "Latin American Reaction to U.S. Policies on Drugs and Terrorism." In *Security, Democracy, and Development in U.S.-Latin Relations,* edited by Lars Schoultz, William C. Smith, and Augusto Varas, pp. 115–136. Miami: University of Miami North-South Center, 1994.

———. "National Security and Drugs: Their Impact on Colombian-U.S. Relations." *Journal of Interamerican Studies and World Affairs* 30, no. 1 (Spring 1988): 133–160.

———. "The Political Economy of Colombian-U.S. Narcodiplomacy: A Case Study of Colombian Foreign Policy Decision-Making, 1978–1990." Ph.D. thesis, Paul H. Nitze School of Advanced International Studies, Johns Hopkins University, Baltimore, 1990.

Trebach, Arnold. *The Great Drug War.* New York: Macmillan, 1987.

Tulchin, Joseph S. "Hemispheric Relations in the Twenty-first Century." *Journal of Interamerican Studies and World Affairs* 39, no. 1 (Spring 1997): 33–38

U.S. Department of Justice. "The Cali Cartel: The New Kings of Cocaine." DEA Drug Intelligence report, November 1994.

U.S. Department of State. Bureau of International Narcotics Matters. "International Narcotics Control Strategy Report." U.S. Government Printing Office, 1995–2001.

———. "Certificación de paises productores de drogas." U.S. embassy, Bogotá, 1998.

———. "Clinton informa al congreso sobre congelación de bienes colombianos." Statement by President Bill Clinton to the U.S. Congress, April 28, 1998.

———. "Clinton pide al congreso mas dinero para contener drogas ilícitas." U.S. embassy, Bogotá, 1998.

———. Bureau of International Narcotics and Law Enforcement Affairs. "The Certification Process." January 4, 1999.

———. Record briefing of Thomas Pickering, undersecretary of state, November 27, 2000.

U.S. General Accounting Office. "Drug Control: U.S.-Supported Efforts in Colombia and Bolivia." GAO/NSIAD-89-24. Washington, D.C., September 1988.

———. "Drug Control: Challenges in Implementing Plan Colombia." GAO-01-76T. Washington, D.C., October 12, 2000.

———. "Drug Control: Counternarcotics Efforts in Colombia Face Continuing Challenges." Washington, D.C., February 26, 1998.

————. "The Drug War: Colombia Is Undertaking Anti-Drug Programs, but Impact Is Uncertain." GAO/NSIAD-93-158. Washington, D.C., August 10, 1993.

————. "Drug War: Observations on Counternarcotics Aid to Colombia." GAO/NSIAD-91-296. Washington, D.C., September 30, 1991.

————. "The Drug War: Observations on the U.S. International Drug Control Strategy." GAO/NSIAD-95-182. Washington, D.C., June 27, 1995.

————. "Justificación de la certificación de Colombia por razones de intereses nacionales." U.S. embassy, Bogotá, 1998.

————. "Promising Approach to Judicial Reform in Colombia." GAO/T-NSIAD-92-2. Washington, D.C., 1992.

————. "U.S. Counternarcotics Efforts in Colombia Face Continuing Challenges: Report to Congressional Requesters." GAO/NSIAD-98-60. Washington, D.C., 1998.

U.S. House of Representatives. Committee on Foreign Relations. "Aid to 'Plan Colombia': The Time for U.S. Assistance Is Now." Report from Senator Joseph Biden, May 2000.

————. Committee on Government Operations. "Stopping the Flood of Cocaine with Operation Snowcap: Is It Working?" August 15, 1990.

————. Committee on Government Reform and Oversight. Hearings on counternarcotics efforts in Colombia, July 9, 1997.

————. Committee on Government Reform and Oversight. Subcommittee on National Security, International Affairs, and Criminal Justice. "Counternarcotics Efforts in Colombia." July 9, 1997.

————. Committee on International Relations. Hearing, September 11, 1996. Witnesses included: Assistant Secretary of State Robert Gelbard, Principal Deputy Assistant Secretary of State Eric Newsom, and Principal Assistant Secretary of State Peter Romero.

————. Prepared statement by General José Rosso Serrano, director of the Colombian National Police, before the Committee on Government Reform and Oversight, Subcommittee on National Security, International Affairs, and Criminal Justice, February 14, 1997.

————. Record briefing on the release of the annual International Narcotics Strategy Control report, Washington, D.C., February 26, 1999. Comments made by: Acting Secretary of State Frank Loy, Attorney General Janet Reno, ONDCP Director General Barry McCaffrey, Assistant Secretary of State Randy Beers, and Deputy Director, National Drug Control Policy, Ton Umberg.

————. Select Committee on Narcotics Abuse and Control. "The Andean Summit Meeting, February 15, 1990." March 7, 1990.

————. "State Department Drug Certification." Testimony by Robert Gelbard, assistant secretary of state, before the Committee on International Relations, March 29, 1995.

————. Testimony by Brian Sheridan, assistant secretary of defense for special operations and low-intensity conflict, before the Committee on International Relations, September 21, 2000.

———. Testimony by Donnie Marshall, DEA chief of operations, before the Committee on Government Reform and Oversight, Subcommittee on National Security, International Affairs, and Criminal Justice, July 9, 1997.

———. Testimony by Robert Gelbard, assistant secretary of state for international narcotics and law enforcement affairs, before the Committee on Government Reform and Oversight, Subcommittee on National Security, International Affairs, and Criminal Justice, February 14, 1997.

———. Testimony by Robert Gelbard, assistant secretary of state for international narcotics and law enforcement affairs, before the Committee on International Relations, Subcommittee on the Western Hemisphere, July 29, 1995, and March 7, 1996.

U.S. Senate. Committee on Armed Services. "Armed Strategy." In *The Andean Drug Strategy and the Role of the U.S. Military.* Washington, D.C.: U.S. Government Printing Office, 1990.

———. Committee on Foreign Relations. "Corruption and Drugs in Colombia: Democracy at Risk." February 27, 1996.

———. Committee on Government Reform and Oversight. Subcommittee on National Security, International Affairs, and Criminal Justice. "Drug Control Policy and Colombia." July 9, 1997.

Van Wert, James M. "The State Department's Narcotics Control Policy in the Americas." *Journal of Interamerican Studies and World Affairs* 30, nos. 2–3 (Summer–Fall 1988): 1–18.

Varas, Augusto. "From Coercion to Partnership: A New Paradigm for Security Cooperation in the Western Hemisphere." In *The United States and Latin America in the 1990s: Beyond the Cold War,* edited by Jonathan Hartlyn, Lars Schoultz, and Augusto Varas, pp. 46–63. Chapel Hill: University of North Carolina Press, 1992.

———. "Hemispheric Relations and Security Regimes in Latin America." In *Hemispheric Security and U.S. Policy in Latin America,* edited by Augusto Varas, pp. 33–65. Boulder: Westview Press, 1989.

———. "Post–Cold War Security Interests and Perceptions of Threats in the Western Hemisphere." In *Security, Democracy, and Development in U.S.-Latin Relations,* edited by Lars Schoultz, William C. Smith, and Augusto Varas, pp. 1–32. Miami: University of Miami North-South Center, 1994.

Vargas, Mauricio. *Tiro Directo.* Bogotá: Espasa, 1998.

Vargas Meza, Ricardo. "The Revolutionary Armed Forces of Colombia (FARC) and the Illicit Drug Trade." Cochabamba, Bolivia: Acción Andina, June 1999.

Walker, William, III. "Drug Control and U.S. Hegemony." In *United States Policy in Latin America: A Decade of Crisis and Challenge,* edited by John D. Martz, pp. 299–319. Lincoln: University of Nebraska Press, 1995.

———, ed. *Drugs in the Western Hemisphere: An Odyssey of Cultures in Conflict.* Wilmington, Del.: Scholarly Resources, 1996.

Washington Office on Latin America (WOLA). *Clear and Present Dangers: The U.S. Military and the War on Drugs in the Andes.* Washington, D.C.: WOLA, 1991.

————. *The Colombian National Police, Human Rights, and U.S. Drug Policy.* Washington, D.C.: WOLA, 1991.

————. *Reluctant Recruits: The U.S. Military and the War on Drugs.* Washington, D.C.: WOLA, 1997.

Watson, Cynthia. "Political Violence in Colombia: Another Argentina?" *Third World Quarterly* 12, nos. 3–4 (1990–1991): 25–39.

White, Brian. "Analyzing Foreign Policy: Problems and Approaches." In *Understanding Foreign Policy: The Foreign Policy Systems Approach,* edited by Michael Clarke and Brian White, pp. 1–26. Brookfield, Vt.: Gower, 1989.

Wilde, Alexander W. "Conversations Among Gentlemen: Oligarchic Democracy in Colombia." In *The Breakdown of Democratic Regimes: Latin America,* edited by Juan J. Linz and Alfred Stepan, pp. 28–81. Baltimore: Johns Hopkins University Press, 1978.

Wood, Bryce. *The Dismantling of the Good Neighbor Policy.* Austin: University of Texas Press, 1985.

Youngers, Coletta. "Waging War: U.S. Policy Toward Colombia." Paper prepared for delivery at the 1998 meeting of the Latin American Studies Association, Chicago, September 24–26.

Zakaria, Fareed. *From Wealth to Power: The Unusual Origins of America's World Role.* Princeton: Princeton University Press, 1998.

Zamosc, Leon. "The Political Crisis and the Prospects for Rural Democracy in Colombia." *Journal of Development Studies* 26, no. 4 (July 1990): 44–78.

Index

183

About the Book

In recent years, Colombia has become the recipient of the third largest amount of U.S. foreign aid—most of it slated for antidrug efforts. Russell Crandall offers a clear and concise analysis of the evolution and present dynamics of U.S. policy toward Colombia, a policy that since 1990 has been driven overwhelmingly by factors related to the "war on drugs" within the United States.

Crandall shows how, in pursuing its drug war–driven policies, the United States succeeded primarily in weakening the Colombian state at the very time that guerrilla groups and paramilitary forces were gaining strength in rural areas. He also considers the roots of those groups and discusses efforts to bring peace to the country. He concludes by assessing current U.S. policy toward Colombia and suggesting directions for future policy.

Driven by Drugs tells a story that is essential for understanding the complexity of the U.S.-Colombian relationship—and that is equally significant as a case study of U.S. foreign policy.

Russell Crandall is MacArthur Assistant Professor of Political Science at Davidson College.

327.7308 Crandall, Russell,
61   1971-
Cra
          Driven by drugs.